CULTIVATING KNOWLEDGE

GLOBAL CHANGE / GLOBAL HEALTH

Elizabeth Olson and Cynthia Fowler
EDITORS

ANDREW FLACHS

CULTIVATING KNOWLEDGE

Biotechnology, Sustainability, and the Human Cost
of Cotton Capitalism in India

THE UNIVERSITY OF
ARIZONA PRESS
TUCSON

The University of Arizona Press
www.uapress.arizona.edu

ISBN-13: 978-0-8165-4025-9 (cloth)
ISBN-13: 978-0-8165-3963-5 (paper)

Cover design by Leigh McDonald

Library of Congress Cataloging-in-Publication Data
Names: Flachs, Andrew, author.
Title: Cultivating knowledge : biotechnology, sustainability, and the human cost of cotton capitalism in
    south India / Andrew Flachs.
Other titles: Global change/global health.
Description: Tucson : The University of Arizona Press, 2019. | Series: Global change/global health |
    Includes bibliographical references and index. | Summary: "An ethnography of rural farmers in
    India that brings to light the devastating consequences of large agrobusiness. This book is the first
    in the new Global Change / Global Health series"— Provided by publisher.
Identifiers: LCCN 2019008296 | ISBN 9780816539635 (cloth)
Subjects: LCSH: Cotton farmers—India—Telangana—Social conditions. | Cotton growing—Social
    aspects—India—Telangana.
Classification: LCC HD8039.C66 F53 2019 | DDC 338.1/73510890095484—dc23
LC record available at https://lccn.loc.gov/2019008296

Printed in the United States of America
♾ This paper meets the requirements of ANSI/NISO Z39.48-1992 (Permanence of Paper).

CONTENTS

List of Illustrations   vii
Acknowledgments   ix

1. Cotton, Knowledge, and Agrarian Life in Telangana   3
2. The Political Ecology of Knowledge in Indian Agricultural Development   34
3. Cotton Colonialism, Cotton Capitalism   58
4. False Choices: The Problem with Learning on GM Cotton Farms   82
5. Opportunism, Performance, and Underwriting Vulnerability on Organic Cotton Farms   115
6. Performing Development: Practice, Transformation, Suicide   143
7. Redefining Success in Telangana Cotton Agriculture   171

References   *195*
Index   *219*

ILLUSTRATIONS

Figure 1. Cottonseed marketing in Warangal   4

Map 1. Map of research area   21

Figure 2. Pesticide spraying for nontarget pests in a GM cotton field   30

Figure 3. Cottonseeds by percentage of households buying a particularly popular brand   85

Figure 4. Farmer cotton field comparison   88

Figure 5. Boxplots for 2013 fad seed yields   90

Figure 6. Average number of years farmers planted cottonseeds 2012–14   91

Figure 7. Spatial patterns of seed fads in Kavrupad and Ralledapalle over time   94

Figure 8. Seed shop in Warangal, Telangana   98

Figure 9. Government seed permit distributed to guarantee seed packets to farmers   102

Figure 10. Boxplot of cotton yields per acre per household of organic and GM farmers   128

Figure 11. Percentage of households receiving material benefits from organic programs 2012–13 for Addabad, Ennepad, and Japur villages   130

Figure 12. Organic cotton murals in Telangana   149

Figure 13. Relationship of yields to Bt adoption in India   173

Figure 14. Cotton insecticide sprays 1997–2013   174

Figure 15. Pink bollworm in Telangana cotton boll   181

ACKNOWLEDGMENTS

I AM VERY grateful to the people and institutions who made this work possible, beginning first and foremost with the many farmers, scientists, academics, and officials who invited me into their homes and onto their fields to speak with them about the ways in which agricultural technologies are changing their lives. Qualitative and anthropological work depends on the generosity of people willing to share their lives, hopes, and fears. Thank you for telling your stories.

In India, Dr. E. Revathi of the Centre for Economic and Social Studies and Dr. R. Ganesan of the Ashoka Trust for Research in Ecology and the Environment provided valuable logistical support, intellectual advice, and helped arrange my Indian research visa. More recently, P. Srinu and George Tharakan at the University of Hyderabad helped me to think through the anthropology of Indian cotton agriculture. Ramavath Bikshapathi and Golusula Rani provided support and friendship as I worked in their villages and beyond. I am indebted to the assistance and friendship of my research assistants: Christine Diepenbrock, Golusula Rani, G. Ranjith Kumar, Arun Vainala Kumar, Shivaprasad Citimar Sonnar, Koduri Karthik, Mutiraj Vykuntam, Jadav Chakradhar, and Barik Rao. Each taught me a great deal about India, provided excellent insights into this research, and was willing to work with me in the often hot, wet, and unpleasant rural conditions that this research required. I am especially grateful to Ranjith and Arun, who invited me into their homes, who helped to arrange further research assistants, and who went above and beyond in their service to this project. It would not have been nearly as fun without them. Dr. Uma Reddy helped connect me with important agricultural data, farmer societies, and alternative farming models. The staff of Prakruti Organic and PANTA were gracious enough to host me and help in this research, particularly Kishan Rao. Arun Ambatipudi and G. V. Ramanjaneyulu helped me understand the complexity of alternative agriculture in South India and introduced me to many dedicated farmers and organic agriculture organizations. Finally, without the support of Ram Mohan Rao and Vandita Rao I would never have been able to conduct this research. They provided contacts, logistical support, a network of tireless friends, teachers, and students through the Rural Development Foundation (RDF), and allowed me to feel truly welcome and at home at Kavrupad. I am especially grateful to Ram Mohan for innumerable book suggestions, terrific conversations, and his insightful perspective on India. Even at my most critical and analytical, I truly believe that their goodwill and tremendous efforts in developing and empowering rural India through RDF are changing Telangana and the world for the better.

This research was funded in part through the support of the United States Department of Education Jacob K. Javits Fellowship, the National Geographic Young Explorer's Grant 9304-13, the William L. Brown Center at the Missouri Botanical Garden, the Washington University Lynne Cooper Harvey Fellowship, the John Templeton Foundation (Glenn Stone, PI), and the American Institute for Indian Studies. I am grateful as well to the Volkswagen Foundation for funding a postdoctoral fellowship during which I could write the majority of this book. Washington University in St. Louis, Heidelberg University, and Purdue University provided logistical support, encouraging colleagues, office space, and plenty of coffee to help me write.

I conceived this project as a PhD student at Washington University in St. Louis, where Glenn Davis Stone introduced me to India, invited me to continue his work on farmer decision-making, and set in motion years of collaborative research and friendship. In addition to supervising my doctoral work and helping me make logistical arrangements in Telangana, Glenn helped to fund the collection of some of the data referenced in this book. His influence guides this book, both through his intellectual guidance in the field of agrarian political economy and his valuable suggestions to track down leads or embrace new approaches. Glenn, thanks for inviting me along for the ride.

At Washington University in St. Louis, I benefitted from the methodological and theoretical training insights of Peter Benson, Iver Bernstein, John Bowen,

Rainer Bussmann, Geoff Childs, Talia Dan-Cohen, Gayle Fritz, Jan Salick, Glenn Stone, Kedron Thomas, and Gautam Yadama. Many friends and colleagues helped me imagine and write drafts of this book, listening to my frustrations and celebrating my breakthroughs. James Babbitt, Carolyn Barnes, Andrea Bolivar, Elissa Bullion, Anita Chary, Kehan DeSousa, Steven Goldstein, Ashley Glenn, Robbie Hart, Alison Heller, Ed Henry, Hazard to Ya Booty, Brad Jones, Josh Marshack, Natalie Mueller, Jennifer Moore, Kelsey Nordine, Joseph Orkin, Efstathia Robakis, Elyse Singer, Christopher Shaffer, Rhonda Smythe, Maggie Spivey, Cindy Traub, Mollie Webb, and John Willman, I am grateful to have such intelligent and supportive friends as you.

While at Heidelberg University, Daniel Münster organized a fantastic space to work and teach, and I am grateful for the intellectual support of the community he brought together. Through conferences and conversations in Europe and North America, Aniket Aga, Eugene Anderson, Shaila Seshia Galvin, Dominic Glover, Himanshu Jha, Theresa Lesigang, Harro Maat, John Marston, Rahul Mukherji, Judith Müller, Ursula Münster, Julia Poerting, Paul Richards, Debarati Sen, Heather Swanson, Marcus Taylor, and Jim Veteto all provided valuable support and suggestions.

I am fortunate to have fantastic colleagues at Purdue University who helped me develop the final stages of this project, especially Myrdene Anderson, Sherylyn Briller, Ellen Gruenbaum, Jennifer Johnson, Riall Nolan, Zoe Nyssa, Melissa Remis, and Laura Zanotti. I am very grateful for the editorial assistance of Steve Pijut and Hannah McLimans, who helped to make this book clearer and easier to read. Allyson Carter has been a terrifically supportive editor at the University of Arizona Press, and I am grateful to Cissy Fowler and Liz Olson for their support and encouragement in including this book in their series. At the University of Arizona Press, I am grateful for the assistance of Rosemary Brandt, Scott De Herrera, Amanda Krause, Abby Mogollon, and Kerry Smith.

Thanks to Joel Flachs and Rita Flachs for providing perspective and support as I spent so many months away rather than coming home to visit you. Thanks to Katie, Srulik, Ami, and Ziv Wojnowich for FaceTime in India and to Rosemary Renshaw for my first introduction to South Asia. Azalea Flachs, I hope to take you someday. Thanks to Laura Geller, Felicity Geller-Kunert, Doreen Kunert, Willie Kunert, and Rosebud Sparer for encouraging this academic endeavor from the beginning.

I could not ask for a more supportive partner than Iris Kunert, who inspired me to pursue this path and has now traveled with me across three continents to see it through. Thank you for looking at so many versions of this. I am so fortunate to have you in my life. My book, like my heart and me, is dedicated to you.

Arguments and figures that I developed in the following articles have been adapted and expanded upon with permission from the following:

Flachs, Andrew. 2016. "Redefining Success: The Political Ecology of Genetically Modified and Organic Cotton as Solutions to Agrarian Crisis." *Journal of Political Ecology* 23 (1): 49–70.

Flachs, Andrew. 2017. "Show Farmers: Transformative Sentiment and Performance in Organic Agricultural Development in South India." *Culture, Agriculture, Food, and Environment* 39 (1): 25–34.

Flachs, Andrew. 2018. "Development Roles: Contingency and Performance in Alternative Agriculture in Telangana, India." *Journal of Political Ecology* 25 (1): 716–31.

Flachs, Andrew. 2019. "Planting and Performing: Anxiety, Aspiration, and 'Scripts' in Telangana Cotton Farming." *American Anthropologist* 121 (1): 48–61.

Flachs, Andrew, and Glenn Davis Stone. 2018. "Farmer Knowledge Across the Commodification Spectrum: Rice, Cotton, and Vegetables in Telangana, India." *Journal of Agrarian Change*. Published ahead of print, September 28, 2018. https://doi.org/10.1111/joac.12295.

Flachs, Andrew, Glenn Davis Stone, and Christopher Shaffer. 2017. "Mapping Knowledge: GIS as a Tool for Spatial Modeling of Patterns of Warangal Cottonseed Popularity and Farmer Decision-Making." *Human Ecology* 45 (2): 143–59.

Stone, Glenn Davis, Andrew Flachs, and Christine Diepenbrock. 2014. "Rhythms of the Herd: Long Term Dynamics in Seed Choice by Indian Farmers." *Technology in Society* 36 (1): 26–38.

CULTIVATING KNOWLEDGE

1

COTTON, KNOWLEDGE, AND AGRARIAN LIFE IN TELANGANA

Think of cotton. It's easy now, but it wasn't once.
—AMITAV GHOSH, *CIRCLE OF REASON*

SEED IS a choice that cannot be taken back. As seeds grow, farmers care for them, continuing to make choices that they hope will lead to yields, profits, and a good life. In Telangana, India, the seemingly simple decision about which seed to plant has taken center stage in a larger debate over two mutually exclusive visions for the future of agriculture: genetically modified organisms (GMOs) and certified organic farming. By asking how cotton farmers learn about their seeds and put that knowledge to use, *Cultivating Knowledge* illuminates the local impact of global changes: the slow, persistent dangers of pesticides, inequalities in rural life, the aspirations of people who grow fibers sent around the world, the place of ecological knowledge in modern agriculture, and even the complex threat of suicide. It all begins with a seed.

Shiva's eyes scan dozens of brightly colored cottonseed packets, each with names and images to ignite farmer imaginations.* There's *ATM*, with an image of a cotton boll in a superhero's cape, shooting white, fluffy cotton out of a money slot. Another seed, *Jaadoo*, Telugu for "magic," bears a chicken laying golden eggs. Although there are three small shops closer to his home where he could buy seeds, fertilizers, and pesticides, Shiva and I have taken a forty-minute

---

* All interlocutor, village, and institution names have been changed in the interest of anonymity. I have not changed the names of official government organizations or bureaucratic offices.

bus ride to the regional capital, Warangal, where he hopes to get a better deal on higher-quality cottonseeds (figure 1). The shop is cramped, a dimly lit room with rows of seed-covered shelves and a low counter where a sales clerk sits in a plastic lawn chair.

Yesterday the second sustained storm of June brought cool respite from the summer heat, and Shiva sighed with relief at this signal. Confirmed by newspaper meteorologists and his elderly uncle, the monsoon rains had finally arrived in earnest. "Farmers who planted too early are now seeing their seeds baked by the sun," he explains. "They have been tricked by this year's late rains."

Today, Warangal's row of agricultural input shops is mobbed by farmers and chemical brokers hawking new technology. The crowd's anxious energy reflects the newest fears that genetically modified (GM) cotton may be losing its resistance to some predatory insects, driving that season's profits down even as labor and pesticide costs rise to squeeze farmer budgets. Shiva, having heard

FIGURE 1. Cottonseed marketing in Warangal. The van pictured here plays a jingle advertising *Jaadoo* and *ATM* while delivering seeds to small shops in Warangal. Photo by Andrew Flachs.

that *ATM* is popular and may be high yielding, opts to buy six one-pound seed packets for his four acres of cotton land.

By seven the following morning, the air in Shiva's village, Ralledapalle, is thick with the scent of cow manure and upturned earth. Harnessing his bullocks, he plows close, single lines, a shift from the sparser, crisscrossed box pattern that he plowed two years ago. This is why it takes six packets to plant four acres, a gamble that sowing more plants per field will reap higher yields from the same soil. The seeds are neon pink, treated with imidacloprid to ward off insects that would attack cotton during its germination. It takes a few hours for Shiva and his wife, Laxmi, to plant the field, two seeds to a hole, one elbow away from each other. I help, in between scribbled notes and photographs.

By the end of October, green cotton plants stretching up to my chest begin to flower and fruit. In time for Diwali, the autumn Hindu festival of lights, farmers sell their first cotton crop and hope that they have recouped their losses—pesticide sprays every two weeks, seed packets, fertilizer applications, hired labor for weeding and picking, hired bullocks or tractors to till the earth, all bet against the vagaries of weather that threaten to flood fields and blow down plants. How farmers learn about their seeds, and how they adapt that knowledge to each year's challenges, determines the fate of their crop and their livelihood. This year, Shiva timed his harvest well. Diwali is a time of celebration, and he returns from the market with cardamom *laddu* sweets, my favorite, and a new saree for his wife. The cotton will continue to fruit and flower, providing more harvests, until February, at which point Shiva and Laxmi will decide if it is worth their continued time and energy to gather the diminishing returns of this crop. If not, they'll burn the field to restore nutrients to the land as it rests for a few months until they sow again next June.

Farmwork does not always proceed so smoothly, and the stakes for a good season can be high. A few years ago, Shiva's neighbor Dharwesh found his cotton stems and the undersides of his leaves covered in whiteflies (*Bemisia tabaci*). Although GM cotton contains insecticidal genes intended to protect against American bollworm caterpillars (*Helicoverpa armigera*), the worst pests, whiteflies and other insects unaffected by that genetic modification, drink cotton's juices and spread disease through Indian farmers' crops. Panicking, Dharwesh borrowed a motorized pesticide sprayer to treat his fields. The machine allowed him to spray faster, but it also leaked and sputtered. A few rows into his field, Dharwesh's machine overloaded and engulfed him in a cloud of smoke and insecticide. He collapsed, awakened minutes later by a neighbor who rushed him to a nearby clinic. Dharwesh recovered, but some of the insecticide was lodged in his left eye for too long. He is now blind in that eye, a fate better, he explains, than it might have been.

Their neighbor, Bhadra, across the road was even less lucky. Rising debts and poor access to credit left him desperate. A cotton farmer who has had several unlucky seasons, lost money to laborers, and borrowed to afford agricultural inputs like fertilizers and pesticides grows increasingly anxious. A young man, Bhadra's marriage prospects, and thus his standing among his peers and his place in the village, were in jeopardy with every insect attack and lost rupee. He heard a rumor that the woman to whom he was arranged to be married was now pursuing other husbands. Overwhelmed, he drank several gulps of the concentrated insecticide that is present in every Telangana cotton farmer's home. Bhadra vomited twice, and died later that day, joining 11,771 Indian farmers who committed suicide in 2013 (National Crime Records Bureau 2014).

A few hundred kilometers west, Mahesh does not decide between different cottonseed brands at a shop. Because his village has decided to sell organic cotton, he is legally prohibited from planting GM seeds, the seeds planted by the vast majority of cotton farmers in India. Indeed, he cannot even find non-GM seeds on the shelves at most Telangana shops! Instead, he receives them at a discount from a nongovernmental organization (NGO) that helps the farmers in his village comply with organic standards and then sells their cotton to interested buyers in Europe, Japan, and North America. Mahesh has reaped lower overall yields than the farmers around him, but he has found greater stability in this uncertain market and a new celebrity as a leader in a village that is bucking the trend of an agrarian crisis defined by suicide, stagnant yields, and pesticide overuse.

FEELING GLOBAL CHANGE ON THE FARM

Farmers, lucky and unlucky, bring cotton to shelves and racks around the world. As I type these words, I am wearing cotton socks, cotton underpants, denim cotton jeans, and a cotton T-shirt. My bed has cotton sheets, cotton drapes hang across my windows, and my towels dry quickly and fluff up because of cotton's absorptive fibers. The fast, cheap, and plentiful cotton products on shelves around the world begin as seeds in fields like Shiva's, Dharwesh's, Bhadra's, and Mahesh's. Social scientists have used cotton and clothing to explore the stakes of modern globalization, from investigative journalism like National Public Radio's

Planet Money T-shirt project (National Public Radio 2013) to stories of the life cycle of cotton clothing (Brooks 2015; Sneyd 2016). As commodity chain studies, these works illuminate the hidden links between those who consume cotton and those who produce it, from textile workers to small farmers. This book engages with similar ideas, but my focus is different. I am concerned with how people live global change on the level of the farm field, and what consequences that has for rural well-being—a profound concept in the academic study of rural life that I will take up further in chapter 2. Well-being calls attention to local definitions of and aspirations to success in rural India, encompassing how farmers think about living well, their efforts to claim opportunities historically denied, and the chance to define the terms of their own development (Escobar 2011; Pandian 2009; Rahnema and Bawtree 1997; Walsh 2010).

While some analysts have blamed GM seeds or insects for the agrarian crisis of South India and others celebrate new technologies and programs as means to empower rural economies, I argue that the biggest impact of technologies like GM cotton and organic certification is in the ways that they transform farmer knowledge. It is from this farm-level perspective on the story of Telangana cotton that I invite readers to learn how new technologies change lives. Every season is set in motion by the seemingly small choice that farmers make when they decide which cottonseed to plant. For farmers like Shiva and Mahesh, these choices take place within a bewildering GM seed market or a strict organic regulatory apparatus. These choices bring some farmers fortune and local renown, and others debt and death. Each decision is not made in isolation but is embedded in a deep history of trade and inequality, a global network where biotechnology and supply chains intersect with a local attempt to live well as a cotton farmer.

One of the strengths of qualitative social science is in using seemingly small things to tell the story of global transformations. Anthropologists have used sugar to explore the rise of class and capitalism in the Atlantic (Mintz 1986) and matsutake mushrooms to search for meaning in ecologically and economically disturbed landscapes (Tsing 2015). Cotton, crisis, and the hope for a solution in India tell a story of how global technologies change how farmers make decisions and pursue success on the farm field. In this book, I use seeds as synecdoches, representative elements of larger technological, ecological, and social relationships, to explore the possibilities created by GM and organic visions of agrarian life.

Fundamentally, *Cultivating Knowledge* investigates rural well-being in the context of global change, using the theoretical lens of agricultural knowledge to explore how small cotton farmers in South India become caught up in seismic economic, social, political, and ecological shifts. This book intersects a wide range of scholarship related to agrarian political economy, suicide, agricultural performance, rural distress, and political ecology. Each of these facets sheds light on a larger theme: my contribution to theories of knowledge in contemporary agrarian life. Understanding sustainable farming by looking to agricultural knowledge allows me to make the following specific contributions:

1. GM and organic cotton farmers' seed decisions in India are a point of departure to understand how farmers make decisions, informing debates over farmer decision-making, the diffusion and adoption of new technologies, and the role of different kinds of learning in a neoliberal context where choices are not always choices at all.

2. Agrarian decisions in these two development systems are best understood as constrained choices and as performances, an anthropological and political ecology view of agriculture that illuminates the parallels and divergences in these two mutually exclusive ways of farming.

3. The opportunities, infrastructure, social relationships, and constraints of GM and organic development programs determine how they might promote sustainable livelihoods in the rural developing world.

As an anthropologist I am interested in the ways that new technologies and ideas are put to use every day on the farm. Organic production and conventional agriculture, including GM seeds, do not exist apart from their social context, and so I argue that it is critical to understand the long-term impact that different kinds of development programs have on management knowledge. However, I do not believe that all development is bad or damaging to indigenous technical knowledge. I am cautiously optimistic about many organic, integrated pest management (IPM), fair-trade, and farmer cooperative initiatives that provide consumers with high-quality clothing and provide producers with enough flexibility in their production systems to engage a development that they themselves have helped to shape. Some such programs even ask farmers to produce less cotton and transition to a more diverse set of crops. I will also argue in chapter 4 that it is not GM seeds themselves, but rather the market in which these seeds are distributed that causes the most egregious problems for farmer knowledge. My observations of both biotechnology and organic agriculture are guaranteed to irritate enthusiasts championing their favored technologies.

Yet the challenges of global environmental change and intensifying planetary interconnection ask scientists, policymakers, activists, and anyone curious about the lasting social impacts of new technologies to look beyond these abstractions and understand what happens in the field, and to whom. As potential solutions to agrarian crisis, GM seeds and organic agricultural programs offer farmers different forms of institutional regulation and socioeconomic success, incentivizing some kinds of agricultural knowledge and performances while constraining others. My approach in this book asks readers to move beyond the futuristic promise of GMOs and organic development and focus on the anthropological question, How are farmers learning to use these technologies every day in the field?

LONG HISTORIES AND NEW PROBLEMS IN INDIAN COTTON

Indian small farmers have grown cotton for more than five thousand years, and Indian cotton has dominated the global clothing trade for centuries. The soft, breathable-yet-warm clothes spun by the Asian cottage industry and sold by Arab traders through the fifteenth century enriched empires in India and drove Europeans west in search of a more direct connection to cotton. Indian cotton was an early global commodity, shipped across the Indian Ocean to city-states like Zanzibar or Baghdad, traded to Mediterranean Europeans through Arab intermediaries, and, through the British, sold to the far reaches of transatlantic capitalism. The combination of early industrial capitalism and slavery allowed American production to surpass that of India in the early 1800s, but by the second year of the American Civil War India was again supplying the vast majority of the cotton consumed by the industrial world (Beckert 2014). Only with the global restructuring of agricultural trade and the rise of fertilizer, pesticide, and water-intensive farming since the 1960s has Indian smallholder cotton been forced to share the market with cotton produced by large farmers in the United States, China, and Brazil. Thus, it is surprising that the ancient and impressive Indian cotton sector would gain international renown for an agrarian crisis defined by pest attacks, yield problems, and suicide at the end of the twentieth century.

Since the 1970s, Indian farmers long accustomed to the native Indian cotton, *Gossypium arboreum* L., have increasingly planted a hybrid blend of North American cotton, *Gossypium hirsutum* L. Not only did the American hybrid boast a longer fiber length, better suited to the industrial machinery that spins cotton into yarn, but breeders also found that it produced higher yields than the native Indian species when supplied with fertilizers. Yet rising yields came at a cost, and farmers discovered that nutrient-hungry hybrid cotton was especially susceptible to Asian insect pest attacks. In response, Indian growers steadily increased their pesticide use through the 1990s (Kranthi 2012), and although India was and is among the world's top cotton planters by acreage, individual Indian planters had and continue to have low yields per acre compared with farmers in the USA, Brazil, or China (USDA Foreign Agricultural Service 2015).

Maintaining this intensive smallholder cotton agriculture is costly. During a national survey of pesticide use, toxicologists P. C. Abhilash and Nandita Singh (2009) found that cotton pesticides during the 1990s accounted for almost half of all pesticides sprayed in India, despite covering only 5 percent of the cultivated land. "You didn't want to go inside," one cotton farmer recalled during the survey and interview fieldwork that forms the empirical basis for this book. "During the monsoon season the houses smelled of pesticide, the fields smelled of pesticide—you couldn't get away from it." Increases in the costs of production combined with the ecological toll of increased pesticide and fertilizer use decreased local biodiversity and left farmers with lower yields and thinner profit margins.

Lower profits, increased anxiety, and a wave of farmer suicides composed a trifecta of agrarian distress. Hundreds of millions of people depend on agriculture to make a living in India, where an engaged rural citizenry makes frequent demands on the immense civil bureaucracy and the press freely pursues stories of agrarian distress to challenge state responses. In 2002, the year that GM cotton would be commercially released in India, public health researchers estimate that farmer pesticide poisoning accounted for a third of all suicides around the world (Gunnell et al. 2007). Like Bhadra above, hundreds of thousands of Indian farmers ended their lives by drinking the very pesticides that drove them to desperation between 1995 and 2015 (Menon and Uzramma 2018). The crisis of pest attack had become a crisis of suicide, speaking to a larger existential catastrophe in rural India. As anthropologist Janet Roitman (2013) has shown, policymakers do not use crisis as an objective judgment but as a tool to organize and respond to the chaos of everyday life. From this environment of need and anxiety, two potential solutions, mutually exclusive because of global regulatory standards, presented themselves to Indian cotton farmers: GM seeds and organic agriculture.

POLITICAL ECOLOGY AND DENATURALIZING SUSTAINABLE DEVELOPMENT

When I explain Indian agrarian distress in this way, the story sounds almost inevitable: fundamental problems with the cotton led to difficulties for the people who grew it. Yet small Indian farmers have grown cotton for millennia. What changed? The blame rests less with the biology of cotton than with sociopolitical systems that determine what farmers grow and how they learn about their crops. Political ecology is a way of understanding and interpreting human-environmental interactions that encourages researchers to pay attention to relationships of money, land, and labor, as well as to the shifting ways that people and institutions exercise power over a landscape. According to this way of thinking, India's cotton crisis is best understood as the product of specific historical and material relationships and not as an inevitable outcome of natural processes.

My favorite example of political ecology's ability to denaturalize environmental questions comes from anthropologist Eric Ross (1998), who examines the political factors of the 1845 Irish potato famine. The famine, Ross argues, did not progress because Irish agriculture was vulnerable to blight or even because the Irish peasantry overrelied on a nonbiodiverse potato stock. These are the wrong issues to focus on. Instead, Ross considers the colonial conditions under which Irish peasants sent goods to the British Empire. Unlike most of the material goods in Ireland, potatoes were not taxed by foreign landlords. As the blight decimated potato crops, administrators did not ease their export quotas, and almost all remaining seed potatoes were eaten rather than saved for the next harvest. This does not mean that the Irish stopped producing food. In fact, Ross notes that at the height of the famine, the Irish sent nearly five hundred thousand hogs to England for slaughter, some of which surely would have helped to stave off famine if not for the unrelenting demands of the imperial directors. The idea that such a crisis is natural or inevitable, stemming from overpopulation or monoculture, ignores the political conditions under which such a famine was possible in the first place. Through a combination of qualitative and quantitative research into GM and organic seed choices, I use political ecology and anthropology to understand the roots of Telangana's agrarian distress and study how farmers adapt potential solutions.

From a political ecology perspective, the cotton crisis I highlight above was completely *unnatural*. This agrarian crisis was not an inevitable outcome of people growing cotton, a natural problem inherent to cotton plants or the farmers who grow them. Rather, it was set in motion by a series of social and political acts, including neoliberal policies, the restructuring of Indian agriculture after the green revolution, the introduction of hybrid seeds, and the unleashing of a pesticide treadmill into South Asian pest cycles. Farmer suicides and rural distress rose in tandem with Indian neoliberal economic reforms (Mohanty 2005; Münster 2012), as they did with the rise of neoliberal policies around the world (McMichael 2007). Following the geographer David Harvey (1991, 2007), I will use *neoliberal* in this book to describe policies that loosened state oversight over the agrarian political economy, rolling back state extension services aimed at small and marginal farmers while simultaneously promoting private knowledge and resource production for agricultural inputs that farmers purchased rather than produced. In the agrarian sector, seed production sped up, global technologies like genetically modified traits became more readily available, and farmers came to think of themselves as consumers in a vast market of purchasable options (Flachs 2019). Where before seeds had been the products of public breeding programs or local farmers, the expansion of commercial agribusiness since the 1990s allowed seeds to become choices in a private marketplace—choices that Indian farmers made as individual consumers who bore the full responsibility for their own success or failure. The pressure to choose the right seeds and maximize profits amid rising costs and stagnant yields is leading farmers to increase pesticide and fertilizer applications, plant their cotton more densely, or seek out new technologies like herbicides to try to close the gap.

Both GM seeds and organic agriculture offer visions for what the future of farming could look like. I will discuss the concept of sustainability as it relates to agricultural knowledge further in chapter 2, but because both technologies make claims to a sustainable agriculture, this begs the question: Sustainable in what context? Sustainable for whom? How do farmers learn and adapt that knowledge when facing market and ecological changes? In the model of the GM seed, agriculture continues along the input-intensive path that it has traveled since the birth of industrial agriculture. Sustainability within GM crops assumes that cash crops, monocultures, and state-corporate partnerships will continue to define the logic of agricultural production. Like a business, a farm would ideally maximize its comparative advantage by growing as much of a cash crop as possible, optimizing a set of input investments, including fertilizers, pesticides, and water infrastructure, to gain a profit. A GM cottonseed is thus a sustainable technological intervention in the sense that it produces its own pesticide, reducing the amount that a farmer would have to spray or purchase. Additionally, this pesticide reduction is a major potential benefit of GM cotton for both biodiversity and public health.

Organic agriculture makes different base assumptions about markets and ideal farm management. Sustainability within organic agriculture assumes that elite consumers will pay premiums for ethical nonchemically managed cotton, while producers will sacrifice higher yields in favor of value-added markets and long-term socioecological benefits. Organic cotton production is sustainable in the sense that synthetic pesticides and fertilizers are largely banned and elite consumers compensate for yield losses with price premiums. Both of these visions for the future of agriculture claim sustainability as a function of technology, be it the hardware sense of a GM seed or the software sense of an organic certification. Yet the opportunities of these technologies, or even their efficacy as measured by scientific tests, are neither natural nor inevitable. Rather, they depend on how farmers learn about them and adapt them to their fields. In fact, when we understand sustainability as the product of technological interventions, we as researchers, development experts, farmers, or simply as engaged global citizens fail to understand that such technologies are always part of a larger daily practice.

No book is an island, and so to make sense of seeds and knowledge in India, I engage with scholarship in anthropology, political ecology, and South Asian studies, each of which has made substantial contributions to our understanding of global agrarian change and rural well-being. I will address this scholarship in greater detail in chapter 2, but much influential research on South Asian agricultural development (Besky 2014; Gupta 1998; Pandian 2009; Ramamurthy 2011; D. Sen 2017; Subramanian 2009) pays insufficient attention to the contingencies of seed choice or agricultural decision-making because it focuses on local political organization and farmer narratives to describe agrarian change. Similarly, many influential political ecology approaches (Kloppenburg 2004; Stone 2007; Scoones 2006; Taylor 2014) underplay the role of social performance in farmer decision-making because that data is not ethnographic or farmer-focused enough. Global technological changes in agriculture have raised national cotton yields, lowered costs for consumers, and provided new markets for agribusinesses that sell farm inputs. They have also exacerbated uncertainty and anxiety in rural communities. I argue that agrarian distress is in this way rooted in historical, material, and emotional factors, not simply pest attacks or pesticide overuse that can be solved through new seeds or organic regulations. We cannot understand these affective, sociocultural factors apart from the material political economy. This book aims to bridge political ecology and anthropology by combining empirical data on both social and material factors in agrarian life. In the following chapters, I will show how the political and economic structures governing cotton agriculture shape the following: what farmers are able to do in the field; how agricultural practice drives farmers' agricultural performances as social, economic, and ecological acts; what kind of adaptive agricultural skillsets farmers build as a result; and how that knowledge serves their frustrations and desires as cotton farmers.

While providing excellent analyses of power and political economy, political ecologists have tended to neglect the importance of social performance in studies of agriculture (Flachs and Richards 2018). As I argue in the following chapters, this is a mistake because a farm is a very public stage upon which farmers perform both knowledge and aspiration. This text contributes to social theories of knowledge by integrating anthropological and political ecology perspectives around the idea of performance, situating the aspiration for well-being amid rural distress as an epistemological moment. Anxiety and desire shape decision-making and therefore shape knowledge on these farms. As such, a qualitative examination of how farmers make decisions and engage development institutions ranging from the state to agribusiness to organic NGOs is crucial to understanding how these technologies might improve the lives of vulnerable farmers.

By understanding agrarian life through a combination of anthropology and political ecology, I explore how the agrarian crisis of India's cotton sector came to be, and how solutions reflect existing structures of power and politics in the natural environment. Political ecology is increasingly concerned with what people do, a question of human-environmental relationships that determine how we learn. In this book, I will argue that the practice of knowledge and the performance of identity are intertwined in the context of agricultural development, leaving measurable traces on the landscape with real implications for rural well-being. This is not an inevitable progression, but one that follows from specific economic and political agendas and spreads through established channels of power.

GENETICALLY MODIFIED AND ORGANIC VISIONS FOR THE FUTURE

Throughout this book I will refer to *organic farmers* and *GM farmers*. I use these terms as a shorthand to reference the agricultural, social, and economic worlds in which these farmers live and to illuminate the parallels between these two systems. Both organic agriculture and genetic modification are technologies that emphasize off-farm expertise, offer paths to development, can destabilize adaptive knowledge, can help farmers live well by growing cotton, and can reinforce existing inequalities. All of the farmers described in this book own relatively small holdings compared to global agricultural producers elsewhere. A large Telangana cotton farmer may own ten acres, but many own fewer than five. Large and small Telangana farms employ a mix of household labor, locally produced technology, and mechanical or chemical management tools sold by agribusiness, and most produce a mixture of market and subsistence crops. It would be equally accurate to call GM farmers fertilizer or pesticide farmers to distinguish them from the organic farmers. I have chosen to refer to seed choice here to call attention to the seed as the first decision that farmers make, one that sets them on a path that includes fertilizers, pesticides, shops, corporate breeders and branders, and defines success through yields and returns on the market. In planting non-GM seeds, organic farmers enter into a different set of social and economic relationships, embracing a variety of socioeconomic safety nets provided by organic developers, a different set of agricultural management strategies, and a vision of agricultural success beyond high yields. Seed choice connects global stories about sustainability to farmer knowledge, local socioeconomic support systems, and the ultimate governance of these agricultural economies.

Seed breeding around the world has become an increasingly technological enterprise conducted not by farmers using local seed knowledge but by scientific and commercial breeders trained in industry and university settings (Kloppenburg 2004). While it is true that the earliest farmers changed the genetic code of plants and animals through domestication and selection, this gradual coevolution is very different from the industry-driven practices of contemporary global agriculture. Far more specific and controlled than traditional population improvement, GM technology gives agricultural scientists exact control over certain genetic traits. For Indian cotton at the moment that I write, this trait is pest resistance. GM herbicide-tolerant cotton is fast approaching, but this trait is not currently widespread in India. GM cottonseeds are also called Bt cottonseeds because they take their name from genes derived from the bacterium *Bacillus thuringiensis*. This soil-dwelling organism naturally produces proteins fatal to insects in the Lepidopteran order—including cotton bollworms. GM cotton has been modified to include those same genes, and so to produce the same insecticidal proteins without the need for insect sprays. At the time of Bt cotton's introduction to India in 2002, Lepidopteran sprays targeting cotton bollworms accounted for most pesticide applications and for the most toxic and environmentally persistent pesticides used on Indian cotton fields (Kranthi 2012; Veettil, Krishna, and Qaim 2016). GM cotton, at least initially, could kill the bollworms without a single spray. "It saved us," recalled Kappa, an elderly farmer who helps her son manage three acres of cotton. Over a cup of tea, she lamented many of the changes she has seen in her village since the 1970s: the family has grown smaller and more separated, labor costs have risen, many of her friends suffer from diabetes, and even the rice (*Oryza sativa* L.) tastes worse than she remembers as a child. Bt cotton stands alone as a beneficial change over that time period, one that raised incomes and yields while reducing pesticide sprays. "Half of the farmers in this village would have committed suicide without Bt cotton," she explained solemnly.

Prior to the introduction of GM cotton, commercial seed breeders became interested in pest-resistant traits because the insecticidal Bt genes could be bred into hybrid cottonseeds, a growing market among Indian farmers. Hybrid seeds, which are not saved but purchased new each year, grow best if farmers also purchase the fertilizers that allow these plants to convert nitrogen, phosphorus, and potassium into a flurry of cotton bolls. In this bargain for higher yields, farmers came to rely on expertise vested in state extension services, universities, input shops, and commercial agribusiness. Farmers who plant monocultures of cotton hybrids bred to respond to the proscribed combination of fertilizers and irrigation rely on pesticides to keep their plants safe from the bollworms, whiteflies, leafhoppers (*Amrasca biguttula biguttula*), and other insects that would feed on their crop. In fact, all of a GM farmer's key inputs are produced off the farm: pesticides and fertilizers purchased from shops, machines leased from local dealers or rich farmers, seeds bred by laboratories, and even planting density recommendations from university extension services.

Seed selection locks farmers into this kind of agriculture, and so the ways that farmers choose seeds is important. As I discuss in chapter 4, farmers are increasingly "herding" (Stone, Flachs, and Diepenbrock 2014) en masse to plant particular seed brands. Advertisements, black-market brokers, and even rich or highly regarded farmers sway villages and whole districts to plant seeds with great enthusiasm. However, the faith that farmers place in those seeds is short lived. Most farmers switch to a different seed brand every year in the search for the best yields, intensifying a process ongoing since at least 2007 (Stone 2007). Like hybrid seeds or mechanical planters before them, GM seeds represent a piecewise commodification of farmer skills (Goodman, Sorj, and Wilkinson 1987) that lead farmers to trade concerns of crop breeding or plant management for concerns of seed brand choice and capital investment (Kloppenburg 2004). Importantly, the knowledge vested in this agricultural innovation rests in boardrooms and biotechnology labs near cities like St. Louis, Missouri, or Hyderabad, Telangana—not on farms.

Information can also be commodified and sold to farmers on certified organic farms. Organic agriculture became nationally institutionalized in 2002, the same year that GM cotton was commercially released to Indian farmers. On all farms, the choices that farmers make pass through many levels of social mediation: caste, gender, farmer holdings size, education, advertising, or scientific development and advising at plant science stations to name a few. But on certified organic cotton farms, Indian farmers must additionally conform to national and international regulations determining how they manage their farms. To secure the certified organic label, farmers submit to audits as well as to visits from donors who want to use their stories of empowerment or development to add value for consumers at the end of organic cotton's supply chain (Franz and Hassler 2010; D. Sen and Majumder 2011). To comply with organic standards, various aspects of agricultural knowledge are not merely socially mediated, but actively taught on these farms. However, this relationship of knowledge and power is complex. While organic development programs teach agricultural methods required for certification, farmers "ground-truth" organic regulations, adapting rules and suggestions to local agricultural needs. Sometimes, those farmers learn to leverage their roles as village intermediaries, gaining special access to off-farm resources and social renown as local celebrities. Their influence and success then encourage others, who may be skeptical, to join the program. The shifting target of success that farmers hope to achieve can depend as much on being a good student or business partner as on being a good land manager, a topic I'll discuss further in chapters 4 and 5.

Anthropologist Sarah Besky (2014), drawing on geographer Julie Guthman, has described how ethical supply chains contribute to a "third world agrarian imaginary." There, American and European consumers imagine the agroenvironment of the Global South as a naturally occurring landscape divorced from any particular history. This allows these consumers to see cropping systems or agricultural crises as states of nature rather than outcomes of sociopolitical histories. Although Besky and Guthman write of organic and fair-trade supply chains, this rhetoric is also true for GM seeds, whose fiercest proponents accuse critics of sentencing farmers in the developing world to death (Paarlberg 2002). Following missteps in European and American markets in the late 1990s, the rhetoric of GM agriculture has shifted from a narrative of logical, modern agriculture for the industrial world, to one of uplifting and promise for the developing world (Jasanoff 2005; Schurman and Munro 2010). This period coincided with the first international regulations guaranteeing value-added organic markets for goods produced across the globe, and so, as a counter to the crisis-resolving narrative of biotechnology, organic agriculture proponents promoted their own vision of agricultural development.

GM and organic crops have become subsumed by a larger debate over the future of agriculture. Organic consumption and GM seed technology both enable supply chains in which supporters promote the health and environmental benefits of cotton consumption (Charles 2001; Guthman 2004; Pollan 2006), the promise of increased wages, and the fight against ecological devastation in the developing world (R. L. Bryant and Goodman 2004; Paarlberg 2001).* As the nation with the largest number of small farmers, a well-established narrative of crisis and underdevelopment, highly developed civil and scientific sectors, and the first developing nation where GM crops would be grown by small farmers, India became the battleground for these two visions.

Although biotech advocates claim that Bt cotton has assuaged the agrarian crisis, GM seeds' role is not totally clear (Kathage and Qaim 2012; Kranthi 2012; Plewis 2014; Stone 2011, 2013), in part because it is difficult to separate the effects of any new seed from other factors in agriculture. GM technology impacts farmer lives only insofar as it is filtered through the social politics of shops, extension offices, laboratories, and caste relationships in which farmers learn. Organic agriculture is similarly dependent on these social relationships. Numerous scientific studies highlight the benefits of household-produced farm inputs and diversified planting strategies (Eyhorn, Ramakrishnan, and Mäder 2007; Forster et al. 2013; Raghupati and Prasad 2009; Desmond 2013) without

---

* Ethnographic work on fair-trade tea (Besky 2014) and coffee (West 2012) has shown that added costs for consumers do not always translate to higher wages for producers.

considering the complex socioeconomic reasons that farmers participate in organic development programs. Such research problematically asserts organic agriculture's success as a technological advancement rather than as a successful partnership between farmers, consumers, and NGO or corporate promoters.

The spread of GM seeds and organic agriculture in India have real, material stakes for farmers around the world. Indian small farmers plant more GM crops than small farmers in any other developing nation (C. James 2015), and the only legal GM crop is Bt cotton. In fact, one third of the land where cotton is grown on Earth is in India, more than any other country (USDA Foreign Agricultural Service 2015), and more than 95 percent of Indian cotton is genetically modified (Cotton Corporation of India 2014). Since farmers began commercially planting GM seeds in India, bollworm sprays have decreased, yields have increased, and suicides have plateaued. Yet despite regulations that prohibit GM cotton from sale in organic markets, even when it is grown without the use of chemical fertilizers or pesticides, Indian organic farmers also produce 74 percent of the organic cotton sold in the global market (Willer and Lernoud 2016). There is no clearer case than India to ask how biotechnology and alternative agriculture create possibilities for sustainable rural well-being in the developing world.

SITUATING TELANGANA FARMERS: SITES, RESEARCH DESIGN, AND METHODOLOGIES

This research is set in a very specific time and place. The crisis surrounding cotton agriculture in the semiarid Deccan Plateau where I began working in 2012 defines my research questions and structures the stakes for knowledge and development. This book focuses on three districts in Telangana, India, formerly the north-central region of Andhra Pradesh. I base the findings in this book on research conducted over sixteen months and four consecutive cotton-growing seasons during 2012–16, as well as a later trip in 2018, which I began as a graduate student at Washington University in St. Louis. In total, I asked 394 GM-cotton-planting farmers about 4,599 seed choices and 108 organic-cotton-planting farmers about 851 seed choices. This longitudinal approach allowed me to see changes in how farmers made decisions about which seeds to plant and to develop long-term relationships with the farmers who were patient enough to share their time and energy with me. Although my work and my errors are my own, I have worked in collaboration with Glenn Davis Stone, my PhD supervisor at Washington University, who conducted research in this area during 2002–10.

The villages where I worked reflect the diversity of social, agricultural, and economic opportunities that Telangana farmers face. Farmers in this area grow cotton, rice, and maize (*Zea mays* L.), along with a number of flowers and vegetables for their kitchen needs. Cotton is typically sown in June, once the monsoon season has begun, and is harvested from November until early March, if farmers are lucky to have several high-quality cycles of fruiting and flowering. Many farmers then plant maize in the three months between cotton harvest and sowing. In the Warangal and Medak districts, farmers often grew one crop of rice in the rainy season and one crop in the winter months, while organic farmers in the Adilabad district grew sorghum (*Sorghum bicolor* [L.] Moench) during that time. After the harvest of each of these crops, farmers bring their wares to urban markets where they haggle with buyers and gamble that today's price will be better than tomorrow's. Because these dynamics vary considerably between organic and GM farmers, I will discuss them in greater detail in chapters 4 and 5. Although I focus on the agrarian economy because this is a book about agricultural knowledge, the communities in Telangana also have an active wage economy. As children across India receive better access to education, they are increasingly seeking nonagricultural work in cities like Warangal, Hyderabad, Bangalore, and Delhi. Many are now sending remittances home, and this new geography of youth employment is sure to reshape India over the long term. Still, agriculture is a major economic sector in the villages I describe in this book. Even youth who have left their rural villages and who have no interest in farmwork maintain important ties to their family's land. Thus do changes in agricultural knowledge impact rural well-being even for members of the household tangential to farming.

The diverse places where farmers work their fields affect their access to markets and the calculations in their decision-making. The villages described in this book represent different soil types amenable to cotton agriculture; differing access to infrastructure, including electricity and irrigation; a range of experience growing cotton; and different ethnic compositions. Differences in proximity to cities and in-village resources enable a range of agricultural possibilities for farmers, including access to off-farm experts or the ease of using agricultural inputs. Finally, the villages practicing organic agriculture in which I worked represent farmers working with NGOs as well as corporations (map 1).

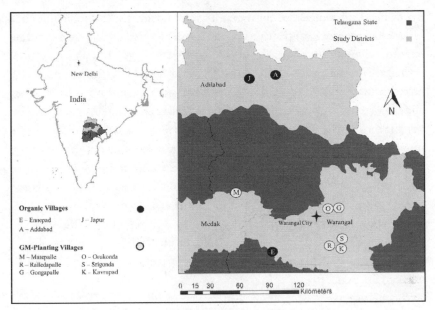

MAP 1. Map of research area.

Attention to this nuance helps me to keep track of the variation in seed choices and experiences among Indian cotton farmers.

Much as race and class influence the geography of opportunity in the Indiana city where I wrote this book, ethnic and caste distinctions in rural Telangana influence where resources and infrastructure are built. Although caste and tribal discrimination have been officially outlawed since the 1950s, historical disenfranchisements ripple into the present in the form of generational wealth, land ownership, influence within agricultural development projects, and other kinds of social status. The Indian census offers three caste categories and a category reserved for tribal farmers not belonging to the formal caste system: scheduled castes (SC), the lowest castes of people formerly called untouchable or harijans; backward castes (BC), less disenfranchised people historically working in commerce and agriculture; and open castes (OC), the majority who do not receive caste-based benefits or reservations in government or university settings based on historical disenfranchisement. Members of scheduled tribes (ST) in rural Telangana live outside villages proper on more marginal land, follow different customs, and often speak a different language than Telugu, the majority language of Telangana. Even fifty years ago, many OC families would have dominated land ownership and skilled labor in the village. This socioeconomic history has a contemporary impact on the infrastructure and resources available to these communities, and each village has its own specific history.

In the Telangana villages where I worked and lived, SC, BC, and OC people tend to cluster near others of similar caste, and each caste area has kiosk shops and minor temples. For example, Kavrupad, a village of several hundred people, has one seed and agricultural input shop, although most farmers prefer to buy seeds from Warangal when given the chance. Kavrupad farmers grow cotton on mostly red clay soil and reflect a diverse caste and socioeconomic spectrum. These villages have regular access to electricity, houses are a combination of concrete and brick, and roads running through the villages provide regular public bus and private autorickshaw transportation to larger cities. In addition to the state-run public school, Kavrupad has an innovative NGO-run school where I myself have taught English to primary school students and donated time and money.

By contrast, tribal communities like Ralledapalle, home to Shiva from the opening of this chapter, tend to live in hamlets (*thandas*) adjacent to villages with poorer infrastructure and poorer access to shops and transportation routes. Ralledapalle is only two kilometers away from Kavrupad, but it is socially a world apart. The road to this village is unpaved, buses have no stops in the *thandas*, electricity is less reliable, businesses are rare, and houses are a mix of concrete, brick, mud-brick, tin, wood, and palm thatch. *Thandas* throughout Telangana are established on more marginal hilly soil, and ST villagers typically travel to towns for most services and for transportation to nearby cities. There, ethnic ST people who speak the state language of Telugu as a second language may face derision from shop owners or higher-caste residents who see them as unwelcome, lower-class others. During my observations in agricultural input shops, sales representatives were often dismissive of or openly hostile to ST buyers, who finished their transactions quickly. After, shop owners would often turn to me and make disparaging remarks about ST farmers, calling them ignorant and backward. Near Warangal, Telangana *thandas* are almost exclusively populated by ethnic Lambadi or Banjara people. Categorized as a criminal tribe under British leadership, speaking a different language, and holding a different set of religious and social traditions, Lambadi people settled outside main Telangana villages after migrating from Northwest India in the early twentieth century (Naik 2000).* The differences in opportunities for travel, school, and infrastructure can be extreme across these ethnic boundaries even when the distances are minor.

GATHERING DATA

A social scientist's research methods always flow from the research question. To understand how farmers learn to make seed decisions structured within village and global manifestations of power, I employ a mix of quantitative and qualitative methods that track different types of learning. Qualitative research methods include interviews, focus groups, and participant observation, while quantitative methods include ethnobotanical counts, geographic information system (GIS) data collection, household surveys of demographic variables, and seed surveys. Data from these survey and spatial instruments provided information that could be statistically analyzed, quantifying farmer decisions in response to yields, costs, or the decisions of neighbors. For instance, I could better understand how farmers learned from each other by seeing how their seed choices changed not only through time, recorded in a survey, but through space, visible with a GIS. However, to know what questions to ask and how to interpret patterns that emerged from these data, I had to conduct interviews, participate and observe in daily life, and walk alongside farmers in seed shops and rows of cotton. These things do not lend themselves to quantification.

In anthropological fieldwork, these data are . . . messy. I relied on farmers to give accurate accounts of their fields and lives in areas where people themselves do not keep written records. The surveys that I administered asked those farmers to then develop justifications for their seed choices, even though I was there to study how difficult it is to decide which seed to plant. When asked to dredge up reasons for their seed decisions, most farmers sighed and said, "*Manci digubadi annakunthunnanu,*" literally, "I'm hoping for a good yield."† On Telangana cotton farms, yield gives some farmers a way to measure a return on an investment and provides a visible signal of their farming prowess, a clear sign of success

---

* The Criminal Tribes Act, enacted between 1871 and 1924, defined ethnic and social communities as habitually criminal, restricting their freedom of movement and in some cases forcing men to report regularly to the police. Their historical disenfranchisement ripples into the present. Anand Pandian (2009) describes the postcolonial struggles of the Kallars, another formerly criminal tribe.
† Although I mostly translate Telugu phrases into English, I will transliterate the most meaningful and important terms.

among rural farmers. What is a farm if not a stage on which to proclaim to one's neighbors? Some are simply trying to make do, earning and working without the imperative to carefully document, analyze, and improve every aspect of their farm management. Others said they were driven by a more anxious desire for success in an agricultural economy where the means to and meanings of success are not always clear. I learned from these conversations that wanting more can be very far from knowing how to get it.

As an anthropologist, I rely on my participation in and observations of daily life in these villages to contextualize the data I collected. In addition to the conversations that inevitably arise when getting to know people, I typically spent hours with each farmer discussing aspects of life beyond the survey questions. Armed with this qualitative information I critically examined the quantitative data I collected on seed choices, and vice versa. The gaps between farmers' professed logic and the years of seed choices that I observed inform my ultimate conclusions on the social politics of farm management decisions. Living in these villages, teaching schoolchildren, photographing weddings, planting seeds alongside farmers, and harvesting the crops gave me insights into daily life and the ways in which farmers approach their work that I would not have been able to document otherwise. Although each survey was likely to turn into an extended structured interview depending on the farmers' time and patience in that particular moment, I also conducted and transcribed more formal interviews with shop owners, NGO officials, plant scientists, key informants on conventional and organic farms, and focus groups of five or more farmers. As a foreign male researcher, interested in decisions made at the household level, the majority (about 75 percent) of the farmers whom I spoke with were men. On these farms, men usually, although not exclusively, purchase seeds and other inputs, plow fields, sow fertilizers, and spray pesticides, while women usually weed and pick the cotton. The discrepancy between these kinds of practices and resulting knowledges is an important part of this story, which I discuss in chapter 4. However, I must acknowledge that my data on these decisions are biased toward the male heads of the household, who felt most comfortable speaking with me. I was able to speak to more women in the context of organic agriculture, in part because these programs make a special effort to include women in the agricultural decision-making process, as I discuss in chapters 5 and 6.

Most days, fieldwork consisted of waking early in the morning and accompanying a research assistant to farmers' fields and houses to conduct surveys. While these surveys allowed me to collect quantitative information and thus to speak to agricultural economists, development experts, and environmental scientists, they served a more practical purpose. Survey work is a legible form of research to Indian farmers, who encounter development experts and rural sociologists in their lives as farmers. Along with my volunteer work at the local school, the survey gave me a reason to be living in these villages for months at a time. Like many anthropologists working in rural areas, my status as a curious outsider was a source of initial confusion: I was not buying cotton, auditing organic producers, converting anyone to Christianity, or giving out government aid. What *was* I doing, and why didn't I leave after a few days like so many other outsiders? Luckily for me, a social scientist is a reasonable thing for a foreigner to be in India. These questions faded over time, as they do in all long-term fieldwork, replaced by the wry teasing that I ought to stop studying, get married, and have children like a normal person. The surveys got my foot in the door, a prelude to a day spent picking cotton, planting seeds, or riding with farmers to the market. Through these tasks, a seed survey can give way to larger conversations about debt, anxiety, hopes and frustrations, or aspirations for children. This mix of research tools is my effort as an anthropologist to triangulate different perspectives on knowledge and daily life in search of the larger question: What are the lived experiences of these visions for sustainable agriculture?

BM SEEDS, PESTICIDE, AND SUICIDE

Despite my intention to confine my research to seed choices, these choices exist within the larger context of farmer suicide. The primary thrust of my academic research has been to understand how farmers manage an agricultural landscape given new tools. This alone has been fertile ground to explore family dramas and development anxieties—seed decisions, far from rational economic calculations, are infused with social and cultural values. Indeed, the bewildering market of cottonseeds reminds me of the largely meaningless choices that I face when deciding among dozens of brands of toothpaste in my local Indiana supermarket. Who cares if I choose minty fresh over whitening? The difference, of course, is that my livelihood and standing in my community does not depend on that choice. Toothpaste does not commit me to a season of economic life. Anthropologists are trained to consider the broader contexts and histories in the communities where we work. While I am not an expert on suicide or desperation, it hangs over this project like summer heat waiting to be broken by a violent monsoon. Farmer suicide is the most dramatic outcome of the agrarian crisis that spurred GM seeds and organic agriculture to reach out to cotton farmers. All nine villages where I met with farmers had stories of suicide because both Telangana and the Warangal district where I conducted most of this research were hit especially hard by farmer suicides. Now, those deaths have become well publicized through local media, international journalism, and academic publications.

Both GM and organic cotton agriculture claim to provide the solution to suicide, a phenomenon far too complex to be reduced to a simple bad harvest. Emile Durkheim, one of modern anthropology's foundational thinkers, explained suicide not as an individual act but as socially embedded and inextricable from cultural context (Durkheim 1897). In this tradition, I do not understand Indian farmer suicides as a direct result of the spread of GM cotton, as would the most vociferous Bt cotton critics (Shiva et al. 2002; Peled 2011). Neither would I argue that GM cotton is a cure for farmer distress and suicide, as would the strongest proponents of that technology (Monsanto Company 2017; Qaim 2010). Instead, I argue, with most social scientists, that farmer suicides and agrarian crisis in India are related to the larger vulnerabilities of neoliberal rural life in India: the economic need to purchase more inputs and produce more profits to satisfy creditors in a transforming web of rural relationships (Gruère and Sengupta 2011; Taylor 2011); the social need to perform well, buy well, and provide well for a community undergoing rapid socioeconomic change (L. Bryant and Garnham 2015; Münster 2012; Pandian 2009); and the ecological needs to secure land fertility, water, pest management, or seed stocks that sustain this long tradition of agricultural stewardship (Gold 2003; Gutierrez et al. 2015; Ludden 1999).

Indian farmers are not unique in experiencing a crisis in the new normal of agriculture. During and following the American dust bowl, American agriculture was transformed through mechanization and the growth in agricultural inputs: purchased seeds, an explosion in hired labor, fertilizer, pesticides, and expertise from the growing agricultural input industry. These transformations led to massive increases in crop yields alongside suicide, ecological degradation, and the destabilization of farming communities. Faced with the industrial image of farms as factories, American farmers increasingly turned to experts for advice and inputs (Fitzgerald 2003). Those who remained in rural communities found decreasing profits and dwindling opportunities as public resources, blue-collar jobs, and political capital moved away from farmer enclaves now struggling with high unemployment, hate groups, drug use, and chronic poverty (Davidson 1996; Goldschmidt 1978; Reding 2009). The green revolution, an international effort led by the United States to introduce this model of capital-intensive agriculture to small farmers in Asia, Africa, and Latin America, brought infrastructure, seeds, fertilizers, and pesticides to millions of new farmers. These resources transformed not just how farmers grow crops, but also relationships between farmers and laborers, the ways in which labor and capital are organized, the calculations that young people make when aspiring to be farmers rather than engineers or doctors, and the role that the state plays in daily life (Cullather 2013; Ross 1998). As international markets liberalized in the 1990s, the globalization of industrial agriculture brought these new social relationships, agricultural inputs, aspirations, and ways to conceive of rural communities to small farmers around the planet (McMichael 2007). It is rarely easy to be a farmer.

The scope of farmer suicides is hard to calculate because the definitions of both farmers and suicides vary between countries. Reports from the United States (Stallones 1990), India (Mohanty 2005), the United Kingdom (Stark et al. 2006), Australia (Judd et al. 2006), and of global rural communities generally (Hirsch 2006; Behere and Bhise 2009) suggest that suicide rates are much higher for farmers than for nonfarmers in many countries. Much of the scholarship in farmer suicide has been focused on India in the wake of neoliberal reforms, where public services decreased and farmers became more exposed to global market forces. Parsing out the exact causal relationships between suicide and cotton agriculture is likely impossible, as each case will have its own idiosyncrasies. As was the case for Bhadra above, it may be equally relevant to discuss neoliberal trade policies, cottonseed uncertainty, and fears of adultery without ever claiming that any one is the single cause of a suicide.

Long controlled by a central government, India's economic policymakers began relaxing regulations and price controls in the 1990s (Mukherji 2014). Seeds, fertilizers, and pesticides were previously distributed at government-mandated maximum retail prices. These inputs were sold by government-controlled shops and rarely distributed equally to all who desired them. With neoliberal reforms, these products received new competition, demand, and innovation from a freer market. As the farmer market grew, so too did demand for credit to fill the gaps in seasonal agricultural work between sowing and harvest. Simultaneously, India's profoundly rural identity experienced new pulls from urban centers offering prestige through not land ownership but university education, technology, brand consciousness, and city living. Rural socioeconomic life, always in flux, experienced a seismic shift in the ways that communities related to each other and to the land.

Debt is a way of life in Telangana farming communities, where seasonal harvests repay seasonal loans. But new expectations of how to live cut deeper than rising costs banked against rising returns. In the mid-1990s, local newspapers, government officials, and NGO workers realized that cotton farmers were drinking pesticide to kill themselves in shocking numbers. Across the central cotton belt, in Telangana and Maharashtra, the problem received special attention as farmers were particularly impoverished and often lacked irrigation infrastructure that would stabilize cotton farming. Farmers described themselves as desperate, squeezed by socioeconomic pressures and cut adrift from government assistance that they had come to expect (Menon and Uzramma 2018; Mohanty 2005; Parthasarathy and Shameem 1998). Large-scale analyses of cotton farmer suicide are cautious, noting that the gradual erosion of public and local safety nets is more to blame for spikes in suicide than cotton agriculture itself (R. S. Deshpande and Arora 2010; Gruère and Sengupta 2011; Plewis 2014), which has existed for millennia in India. As statistician Ian Plewis (2014) shows, Indian farmer suicides are highly variable across India, shifting not as a function of GM cotton adoption but of local state resources and community support. Yet suicides crested and then plateaued in 1998, providing an opportunity for GM seeds and organic agriculture to present themselves as solutions to farmers.

GM seeds continue the agrarian problem above. They are not, as some critics charge, a cause of it. Yet GM seeds are often fertilizer and water intensive, and the seeds themselves are slightly more expensive. Farmers rapidly switch between seed brands in a desperate search for the best and most popular brand, with little understanding of what this means or how to judge it. The seeds are not, in this sense, innocent. Such seeds are hardly "terminator" (Shiva et al. 2002) seeds in the sense that they produce sterile cotton or threaten the reproductive capabilities of other crops. But they may be approaching what anthropologist Ann Gold (2003) calls vanishing objects, relational things no longer fully embedded in a world of cyclicality and reciprocity. Farmers buy these seeds to gain profits, reducing agricultural work to a search for the biggest and best yields, and they see the failure to achieve this limited vision of agricultural success as a failure to achieve as a farmer in general. Anthropologist Elaine Desmond (2017) has shown how cotton farmers accept these new limitations on rural life, including both neoliberal markets and poorly understood GM seeds believed to damage the landscape. More damning than increased costs are the increasingly narrow possibilities for living well as a cotton farmer.

One final note demands clarification if we consider GM cottonseeds in the context of global environmental change and health: pesticide contamination. Undeniably, sprays for bollworms, the target pest of Bt cotton, have decreased dramatically since Bt cotton was adopted by farmers across India. Bollworm sprays were among the most toxic and persistent pesticides in cotton fields, and GM cotton is rightly credited for this dramatic reduction (Veettil, Krishna, and Qaim 2016). Yet since the late 2000s, when most farmers adopted Bt cotton, total pesticide sprays in the cotton sector have actually increased over their pre-GM levels (Kranthi 2014), the result of increases in sprays for nontarget pests. The logic of pesticide sprays transcends ecological necessity, as was explained to me during one interview with a farmer named Malothu. "You have to treat the crop like it's your child, working hard and being attentive to its food and protection." I was sitting in the shade with Malothu in the late summer, when cotton flowers were beginning to give way to fat cotton bolls. Humans wait eagerly for these bolls to erupt into white, fluffy cotton, and insect pests match their enthusiasm. His field was not yet under attack, but he was preparing to spray nonetheless because the farmer who owned the field next to him was preparing to spray. To avoid spraying on a day when his neighbors sprayed would broadcast his laziness to the rest of the village, signaling his unwillingness to work toward the communal good of killing insects lurking nearby. There is a competitive edge to this, of course, in a place where success is tracked so closely to yields. "You should always seek to produce more than your neighbors. If they spray four times, you have to spray five. That way, you'll always have the best yield," Malothu explained.

Globally, hundreds of thousands of people die each year from acute or long-term pesticide poisoning, not counting those who ingest it as a form of suicide (Dawson et al. 2010; Maumbe and Swinton 2003; Rupa, Reddy, and Reddi 1991). This can be difficult to explain to a readership in a society where toxic risks are labeled and warnings generally obeyed. On Telangana cotton farms, spraying, weeding, and picking cotton is done by hand, most often by poorer and lower-caste people without land of their own; by young people; and by women. The problem is not that farmers are simply too stupid to realize that the pesticides are harmful—pesticides are often deceptively labeled, farmers lack access to masks or full-body protective gear (let alone to protective clothing suitable for spraying by hand for hours in tropical heat and humidity), and the immediate threat of insects often takes precedence over the long-term threat of pesticide poisoning for heavily indebted farmers. Like the farmers described by geographer Ryan Galt (2009) and anthropologist Seth Holmes (2013), Telangana cotton farmers describe incidences of "bad faith," in which they knowingly experience pesticide exposure but choose to believe that it will not cause long-term harm. What else, farmers have told all of us, can they do?

Bt cotton mitigates exposure to the most devastating pesticides by reducing sprays necessary for tobacco bollworms, but pickers and farmers are still exposed to pesticides that persist on plants, skin, and clothing, where they cause headaches, nausea, dermatological damage, and DNA damage (Venkata et al. 2016). Pesticides fall on the exposed feet of farmers who spray in open-toed, bright, plastic flip-flops; they spill when stored inside one-room homes shared by the whole family; they drip off of the hands that farm workers use to eat meals during farmwork; and they are washed into the rivers where people bathe and fish. Sometimes a farmer will spray with a hand crank, limiting their exposure to pesticide mist. Other times, a farmer will employ a motorized

FIGURE 2. Pesticide spraying for nontarget pests in a GM cotton field. Photo by Andrew Flachs.

sprayer alongside two friends, relatives, or hired workers. The sprayer, typically a man, carries a fifty-pound pack through the cotton field, producing
a steady stream of pressurized poison that settles both on the cotton and on
his clothes; another person walks behind him carrying a metal pot of water
mixed with pesticide to refill the pack when necessary; a third person is tasked
with bringing pots of water from pipes to the center of the field where the
pesticide is mixed. Within minutes, everyone is covered in a fine pesticide mist
(figure 2). In exchange for a photograph with his prized bullocks, one farmer
allowed me to watch as he took over four hours to spray his six-acre field.
Worried that the monsoon rains would wash the pesticide off his cotton, he
had hastily bought a cheaper, generic-brand poison from a local shop known
to carry expired chemicals. "It was a waste," he told me bitterly a few days
later. The pesticide had only killed about a third of the insects eating his crop.
Worried about future losses, he ultimately had to travel to a larger town with
a better agricultural shop to buy a more powerful pesticide. "What if this one
doesn't work either?" I asked. He shrugged. "I'll have to get something even
stronger," he answered, stating the obvious.

Most cotton fields are sparingly intercropped with food crops and small
fruit trees to take advantage of the field gaps where cotton fails to germinate
(Flachs 2015). While providing a reservoir of agrobiodiversity and food security,
such crops are also covered in cotton pesticides when farmers spray. When confronted with the potential danger of eating recently sprayed cherry tomatoes
grown next to his cotton, one farmer turned over a cotton leaf to reveal leafhoppers, saying, "Look, the sprays aren't hurting the insects, and they won't hurt us."
Looking at children in other fields gathering vegetables for the evening meal,
we ate the tomatoes. Modern life in a neoliberal state, as Ulrich Beck (1992)
has described, demands that we accept these risks and their lack of governance.
Each of us begins to see these risks as individual choices rather than political
structures. Political ecology, with its denaturalizing lens, and anthropology, with
its attention to daily life, help to illuminate what is at stake as we navigate the
world of what seems logical, natural, obvious, or inevitable.

CHAPTER SUMMARY

As a field balanced between social science, natural science, and the humanities, anthropology draws liberally from different disciplines to make arguments

about the ways that people live their lives. The arguments in this book draw from social theories of performance, identity, knowledge, and political ecology, and I will reference different kinds of data, data collection, and analysis in each chapter. This is because a topic as diverse as "knowledge" requires a triangulation of both qualitative and quantitative methods. Ultimately, farmer learning is a lens to understand how people understand, adapt, and react to global trends like capitalism and agricultural development. To establish the theoretical vocabulary of this book, the second chapter contextualizes the intellectual history of the anthropology of knowledge, subjectivity, and practice that I will be engaging throughout.

The third chapter places these latest developments in the cotton sector into a historical trajectory. To understand the importance of cotton agriculture for India and development projects writ large, it is helpful to see the development of the networks of trade, finance, labor, germplasm, and expertise that have accompanied cotton over the last thousand years. Beginning in the mid-1800s but accelerating after Indian independence and the green revolution, American and European foreign policy has played an important role in agricultural development in India. The spread of both GM and organic technologies reflect a newer push for sustainable agricultural development, and the foreign regulatory structure of both agriculture systems has adjusted in response to India's uniquely contestable and regulatory apparatus.

The next two chapters contrast the specific experiences of farmers growing GM cottonseeds and farmers participating in organic cotton development programs. Chapter 4 describes how and what GM cotton farmers learn given the extreme constraints on their seed knowledge. GM cotton agriculture provides an especially poor set of conditions for agricultural experimentation, but this breakdown in the creation and adaptation of agroecological knowledge stems from cotton's neoliberal market. Chapter 5 discusses the ways in which farmers learn to work with new kinds of plants, authorities, and incentives that underwrite their production on organic farms. Here, more than among GM farmers, learning to perform for visiting buyers and learning how to work with agricultural institutions is just as important to farmer success as making well-informed seed choices. Both chapters 4 and 5 draw heavily on data collected as a participant observer of farmer experimentation and on survey data. Each chapter measures yields and seed choices with some degree of statistical analysis while placing those numbers in their ethnographic context.

The following chapter provides a qualitative description of the ways that farmers navigate the social politics of agricultural development in Telangana. This leads me to explore the concept of performance, investigating how social capital, charisma, or cries for help shape the narrative of agricultural development. I am agnostic about organic development as a way to make a living, arguing that performance and transformation can be paths to a new and promising way to make a living by growing cotton.

Seeds in India make possible different paths in rural life, determining how farmers can aspire to success or contemplate suicide. *Cultivating Knowledge* is set in India because the stakes are high there for the millions of small farmers experiencing global change while aspiring to live well. Farmers make similar choices, beginning with their seeds, in fields everywhere. While fewer people around the world engage in agricultural work, agrarian life stretches out to all of us in increasingly complex ways. This book dives into the lives and knowledge of the people who grow these seeds on the front lines of global change.

2

THE POLITICAL ECOLOGY OF KNOWLEDGE IN INDIAN AGRICULTURAL DEVELOPMENT

N THE course of examining farmers' experiences with GM and organic agriculture, I convened several farmer focus groups on the subject of seed choices. Politicians or newsmakers use focus-group settings to gather a wide range of opinions, testing public responses to policy statements or a televised debate performance. For anthropologists, focus groups serve two purposes. First, like politicians and newsmakers, focus groups help us understand local opinions in a setting where multiple people can debate the finer points of an important idea. Convening a focus group in rural India during the agricultural season was no easy task—the schedules I am used to in American academic institutions and schedules for Telangana farmers are very different things. I had to arrange tea and cookies, building in time for farmers to show up late and leave early as their work demanded. We had to find meeting places that would make everyone feel comfortable: the courtyard of a well-respected farmer, in a school, near a bus stop, and, once, a log next to a water pump where farmers liked to gather. When it rained, we had to cancel because the sound of voices was drowned out by monsoon raindrops on tin roofs.

When the skies cleared, I would lean forward to ask what new cottonseeds farmers had heard about. Farmers planting GM seeds might shout out dozens of names. When they named new seeds, the crosstalk would overwhelm my small recording device as farmers debated information from advertisements or shops. Rarely did farmers possess firsthand information about how these new brands fared in their own fields. One farmer explained, "If it is a new seed, we'll remember the seed name and plant it. And if we get a good yield, we plant the same seed next year. Year after year the seed will reveal itself. But if [the yield] decreases, then another new seed will be produced." Another contradicted him, saying, "Those seeds might be very good in the advertisements, but all the companies sell fake seeds. When we get those, we're not even getting our investment back!"

This kind of exchange underscores the second purpose that focus groups serve for anthropologists. Focus groups don't just provide a space for several people to give a variety of opinions—they reveal how a community frames an argument. Asking a group of Telangana farmers which cottonseeds are popular is an entry point to learn what kinds of lives cotton farmers desire, and why. The knowledge that farmers planting GM seeds expressed during one-on-one interviews, shared during observations in fields and shops, and debated in focus groups like this most often circles back to producing as great a yield as possible. While this is a laudable goal for farmers trying to make a living by growing a commodity crop, this new vision of success, which values particular kinds of knowledge and practice, neglects other paths to living well in rural India. In many ways, yield trumps stability, relative profit margins, land stewardship, the hope of passing land forward to children, or other ways of living well as a farmer. Narrowing the possibilities for living well exacerbates the uncertainty and anxiety that can lead to suicides in rural India. Crucially, this is a problem with its roots in farmer knowledge.

LEARNING ABOUT GOOD YIELDS AND GOOD LIVES

Both GM crops and organic agriculture make claims to a version of sustainability, and I would like to briefly address this term. Because both technologies respond to India's agrarian crisis, their claims to sustainability address the proximate causes in public discourse: suicide and pesticide use. To keep farming sustainable—that is, to continue to make cotton agriculture a viable livelihood across this agrarian landscape—each technology intervenes in rural life. Sustainability here has both socioeconomic impacts, in that farmers can afford to manage their fields and live fulfilling lives while doing so, and ecological impacts, in that farmers either use fewer pesticides (GM seeds) or none at all (organic agriculture). In academic literature on environmental and social science, sustainability has become a multifaceted term, as Johnson et al. (2018) discuss. This, the authors continue, makes it all the more important for researchers to be explicit about what we mean and assume by sustainability. Introduced as a definition of how to meet the needs of the present without compromising the needs of the future (World Commission on Environment and Development 1987), sustainability now encompasses not only continued growth but questions of justice and vulnerability (B. L. Turner et al. 2003; D. Sen 2017), policy responses (Taylor 2014), adaptability (Berkes, Colding, and Folke 2000), and transformational change in social, ecological, political, and economic systems (Forsyth 2002; Cote and Nightingale 2012).

In this book, I discuss sustainability in the broad and normative sense that a practice can continue and allow farmers to live the kinds of lives they want to live. Leach, Stirling, and Scoones (2010) call for a vision of sustainability that attends to power (which actors and networks control narratives of growth and well-being) and to well-being within environments like farms that are defined by change rather than stasis. Following their lead, sustainability in this book is a function of the extent to which farmers produce adaptive, flexible knowledge and engage with a development that helps them live the lives that they aspire to live.

Related to this idea of sustainability is another normative concept with deep roots in agrarian studies: rural well-being. Key scholars in agrarian studies (Batterbury 1996; Brookfield 2001; Netting 1993; Richards 1985; Wilken 1987) recognize an adaptive skillset, socioeconomic flexibility, and improvisational capacity in the field as paramount to making a living as a smallholding farmer. Farmers must be able to pay taxes, save a surplus, grow enough for both eating and selling, and bounce back from a drought or a fertilizer strike. To do all of these they must have a knowledge base that can support such dynamic changes in the field. In this sense, to live well is to learn well. Scholars of agricultural development, particularly focusing on the Latin American concept of *buen vivir* (good living) (Escobar 2011; Gudynas 2011; Walsh 2010), have expanded on this idea to situate knowledge and living well not just within individual well-being but within the particular and dynamic context of social and ecological community. As with sustainability above, there is not one way to live well. Living well is defined through the aspirations and possibilities of the community in question. This is a view of human rights and capabilities rooted in the writing of philosopher Martha Nussbaum (2006, 2002) and economist Amartya Sen

(A. Sen 2005; Nussbaum and Sen 1993). While there is not space in this book to do justice to the large volume of work on human rights, justice, and capabilities that Nussbaum and Sen have written, the authors generally advocate for a flexible and culturally specific path to dignity, access to the resources one needs to thrive, and the right to a community in which to pursue these aspirations.

Drawing from both this capabilities approach and *buen vivir*, I discuss living well as a means to pursue dignity, success, and a socioeconomically sustainable future as a cotton farmer. For relatively poor farming communities like those described in this book, sustainability and living well is a function of how well farmers can balance sociopolitical or ecological changes that threaten their ability to continue to make a living as farmers (Ploeg 2013). As I argue in this book, that balance fundamentally hinges on farmers' knowledge and its performance in the field.

Exactly how farmers or farming communities come to imagine the lives that they ought to live in the first place is a question that Anand Pandian (2009) explores in his book *Crooked Stalks*. My discussion of rural well-being asks not how people come to live as they ought to live, but how their agricultural knowledge allows them to imagine success and well-being as cotton farmers. It is through these benchmarks of sustainability and well-being that I analyze agricultural knowledge on GM farms in chapter 4 and organic farms in chapter 5. To be sustainable and to promote well-being, I argue, these systems must provide the right conditions for farmers to learn and to adapt that knowledge. As I discuss in this book, some organic agricultural development programs are able to help farmers strike this balance. On the contrary, the confusing market and regulatory structure of GM seeds has made this balance very difficult for most GM cotton farmers.

The kinds of knowledge practiced and valued and the experts and influences invoked on organic farms look different. Very few farmers save their cottonseeds from year to year—in fact, I only met one organic cotton farmer who consistently saves his seeds during my fieldwork in Telangana. Walking with farmers to tour their fields, helping to harvest cotton, interviewing farmers, and conducting more focus groups, I found that most organic farmers do exactly what their nonorganic neighbors do. They ask the people selling the seeds, in this case not private shop owners but organic development program workers, what seeds they ought to plant. The seeds may not be genetically modified, but the interaction is essentially similar—with one key difference. Farmers who buy GM seeds on the open market enter into a local political economy defined by achieving the greatest yields possible through fertilizers, pesticides, labor, and the debt required to pay for all of these. Despite frequently switching seeds, farmers rarely make a profit, recouping their losses on average in this region every fourth year with a bumper harvest (A. A. Reddy 2017).

Virtually every farmer claims to be switching seeds in the hopes that their new seed will bring a good yield: *e samvacaram manci digubadi annukunthun-nanu* (Telugu: "I'm hoping for a good yield this year"). This goodness can be defined by crop health, boll size, pickability, number of flowers, and insect resistance, but all of that is subservient to a seed's potential to yield a large amount of undamaged, heavy cotton that will fetch a good price in the market. The search for a good yield takes on an outsize importance in signaling to one's neighbors, or even one's self, that a farmer is successful. In contrast, many organic farmers receive a variety of program incentives that diminish the importance of yields above anything else, learning that their participation can bring better infrastructure or new media attention to their villages. Such organic farmers have learned that they can achieve far greater rewards on the farm and for their community by learning how to sustain that social network, cultivate local celebrity, work with development programs, and practice the kind of agriculture that organic program directors and their sponsors want to support.

In both cases, the consequences for agricultural management, biodiversity, crop yields, and rural health stem from how farmers learn. My aim in this chapter is to establish a vocabulary to describe farmer seed choices that builds on scholarship covering the spread of technological innovations, the dynamics of learning generally and on farms, the performances of everyday life in post-colonial India, and the daily practice of agriculture.

Cultivating Knowledge contributes to social theories of knowledge by integrating anthropological and political ecology perspectives hinged on this idea of performance. The decisions that farmers make on fields are vitally important not because they are free choices in a market but because they shape agrarian possibilities. While individual decisions are important in the context of farmer decision-making and the creation and adaptation of ecological knowledge, this focus can depoliticize the logics that govern why and how people make decisions in the first place. Rather, the more useful and immediately relevant perspective must consider the larger historical and material conditions that structure agricultural performances within the reality of postcolonial agrarian life.

Seeds are windows into a larger network of knowledge and land management entangled with a political economy on local and global scales. A decision to plant a GM seed or participate in an organic development program is not separate from the local caste hierarchies and labor networks that determine how farmers work and learn in their fields, nor can it exist apart from state subsidies on cottonseeds or the regulations that govern both GM seeds and organic certification. Cottonseeds that farmers plant are commodities, purchasable objects embedded within social, economic, and ecological worlds that have brought them to the shelves where farmers find them. These seeds enable a future where farmers can practice a set of agricultural knowledge, ranging from pest control to water management. Through this daily practice, farmers learn and adjust that knowledge, developing as well the tools to pursue aspirations to farm well, be modern, and live well. In planting, farmers commit themselves to paths where success is defined by yield or celebrity, and where failure can mean committing suicide.

The process by which seeds have transformed from things, saved by farmers with a deep knowledge of their selection and care, into commodities, purchased by consumers hoping to make a profit, is part of a global transformation in agriculture during the twentieth century. Farmers around the world have traded household labor and knowledge for expert guidance and purchasable inputs, including chemicals, machines, and seeds (Brookfield 2001; Goodman, Sorj, and Wilkinson 1987; Kloppenburg 2004; Magdoff, Foster, and Buttel 2000; Netting 1993; Pollan 2006). These transnational pathways have brought Indian farmers new seeds and new reasons to grow them, redefining what farmers need to learn in order to be successful along the way.

COMMODIFICATION AND EXPERTISE IN AGRICULTURE

Farming in rural Telangana involves learning how to work with the scores of expert intermediaries, including shop owners and extension scientists, who connect farmers with inputs. As agriculture becomes increasingly commodified, farmers act increasingly like consumers seeking out the newest and best products. A relatively small village, Kavrupad nonetheless has an agricultural input shop owned by a high-caste family. The shop sells several dozen cotton, rice, and maize varieties, but the real money comes from sales of fertilizers and pesticides. People in the village come to the shop to learn what they should plant and how they should care for it, an important question as new brands offer new opportunities to succeed in rural Telangana. Because he sells them and is himself a farmer, shop owner Vikram Rao has become locally regarded as an expert on the new brands of these various inputs. "People trust me because I know everyone in Warangal and at the extension office," he brags, twisting his thick mustache. This is not entirely true. Because he has been known to sell expired pesticides at a discount and push brands that he gets a larger profit from, farmers have also learned to be skeptical of his advice. "Vikram's shop is very convenient, but Naniram [who manages a cooperative shop in nearby Srigonda, a comparatively wealthier town] sells better products," explains Chanda, a Kavrupad farmer, with a shrug. "You have to buy your seeds somewhere." This is a telling statement. All farmers know that plants produce seeds. Farmers know to apply mixtures from locally growing neem (*Azadirachta indica* A. Juss.) leaves and fruits as a pesticide. Fire and readily available cow manure provide more than enough fertilizer. And yet Telangana farmers most often purchase seeds, pesticides, and fertilizers from experts whom they may or may not trust. The process by which agricultural knowledge has transformed from a daily practice into a purchasable commodity in rural India is one piece of a larger global transformation in the ways that we produce and consume food and fiber around the world.

Rural sociologist Jack Kloppenburg (2004) explains that the commodification of agricultural knowledge began with the seeds themselves. Seeds are inherently tricky to commodify, as they reproduce themselves, and farmers are a uniquely bad market, as farmers tend to know better than anyone what will grow in their fields. To sell to this population, agricultural input companies had to develop a seed worth buying.

The breakthrough in this market came from the United States, where agricultural input companies realized they could sell more fertilizers if they bred plants that produced larger seed heads, or cotton bolls, when supplied with fertilizers. Furthermore, by breeding child lines back with parent or grandparent lines, seed breeders could create hybrid plant lines that would bountifully express those overproductive genes for a single generation. This phenomenon is called hybrid vigor, but it comes at a cost to farmers—seeds from hybrids cannot be saved or replanted because they will lose those desirable qualities and underproduce in subsequent years. This new way of farming required not just new technology but a reimagining of farming as a capitalist enterprise. Historian Deborah Fitzgerald (1993, 2003) argues that American farmers buying hybrid maize seeds became alienated from their land and labor as their specialized crop knowledge was subdivided and appropriated by agribusiness managers. When saving maize seed, farmers had to learn to "read" crops, translating values of color, texture, or taste into agronomic qualities of yield, quality, insect resistance, or other values. But with the development of new seeds and new lines of credit that encouraged farmers to plant cash crops above all else, farmers abandoned this knowledge in favor of new practices that suited the needs of their industry. Farmers became savvy buyers, mechanics, marketers, and economists, leaving the skillsets of crop saving to others. This new agricultural normal defined success through scientific modernity and higher yields, while the sheer scale and sophisticated monitoring of these breeding programs excluded farmers from the seed production process. Fitzgerald (1993, 339) cites one 1936 catalog, in which Funk Bros. Seed Co. advised farmers not to worry if they didn't know which hybrid strain to order: "Just order FUNK'S HYBRID CORN. We'll supply you with the hybrid best adapted to your locality," it reassures farmers. This is an industrial logic applied to agriculture (Fitzgerald 2003), where farmers adopt a set of interrelated innovations managed by experts external to the farming household. In India, all GM cottonseeds are hybrids.

This process was so successful in driving down consumer prices for food and fiber and creating new markets for agricultural products among rural communities that state and private breeders concerned with scarcity and political unrest around the world brought new seeds to farmers across Latin America, Africa, and Asia after the 1960s, a process known as the green revolution (Cullather 2013; Perkins 1997; Yapa 1993). In dissociating that breeding knowledge from the farmer and placing it into a purchasable commodity, Kloppenburg and others (Magdoff, Foster, and Buttel 2000) argue that agribusiness used new seeds as the first hook in getting farmers to buy agricultural products. When that wasn't enough to entice farmer-consumers, state and private breeders incentivized production directly through free services, gave out national awards that built social prestige, flooded markets with seed varieties, and subsidized the production of commodity crops.

By the mid 2000s, anthropologist Glenn Stone (2007) argues that Indian cotton farmers like those mentioned in the focus group above had become unable to differentiate between cottonseeds and now planted them with little knowledge of their potential for success. GM seeds exacerbate this industrial hybrid seed logic in Telangana. Agricultural commodification ripples across the rural landscape, because changes in products make possible changes in the larger agricultural system. Seeds both demonstrate how discrete elements of farm production are transformed into industrial activities (Goodman, Sorj, and

Wilkinson 1987) and lay bare the entire social context within which farmers make agricultural decisions.

Much agrarian-studies scholarship describes the deleterious effects of capitalism on local ecological knowledge. In this book I am concerned with how farmers make decisions given confusing markets, strict regulatory systems, larger changes in agricultural development since the green revolution, and their own aspirations. No matter how messy life can get with these different pressures, farmers are still selecting and sowing seeds. These daily practices, performances, and shared visions for the future determine successes and suicides in rural Telangana. As put elegantly by Robert Netting in his landmark study of small-scale agriculture, people who make a living from small-scale farming "must *do* more and probably also *know* more" (Netting 1993, 50). The same farmers who struggle to differentiate cottonseeds save seeds from vegetables and flowers. Particularly brilliant local varieties of golden French marigold (*Tagetes patula* L.) or brilliant red cockscomb (*Celosia cristata* L.) are painstakingly cultivated and offered during holiday pujas. Farmers can get competitive when claiming that their flowers are the most colorful or robust, while seeds that are given as gifts are treasured as an extension of the giver much as I keep my grandmother's books to remember and feel close to her.

If farmers know more by doing more, then when farmers are asked to do less or to do differently, they will know less or know differently as a result. Even if farmers were able to stay abreast of all the possible changes in GM cottonseed brands, black-market sales and misleading marketing would still stymie their attempts at experimentation. On organic farms, farmers are usually just given seeds, and so have no reason to learn how different varieties respond in their fields. Farmers in both contexts, for different reasons, have learned to interact with cottonseeds as branded commodities outside of their expertise. To best understand this long process of commodification, it is useful to turn to social theories describing how such technology spreads.

LEARNING AMID GLOBAL TECHNOLOGICAL CHANGE

How do we make decisions about new technologies? And how do those new technologies affect what we do and know? Perhaps the most cited work in scholarship on the diffusion of innovations is Bryce Ryan and Neal Gross's (1943) 1936–39 study of the adoption of hybrid maize seed in Iowa. Ryan and

Gross sought to explain why more than 75 percent of Iowa farmers, a population thought to be conservative and risk averse, were planting hybrid seeds by 1939. Could the rapid spread of hybrid maize seed be described by environmental learning (Boyd and Richerson 1988), in which a superior product was recognized as such by increasing numbers of farmers? Or did social factors complicate this smooth and rational evaluation process? This was a question of supreme importance to seed companies hoping to crack the agrarian market and to the United States Department of Agriculture (USDA), hoping to understand this watershed change in agricultural practices. When studying how farmers made these seed decisions, Ryan and Gross discovered that virtually every aspect of the decision had a social component.

While farmers were certainly aware of the possibility of higher yields that hybrid maize allowed, they needed social information to help them decide if the seeds were really worth the investment in new farming practices and new technology. The earliest adopters of hybrid maize planted it tentatively, in experimental plots. Only when these early adopters started sharing their stories of high yields did later farmers plant larger percentages of their holdings with the seeds. Despite the impressive statistics listed by salespersons and extension workers, farmers were more strongly influenced by neighbors who bragged about successful seasons. This analytical work on the role of personal experience and social emulation as a basis for decision-making laid the foundation for the study of the diffusion of innovations (Rogers 2003), a socioeconomic theory to explain how new technologies succeed or fail to enter our lives.

In his review of studies in the diffusion of technology, Stone (2016) argues that research has tended to emphasize two kinds of learning. When analyzing the large-scale spread of technology through a political economy—*environmental learning*, learning through experience, experimentation, and iterative correction—assumes that people can evaluate technology by weighing the costs and benefits of a new decision (Griliches 1957, 1980; Herring and Rao 2012). Anthropologists like myself tend to be critical of such approaches because they assume that people regularly and accurately weigh the costs and benefits of each decision they make. Telangana cotton farmers making decisions about their seeds rarely make such informed, dispassionate calculations. In *social learning*, people defer to the choices of others and ultimately emulate them (Boyd and Richerson 1988). In some situations, social learning allows adaptive strategies to diffuse quickly through a population (Boyd, Richerson, and Henrich 2011) as people copy each other to learn about a beneficial new technology. In others, social learning falls flat when good ideas come from people with low standing in their communities, such as women whose ideas are ignored in a male-dominated field (Henrich 2001). Social learning is inextricably bound to the biases of norms, status, and deference in a larger community.

It is easy to see how social and environmental learning might inform each other. Farmers who socially copy others or go their own route likely have some environmental reason to do so. Similarly, the absence of environmental feedback can explain why various kinds of social learning are fragile, such as faddish consumer behavior (Bikhchandani, Hirshleifer, and Welch 1992, 1998). Some useful innovations do not diffuse because the innovative people are of low social status (Henrich 2001; Tripp 2005), and a crowd mentality can lead people to double down on economic choices that provide suboptimal returns (Richerson and Boyd 2008). In many situations, the earliest adopters are often those people whom others look to because they are expected to do well in the first place (Rogers 2003; Stone and Flachs 2014). In Telangana, a large farmer with connections to regional experts is someone to watch!

Furthermore, anthropologists recognize that no social or environmental knowledge takes place in a vacuum—the local and global political economy structures what knowledge is available for farmers to learn and copy in the first place. As Stone (2016) points out, these institutional channels, which he calls didactic, were present even in Ryan and Gross's hybrid maize study. Seed companies and university extension agents aggressively pushed hybrid seeds, but the authors did not integrate that institutional urging into their theoretical model. If a new technology makes any headway in a village, we would expect that the instructors carry some social weight by virtue of their class, gender, ethnicity, expertise, or other social status. These institutions vary, including trustworthy vendors like Naniram and untrustworthy vendors like Vikram.

The farmers in my study, like all farmers participating in a globalized economy, need to try to stay abreast of changes in their own fields, the myriad changes in the confusing seed market, and changes in neighbor fields. Like farmers everywhere, they have succeeded in some ways and failed in others. Why rely exclusively on one's own field when one lives in a landscape with a wide range of input choices that could not be trialed by any individual? Such isolation would be absurd in actual cotton farms where individual farmers see other fields, speak to family and neighbors, read the newspapers, consult with trusted friends, and form their own opinions. Thus, to get at the heart of seed choices, I investigate how these forces influence moments of decision-making: the daily practices learned and refined every time farmers go into their fields.

LEARNING THROUGH DAILY PRACTICE ON THE FARM

This book argues that the true measure of socioecological sustainability on GM or organic farms is knowledge: the fundamental questions of how individuals and communities learn, how that knowledge is built through daily practice, and how it is used to manage socioenvironmental change. Notable theorists of smallholder agriculture (Brookfield 2001; Netting 1993; Richards 1989; Scott 1998) maintain that it is the active practice of such knowledge and its capacity to change that allows smallholding farmers to be successful in a mixed-market and subsistence economy. Tools do not define sustainability so much as the ways that these tools are put to use. Of course GM cotton and organic cotton *might* be sustainable and valuable tools to improve farmers' lives. Their potential rests in how they become a part of daily life.

The importance of this adaptive, improvisatory, practice-based learning has deep roots in social theories of knowledge. Environmental learning, the application and extension of knowledge by skilled practitioners, is what Aristotle would have called a virtue: a complex and cooperative activity seeking interactive and systematic improvements that is developed through iterative practice (Aristotle 2016; MacIntyre 2007). Aristotle's *Nicomachean Ethics* differentiates *epistêmê*, translated as scientific and universal knowledge, from *techhnê*, translated as craft and artisanal knowledge. *Epistêmê* underlies the universalist logic of international development and especially of technological interventions in agriculture, in the Aristotelian sense that "every science is thought to be capable of being taught, and its object of being learned" (Aristotle 2016, 93). Such knowledge is not concerned with local variation but with universal theory—thus can a test plot of GM cotton (Qaim 2003) or organic management practices (Forster et al. 2013) effectively prove the viability of either technology for farmers in India, and in the developing world generally. *Techhnê*, along with the Greek *phronesis*, describes practiced-based knowledge, and so takes into account local variation, experience, and inspiration. Such knowledge requires a familiarity with scientific knowledge but is more concerned with its application in the workshop or farmer's field. Nonetheless, it is precise and codified, drawn from universal scientific knowledge as a form of deductive reasoning. This knowledge is actively sought, not merely troubleshot.

Philosophers Marcel Detienne and Jean-Pierre Vernant (1991) emphasize a different way of knowing, *mêtis*, that is particularly popular among social scientists studying local variations in practice-based knowledge (Freidberg 2004; Scott 1998). While *technê* requires local adaptation and variability, it can still be explained and rationalized to other informed experts. As political scientist James Scott (1998) argues, it is the logic of *epistêmê* and *technê* that has allowed utopian and state schemes to claim a universal truth in agricultural development built on scientific modernism. However, in examples spanning agriculture, architecture, forestry, and resource management, Scott argues that "a mechanical application of generic rules that ignores these particularities is an invitation to practical failure, social disillusionment, or most likely both. . . . The more general the rules, the more they require in the way of translation if they are to be locally successful" (Scott 1998, 318). Instead, *mêtis* is the knowledge of improvisation and course correction. Like riding a bicycle, telling a joke, or playing the right fill in a twelve-bar solo, agricultural work requires practitioners to keep track of too many factors that defy codification and universality.

Experimentation is important to this kind of learning, as it builds a relational knowledge in which learning and discovery emerge from a series of social and environmental interactions. This is true of all practice-based, variable knowledge. Take cooking, suggests anthropologist Tim Ingold (2011). It is virtually impossible to learn to cook from a recipe. Cooking comes through a combination of instruction, environmental learning, and emulation, from which the cook learns exactly which shade of brown the butter should be or the sound a properly thick egg makes when tapped against the pan. In Ingold's example, it is not that encoded meaning, the essence of Aristotle's universal, teachable *epistêmê*, is irrelevant to learning. Rather, people who learn to improvise don't really learn such universal information. They learn how to practice. I argue that when enacting knowledge during a practice like seed saving or plant management, novices learn new tasks that, through practice and course correction, become variable *mêtis* knowledge.

On the farm, in the absence of adaptation during an iterative learning process, farmers turn to social or institutionally driven learning. This moves the locus of knowledge off the farm field and thus, even when conducted under favorable conditions or as part of a promising intervention, interferes with long-term sustainability in agriculture. Farmers who cannot use knowledge about particular seeds to inform their seed choices or who develop knowledge that does not help them strike a fair price in the market might be learning plenty, but they are not learning the skills to succeed within their agricultural regimes. Through these practices, farmers create and adapt knowledge that can help them succeed in a world of environmental and technological change—or can shut out alternative paths to success.

THE POLITICAL ECONOMY OF LEARNING

Although I center this research on individuals' and communities' ability to learn from their own actions, I do not want to obscure the structural power dynamics of this postcolonial landscape and reduce rural life to a series of calculated, individualist acts. Seed decisions do not happen in isolation. *Cultivating Knowledge* considers two checks against this reductionist logic.

One useful check is to consider the adoption of technologies and their associated knowledge as part of larger structural changes in the political economy of agriculture. Both organic and GM cotton agriculture fall into the trap of considering economic models decontextualized from the political economy. GM cotton proponents from science, industry, and the public sector (Kathage and Qaim 2012; Herring and Rao 2012; *Hindu* 2013) cite high rates of GM seed adoption in India and increases in overall yields as evidence that farmers are making well-informed choices in a free market with objective, uncomplicated benefits. But these celebrations elide other complications in the GM seed market. If choice is free and welcomed, why are economists and policymakers not horrified when locally desired seeds are plagued by periodic shortages of popular brands (Wadke 2012) or an influx of spurious seeds (Herring 2007)? Why should we be surprised that the addition of a Bt toxin has no greater effect on long-term pest resistance than any of the previous pesticides introduced to the cotton sector (Tabashnik et al. 2014)? If yield is so important, how can observers separate the influence of Bt cotton from new pesticides, fertilizers, and denser planting on yields and pesticide applications, (Gruère and Sengupta 2011; Stone 2013), let alone from the increasing costs and competitiveness that influence agrarian distress and suicide (R. S. Deshpande and Arora 2010)? As I discuss in the next chapter, the most marginal farmers with the least access to environmental or political support suffer the hardest losses of India's agrarian crisis (Gutierrez et al. 2015; Vasavi 2012)—a sociopolitical and not a technological root problem. These challenges ripple through both the global and local political economy.

Similarly, although numerous economic models have suggested the superiority of organic cultivation, especially for resource-poor, small cotton farmers (Eyhorn 2007; Forster et al. 2013; Panneerselvam et al. 2012), this technology has been slow to diffuse. Frustrated, pro-organic researchers extol the clear benefits of organic agriculture in profit margins and quality of life, showing that organic cotton has the potential to reach yields comparable to GM cotton. The problem, they lament, is the farmers. Farmers are suspicious of the schemes, do not want to learn new methods, do not want to abandon their personal cultivation knowledge, do not want to join an agricultural program that will separate them from other farmers, or otherwise decide that organic production is not worth the poor yields they expect to see (Eyhorn 2007, 17). Many farmers participating in these studies did not want to abandon known agricultural logic in favor of a new technique, in part, as each study recognizes, because they did not fully trust organic programs to follow through with their promises (Prashanth, Reddy, and Rao 2013). Promise alone was not enough to sway farmers to an alternative way of making a living. Rather, farmers demanded that organic projects prove that they would follow through on their claims. By taking seed choice as a starting point and then asking how knowledge is put to use in this social and economic context, my approach allows me to attend to these seeming paradoxes of yield and farmer decisions. I argue that we need to pay attention to knowledge not in the abstract but as it is performed on the field.

A second useful check is to draw from postcolonial theory to explore subjective performance in the quotidian practice of knowledge. Sociologist Erving Goffman (1959) noted that all people perform a version of themselves in everyday life to various audiences, but when applied to agriculture, performance considers improvisational responses in farm fields that deviate from plans or predicted behaviors (Crane, Roncoli, and Hoogenboom 2011; Richards 1989, 1993). Performances of agricultural knowledge reflect what happened in a field and how a farmer responded, whether that refers to iterative responses to new insect pests or to the sociocultural emphasis on making the field look attractive to a neighbor. Cotton fields are public stages that show how some farmers reap great harvests, care for their fields, and by proxy will be able to buy gifts or afford expenses for their families. It is demoralizing to know that one's field has fallen short in the village. This becomes complex in a postcolonial context, where the audiences include not only changing ecological conditions but a shifting network of experts, states, and transnational governance.

Anthropologist Anna Tsing (2005) revels in these myriad ironies and incomplete reworkings of global capitalism. The path to modernity and capitalism is not smooth or inevitable but slowed and redirected by what she calls friction: the local responses produced by awkward, unequal, unstable, and creative forces of international connection. Postcolonial development and the friction of modern capitalism are keenly felt in India, which has pursued a modernist industrial development oscillating between forms of capitalism and socialism. A nation of small farmers, India has largely pursued this agenda through agricultural development that aims to both promote mechanized commodity farming and move people from agricultural to industrial sectors. Farming well is one legible path to these promises of postcolonial modernity among Indian farmers, as shown by previously criminal castes seeking rights as responsible landholders (Pandian 2009, 2011) or Madhya Pradesh farmers who found new and creative ways to use electronic pricing information to their advantage in the soya (*Glycine max* [L.] Merr.) market (Kumar 2015). Indeed, the failure to achieve these goals and neoliberal India's narrative that crop failure is an individual, not systemic problem, keeps suicide rates stubbornly high in rural India (Menon and Uzramma 2018). The modernity faced by industrializing American farmers (Fitzgerald 2003; Kloppenburg 2004) was configured to particular notions of capitalism, success, and stewardship. While many factors are technologically similar, agrarian change in India works within its own fragmentations and opportunisms of caste, gender, and village politics (Agrawal and Sivaramakrishnan 2000).

Postcolonial scholarship draws attention to the ways in which colonialism creates a pervasive sense of underdevelopment and a moral and material aspiration to overcome these deficiencies. As I'll discuss in chapter 6, agricultural development is complex, and I am not trying to construct a straw man argument about the totalizing and Western nature of development. However, development is one of many forces through which new technologies and practices foster new knowledges, frustrations, and opportunities for small farmers. Some ways of engaging development align with local traditions, such as South Indian ethics that link agriculture with the pursuit of a virtuous life (Pandian 2009). The performance of stewardship and care are enduring moral values in South Indian agrarian landscapes, and farmers have been shown to hybridize elements of development programs with existing management practices and ways of viewing themselves (Gupta 1998; Vasavi 1999). This is an example of reconciling local *technê* or *mêtis* within a state or agribusiness *epistêmê*. Other engagements with development result in new values, as shown by farmers who report that their preintervention lives were defined by ignorance and apathy (Escobar 2011). When this logic becomes internalized, it can become a form of self-discipline (Agrawal 2005b), leading postcolonial subjects to view state-sponsored environmental management as in their own interest. These practices and professions of transformation are always performative, opening doors to certain agroecological strategies and closing others.

This interrelationship of performance, knowledge, and commodification represents both agricultural and existential consequences for agrarian crisis and success. For GM farmers lacking an environmentally learned basis for decision-making, *manci digubadi* gives a stage direction to farmer performances. This is a fragile shared goal, especially because the quantitative measure of a "good yield" is far from certain. Yet this logic echoes the broader desires of technocratic neoliberal development, as I discuss at length elsewhere (Flachs 2019). Ann Gold (2003) observes that seeds make social worlds possible, bringing together families and even fulfilling religious duties. Cotton in particular holds a special place in the Indian imagination, showcasing beauty and status (Herring and Gold 2005; Ramamurthy 2003) alongside national aspirations in the global commodity economy (S. Guha 2007; Beckert 2014). The alternative paths in rural society, in which agricultural success is imagined as the preservation of heirloom tastes or low costs to the household, remain open to farmers when they grow commercial rice and heirloom garden vegetable crops (Flachs 2016c; Flachs and Stone 2018). As performances and practices shift to align with new audiences and stages, knowledge, management, and aspirations shift too. Just as the ability to trial and discover is key to the creation and iterative adaptation of knowledge, recent work in postcolonial studies asks that we consider knowledge and the daily practice of knowledge as a function of the people and practices that create it.

IMPROVISING KNOWLEDGE IN EVERYDAY LIFE

Looking to the ways in which small farmers develop adaptive, improvisatory strategies to solve agricultural problems, Paul Richards (1989; 1993) likens agriculture to a musical performance: like improvising musicians, farmers make agricultural management decisions by drawing on a collection of agroecological knowledge that forms a repertory system. In practice, many of these variables depend on factors in the global political economy, such as the price of agricultural commodities or structural adjustment loans that reduce small farmer subsidies. They may also depend on local networks of labor or prestige that govern who gets credit from the bank or whose concerns are taken seriously by extension scientists (Batterbury 1996). Performance is a versatile metaphor in social theory, describing how power is enacted through social rituals (V. Turner 1970, 1980), how social values are made real, surveilled, and challenged through quotidian acts (Butler 1990), or the ways in which people present strategic versions of themselves to navigate complicated social spaces (Goffman 1959, 1956). For farmers and agricultural scientists, performance often refers to the economic value or yield of a crop that a farmer grows. I use performance here to refer to an active engagement between individuals and audiences who interpret their actions. A musical performance provides a useful analogy. Like many social scientists who study environmental issues, I have some experience as a performing musician. The connection between farmers and musicians may not be immediately clear, but allow me to provide an example.

If I perform a piece of music on a stage, some elements of this performance require careful planning. I probably would not play if my local town does not support live music spaces, if there is no parking lot or local bus line to carry my audience to the venue, or if most people are skimping on ticket fees because of an ongoing economic crisis. This is how my political economy structures my performance. Were I a farmer, I would be beholden to the seeds I can grow and the commodities that my local buyers want to purchase. As a local community member, I need to be sure to invite my friends, to name a catchy drink special so that the bartender will invite me back, and to practice my music. Some elements of my performance may be improvisatory, or at least idiosyncratic. Farmers cannot plan for storms or pest attacks, but they must be ready to spray, pick early, or build berms that curb erosion. Depending on the songs I heard earlier in the day, I may reference their melodies and rhythms, or I may decide that the acoustics of the room better support a quieter composition than I anticipated. During each performance, I take on a stage persona, and outside observers may mistake that performance for my true, authentic self. Though they would be incorrect to say that I am no more than that performed persona, I am certainly a little different for having performed in this way. Through repeated performances, I may come to identify more and more as a musician, which might shape the knowledge I use and the aspirations or frustrations that define my life. With each new crop season, chance for a spotlight in the newspaper, or chance to work with an interesting NGO, farmers' calculations shift around what it means to succeed.

My performer persona is what Goffman would call my front, my presentation of self in this situation. However, as a complex person with many sets of knowledges and identities, my performance is subsumed within what philosopher Judith Butler (1990) would call performativity: the practices that reproduce power in social situations, thereby enabling some identities and disciplining others. My upbringing, which included not only material benefits like music lessons and access to instruments, but also sociological benefits like the confidence to enter new spaces and call attention to myself as a white man in the United States, helped to make and reinforce my position as the performer.

On the farm as on the musical stage, our practices reinforce our knowledge, made easier or more difficult by the political economy and the discursive power that defines our options as performers. Over time, performances and practices shape identity as much as they shape environmental management. The separation between performer and performance becomes blurred with repeated practice and the building of skill until performer and performance simultaneously create one another (Ortner 2005). These presentations of self, like improvised responses to agricultural stimuli, are fundamental elements of the learning process because they represent iterative social feedback that determines what is learned and how that knowledge is put to use in the future.

Performance calls attention to several aspects of agrarian life: the ways in which farmers adopt practices based on the response of different audiences, including demands of modernity from corporate or state actors as well as the need to be seen as a good and responsible farmer by the village community (Pandian 2009); how these presentations of self are contingent on the resonance of that interaction or one's assessments of risk and failure (Bardone 2013; Schieffelin 1998); the iterative function of a performance in an agricultural context that reflects (Richards 1993) and creates (Netting 1993) knowledge; and the ways that farmers develop catchphrases like *manci digubadi* to order their experiences and articulate acceptable ways to respond to social, economic, and ecological problems (Flachs 2019; Vanclay and Enticott 2011). Both the performance of a self in this agrarian development context and the flexibility of practices that can be used and learned on the farm contribute to the daily practice of knowledge. In South India, these performances are linked to a specific postcolonial history that demands certain kinds of progress, strategic presentations of self and knowledge, and uncomfortable combinations of knowledge and identity in a globalized world.

PERFORMING *MÊTIS*

The edge of Brahma's cotton field in Ralledapalle is planted with pigeon pea (*Cajanus cajan* [L.] Huth), a delicious bean used as a base for the *sambar* soup that accompanies rice and vegetables across much of South India. I prefer it boiled and salted like edamame, but this is a minority opinion in Telangana. "These plants are nitrogen fixers," Brahma explains, showing me how pigeon pea and other legumes draw in nitrogen from the air with the help of bacteria living on nodules in their roots. "I make sure to rotate a field of pigeon pea or mung bean (*Vigna radiata* [L.] R. Wilczek) every few years in our cotton fields to keep the soil fertility high." Brahma has a master's degree in biochemistry and is now working toward his doctorate in Hyderabad. He helps his father choose GM cottonseeds by parsing through agricultural reports in local newspapers and accompanies him on trips to Warangal to buy seeds, where his education helps to counter the family's identity as poor farmers belonging to the historically marginalized Banjara tribe.

Yet when it comes to his pigeon pea and the sorghum that his family grows to grind into flour for chapati, Brahma speaks in less scientific terms. "We chose these seeds because the plants grew strong and yielded very well," he says, touching the leaves and curling a particularly long bean pod so that I can take a photograph. He smiles. "I love the colors, these bright greens and yellows, along with the bright reds and purples." The same is true of his sorghum. Grabbing a particularly thick and full seed head, he says, "By eating strong food like this, we can work all day without getting tired. This has much more energy." Brahma pauses, considering that statement. "This sorghum has more *balam* than the rice they eat in Kavrupad."

Although his English is perfect, Brahma's use of the Telugu word *balam* is telling. *Balam* connotes not just nutrition but strength and power, the ability to persevere and endure a long day of work in the field. Gone are the references to the nitrogen cycle or his close reading of relative yields in the newspaper. Instead, Brahma references color and strength. He disparages rice, a grain so important to Telangana that the word for rice, *annum*, is the same word for "food." He takes pride in these plants as something distinct to the *thanda*, or tribal village, outside Ralledapalle where he lives, something that people a kilometer away in the majority Telugu caste village of Kavrupad would not eat.

Brahma steps inside to show me how his family stores saved seeds, in sealed bamboo casks with handfuls of neem leaves to discourage insects, and points out likely candidates for seed saving in the field. This one, with a strong stalk and large seeds, but not this one, which looks healthy to me but whose leaves are too yellow—perhaps indicating a nutrient deficiency or virus—for his liking. This one, with a tightly bound seed head, but not this one, which has slightly larger seeds that stretch away from each other, suggesting that it may be more difficult to harvest or that the seeds might blow off in a heavy storm. These and other observations reveal a wealth of practice-based knowledge and a fair bit of improvisational *mêtis*: plant health, resistance to pests, soil fertility, nutrient quality, the robustness of seed heads, or simply their look and feel. Brahma employs both his knowledge of biochemistry and his attention to these learned details in the field. These sets of knowledge have a complementary logic, but they can be awkward to combine, as when nutritional descriptors fail Brahma and he emphasizes that his homegrown sorghum has *balam*. Most importantly, this example illustrates how place-based and community-based knowledge allows for different sets of values, perceptions, and management strategies. Brahma consults with his family and draws on his years of experience growing food crops to make decisions about sorghum and pigeon pea, but those observations and social networks are not necessarily useful in the fast-paced world of GM cotton cash cropping.

By emphasizing interpersonal reflections and skills learned in the field, I call attention to the audiences of these performers, arguing that knowledge is cultivated through a socially reinforced process of performance. Farmers improvise in the field, but they also strengthen or strain social relationships when their performances are viewed by NGOs, neighbors, family members, or scientists, or when they receive negative feedback from the soils, waters, plants, and animals in their care. These elements reinforce each other and allow us to investigate a deeply personal knowledge connected to the political economy. The practice of *mêtis* demands that these performances become part of one's personal history and sense of self. These are not merely course corrections but part of the farmers' personalities and habits. Contemporary understandings of performance do not see clear separations between the performance and the performative self who gives it.

In the context of performance, *mêtis* describes the subtle shifts that farmers undergo when deploying a postcolonial identity strategically to gain better access to state resources (Subramanian 2009) or to take on more favorable environmental roles as conservators of forests (Agrawal 2005b) or soils (Galvin 2014). James Scott (1998) saw *mêtis* as a check against central planning or expertise that eroded local knowledge and practice, while geographer Susanne Freidberg (2004) warned against the devaluing of *mêtis* through commodified food safety standards that would satisfy safety regulations but render obsolete the knowledge of the taste of a good carrot. This kind of knowledge is especially sensitive to changes in technology, self, and governance. When codified, *mêtis* pays only an ineffective lip service to the dedication and holistic knowledge necessary for its continued production. However, an overly localized *mêtis* is a double-edged sword because "this limitation of perspective renders people prey to outside political interference in the name of conservation of biodiversity, land resources, or even global environmental protection" (Sillitoe 1998, 233). Flexible enough to adapt to changing socioecological conditions but rigid enough to face direct challenges from hostile institutions, *mêtis* is key to understanding how agricultural development is reshaping rural India.

BUILDING THEORY IN THE ANTHROPOLOGY OF KNOWLEDGE FROM COTTON FARMERS

The visions of development offered by GM crops and organic agriculture ask farmers to commit to different possible futures, opportunities, and constraints. This commitment is performed to an audience of visitors, shops, experts, and neighbors on the public stage of the farm field for all to see. The performances allowed and encouraged by divergent governance and audiences in turn affect, full circle, how farmers come to see themselves and come to practice their knowledge each day.

The literature in the diffusion of innovations above shows how complicated it can be to test an agricultural technology in the field, and Bt cotton's anarchic market adds to this difficulty (Herring 2007; Stone 2007). When I began working in Telangana in 2012, I had no reason to expect that environmental learning was a salient factor in Indian farmer Bt cotton choices. However, this was a testable question: How do farmers balance and fail to balance various forms of learning in their cotton choices? As I show in chapter 4, farmers do indeed conduct the kind of evaluations that economists (Herring and Rao 2012) claim. Yet the ultimate usefulness of these trials on GM or organic fields is not always clear. As farmers continued to choose seeds and learn environmentally based information, they did not appear to be learning anything that informed their future decisions. Knowledge, and the performances that create it, is a function of GM or organic cotton's agricultural and sociopolitical needs.

GM cotton farmers' preferred justification, *manci digubadi*, is the obvious answer to a question about seed choice for a cash crop like GM cotton. But when viewed as an iterative performance, it also provides a structured response, a way to justify a choice when there may not be a straightforward answer. Ethnographer Priti Ramamurthy (2011) has called this kind of rationalization the vernacular calculus of the economic, in which smallholders aspire to the possibilities of upward mobility through cotton agriculture. This is an economic calculation informed not by cost-benefit analyses so much as by aspiration to overcome historical marginalization and generational poverty. This view of learning and rationalization is an insight into both an agricultural decision and the subjective postcolonial stakes behind its rationalization—what kind of farming is made possible by the neoliberal choices of the seed market, and how do farmers adopt the discourse of modernist agricultural development in coming to terms with those new possibilities? Crop scientists and policymakers celebrate cotton's high yields, so why shouldn't farmers? The agricultural performances around the "good yield" script have limited other ways to be successful as a cotton farmer. Simultaneously, it erodes a larger repertoire of environmental information from which to improvise. While this has been a boon for seed companies seeking greater penetration into the cotton market, it has limited GM cotton farmers' options for putting their knowledge into practice.

On organic farms, institutionally driven learning must transition from initial education to environmental and social learning relatively quickly. As I'll discuss in chapter 5, many organic farmers try to balance, on one hand, a positive relationship with their sponsoring organic program against, on the other, farming in a way that allows them to generate and adapt knowledge. Farmers take up a variety of learning strategies on the certified and uncertified organic farms that I visited. For their part, organic programs often rely on early adopting farmers as spokespeople to convince others to follow suit. This can create new and fascinating systems of obligation between farmers and organic field agents. Ideally this active teaching gives way to social learning, and the intervention can become self-sustaining. Environmental learning persists among farmers who work to locally adapt pest control methods to the availability of trees, water, and electricity in the villages. These farmers then teach modified versions of organic agriculture to the rest of the village in their own words. Other farmers refuse to adopt organic methods in total, keeping a diverse skillset in which they work with programs to some extent and ignore them in other management decisions. For many farmers, the active instruction of organic agriculture is ignored in favor of social learning because the programs can be uninteresting and time consuming. Preferring to learn from others in the village who attend planning meetings and distribute seeds, these farmers treat organic knowledge and inputs as commodities brought to them at a discounted price. As with many GM cotton farmers, organic farming's objective environmental benefits are less influential than the social weight of the people promoting it. This is not a universal, *epistêmê* development knowledge, but a more contingent, locally flavored, performative *mêtis*.

These performances are central to the ways in which farmers, and the rest of us, navigate our worlds and produce improvisations on repertory knowledge. In turn, this complex performance affects the daily practice of knowledge, its iterative creation, and its adaptation in the field. In a rural Indian context, where farming is a moral as well as an agricultural process, the performance of a development identity in everyday life informs the repertoire of knowledge that guides farmer decision-making. These performances shape management practices and ideas about good farming, a nexus of identity, practice, and improvisatory *mêtis* that creates knowledge alongside new social and ecological stimuli. As such, these affected performances determine what knowledge gets built and how technological innovations are used in the field to combat agrarian crisis—the key question of this book. As much as a universal expertise or commodified knowledge seeks to supplant farmer skill, the daily practices of both self and agriculture continually create a knowledge in conversation with the audiences of governance, environment, market, and village that define agrarian life. The resulting improvisation, a performance drawing on self, practice, and the unexpected, is the essence of a knowledge that is not taught but lived.

3

COTTON COLONIALISM, COTTON CAPITALISM

THE GLOBAL history of cotton is the history of capitalism, empire, and slavery, told across thousands of years of transnational connection. This international trade began in South Asia, where farmers domesticated cotton and traded fibers throughout Asia, Africa, and Southern Europe. Cotton from India buoyed the Indian Ocean trade that drove Europeans to sail west; cotton fueled the rise of mills in Manchester and Boston; cotton clothed displaced and enslaved African people, who grew cotton in American plantations so that their European and American slavers would grow wealthy; sharecroppers grew cotton across the world during the late nineteenth-century colonial period. Today, cotton's long and complicated supply chain has embraced neoliberal factory conditions throughout South Asia that concentrate wealth in former colonial nations. The ways in which cotton production created opportunities for trade and power have helped to shape the global economy, in which farmer budgets are squeezed in countries like India so that clothes are cheap in countries like the United States. This long history has built the foundations for a long-standing agricultural knowledge, a knowledge that has been devalued and manipulated to serve larger global forces. Previously, British colonialism used Indian cotton expertise to clothe an empire. Now Indian cotton is the test case for GM crops and organic farming as visions for the future of agriculture.

At each step, farmers, states, businesses, and private interests looked to use or change ecological knowledge.

Just as India is at the center of this sweeping textile history, cotton is central to India's identity. India is synonymous with beautiful, vibrant clothing like sarees or kurtas that billow and breathe on warm summer days; cotton worker strikes formed the backbone of the Quit India campaign that cemented India's independence from the British Empire; handloom and Mysore clothing, often spun by small-scale artisanal weavers from cotton species indigenous to Asia, are sold on every street corner and are part of every middle class wardrobe; cotton clothes and sashes are traditional gifts for holidays and for guests. Small shops, artisanal weavers, farmers, and national corporations all embrace cotton as a quintessentially Indian crop through which India has helped to shape the world.

Botanical, economic, regulatory, and political links bind Indian cotton production to the global economy, as they have for centuries. In this chapter, I document the deep history of the global cotton trade through the long-standing agricultural links between the United States, Europe, and India. Especially important to this discussion is the industrial and postcolonial political economy that established a flow of resources and expertise between these regions. This pattern repeated itself during India's green revolution and has now returned with the twenty-first-century spread of organic and GM technologies out of the United States and Europe. Despite centuries of global connectivity (Chaudhuri 1985; Ludden 1999) and fifty years of agricultural development (Cullather 2013; Perkins 1997), India has gained a reputation for famine, poverty, and underdevelopment. A larger crisis narrative, which often leaves out the deep colonial or neoliberal roots of farmers' vulnerabilities, makes interventions like GM cotton and organic production seem not just possible but absolutely necessary. This is not to say that suicide, generational poverty, pest attacks, and pesticide overuse are not real and immediate problems for India's cotton sector. However, these technological solutions are not always well suited to addressing the underlying causes of agrarian distress because they continue to divest farmers of knowledge and control over their local agroecology. At worst, the larger narrative of the technological fix can portray India as exotic or inherently underdeveloped rather than structurally disadvantaged because of technologies and policies designed off the farm. India's agrarian distress stems from this long-standing historical and material inequality, felt by rural Telangana farmers seeking to live well in a state with inadequate infrastructure, a hierarchical social geography, and a global political economy that attaches low prices to raw agricultural products from the Global South.

COLONIAL COTTON

Cotton is so ubiquitous in our lives that it is difficult to imagine living without cheap, fast access to clothes, sheets, bags, diapers, or, for U.S. Americans, our cotton dollar bills. In 2018 the world produced about 120 million bales of cotton, enough to make 146 billion T-shirts (National Cotton Council of America 2018). I can buy a pack of three white cotton T-shirts for ten dollars at my local retailer in Lafayette, Indiana. This is a good deal, considering that cotton evolved in the neotropics; is grown by farmers in places like India, Turkey, and the United States; is spun, dyed, stitched, and sewn by factory workers primarily in Southeast Asia; and comes to me in time for the four, six, eight, even twelve fashion seasons in which I need to stay trendy (Brooks 2015). Not included in my ten dollars are the costs of water contaminated by cotton dyes, clothing factory collapses, pest attacks, soil salinization from irrigation projects, chronic pesticide exposure, suicide, biotechnology infrastructure, or multinational trade agreements.

This is a mind-boggling feat of our contemporary global economy. All of these issues demand inquiry and critical thought, but in *Cultivating Knowledge* I focus on the fate of agricultural knowledge in this system. To fully understand the human experiences behind my ten-dollar T-shirts we need to begin five to ten million years ago, when a member of the Malvaceae plant family, which includes okra (*Abelmoschus esculentus* L.) and our common ornamental hibiscus (*Hibiscus rosa-sinensis* L.), branched off to evolve unusual epidermal seed hairs. These fibers may have been intended to enlist birds in dispersing the seeds of this new *Gossypium* genus, they may have been a ploy to catch the wind like dandelion (*Taraxacum officinale* L.) seeds, or the waxy hairs may have helped to repel light rains and discourage seeds from germinating prematurely (Wendel and Grover 2015). Yet as this plant continued to evolve, it attracted an unexpected champion drawn to those threads—us.

Archaeological evidence suggests that people in the Indus valley, the Levant, the Andes, and North Africa all gathered wild and semicultivated cotton fibers 8,000–6,500 years before the present, twisting them into clothing, bags, nets, and ropes long before farmers domesticated the plant. Ancient cultivators in the

Indian subcontinent began growing *G. arboreum* L. and *G. herbaceum* L. intentionally at least 5,500 years ago (Zohary, Hopf, and Weiss 2012) and became the world's first cotton farmers (Oosterhuis and Jernstedt 1999; Dillehay et al. 2007). Within cotton's botanical Gossypieae subfamily, four distinct species from South Asia, the Middle East, the Andes, and Central America have evolved, been domesticated, and undergone parallel evolution at different times and places to become agricultural cotton. The earliest evidence for domestication, the combination of physical and genetic changes that arise from a coevolution between humans and other species, appears approximately 4,300 years ago in South Asia.

Cotton was attractive for a number of reasons. Fiber plants like flax or hemp require a time-consuming rotting process to extract the fibers that can be woven into textiles. Sheep and other fiber-producing animals have to be fed and cared for. Cotton fibers can be harvested and processed directly from the plant. From South Asia, cotton spread to the Levant and the circum-Mediterranean region first as a traded fiber commodity and later as a domesticated plant (Oosterhuis and Jernstedt 1999; Zohary, Hopf, and Weiss 2012). India, home to cotton farmers and weavers with local and traditional skillsets, lay at the center of this global trade, spreading high-quality clothing north to China, east to Southeast Asia, and west to Rome, North Africa, and East Africa (Beckert 2014).

In South Asia, cotton's durable, breathable, easily spun fibers provided the raw material for households across the subcontinent to produce textiles. As subjects in empires in modern-day India and Pakistan, those households paid taxes that built palaces, armies, infrastructure, and civil bureaucracies that ruled Asia through the fifteenth century. Arab and central Asian traders gained power and wealth by selling those same textiles, along with spices and minerals, to Europeans and Africans eager for Asia's riches. Asian states and empires offloaded their surplus production at a profit, while trader entrepreneurs and the states that taxed them concentrated the wealth from this global exchange of goods (Chaudhuri 1985). The notion of a plant capable of providing faster, cheaper, lighter, and higher-quality textiles so captivated the imaginations of Europeans used to wool and linen that naturalists and clothes wearers alike, aided by the writing of adventurers like the thirteenth century's Sir John Mandeville, imagined cotton as a tree that bore tiny lambs who bleated from its branches (Lee 1887). That particular misconception survives in the German *baumwolle* (literally, tree-wool), although most Europeans take their words from the Arabic *qutun*, in honor of the traders who brought it to their shores.

By the mid-fifteenth century, the balance of geopolitical power had begun to shift toward Europe. Europeans saw in cotton the opportunity to build a new kind of empire, one based on the extraction of commodities, land, and labor from colonial regions that fueled urban manufacturing back in the core of the nation. At a time when Indian and Chinese empires lacked consolidated states willing to secure business interests through military conquest, European states began enclosing the peasantry in cities where they could provide cheap labor (Wood 2000). Centralized and hungry for resources, European empires turned their attention to Africa, Asia, and the Americas in the sixteenth century.

Historian Sven Beckert (2014) describes this expansion as *war capitalism*, a new and violent process where racial others produced a surplus extracted by the European capitalist class: "Cotton from India, [enslaved people] from Africa, and sugar from the Caribbean moved across the planet in a complex commercial dance. The huge demand for [enslaved people] in the Americas created pressure to secure more cotton cloth from India" (Beckert 2014, 46). Soon, English industrialists realized they could make far more money by buying cheaper, raw cotton, weaving it in an English factory, and then selling the finished clothes at an increased price to subjects throughout the empire. By the 1700s Indian cotton clothed enslaved people and European industrial workers alike, sewn in factories in colonial cores, such as Manchester or Liverpool, England, or in the periphery nations, like Lowell, Massachusetts. To suppress indigenous weaving systems in colonial nations, England and France enacted tariffs against and ultimately outlawed Indian-produced textiles. Difficult to imagine in our era of fast, cheap clothing, the stakes for cotton were life or death. Beginning in 1726, French cotton smugglers were imprisoned and could face execution. Embracing violence and industry, European states reorganized global production around colonial extraction.

To clothe the empire and feed industrial mills, British entrepreneurs established North American cotton production in the American Southeast, where the American combination of stolen land, New World *Gossypium barbadense* L. and *Gossypium hirsutum* L., and enslaved labor outcompeted British production in Australian, Indian, and African cotton-growing colonies. As plantations produced more cotton that could be spun by more factories, the supply chain produced capital for the wealthy classes who owned factories, ships, and land. In 1776, American colonies disrupted this neat system by removing themselves from this insular political economy. Now, instead of profiting from every step of production, the British would have to pay for American cotton. This was a problem—mercantilist economics of the time assumed that closed production systems, where states controlled and taxed each step of the production process, were the most efficient path to wealth and power.

To regain their standing in the cotton trade, British merchants turned to cotton sources in Egypt and South Asia. Compared to the American industrial infrastructure, these sites were woefully underdeveloped. While extreme rural poverty and rigid local hierarchies were useful in enabling colonizers to extract taxes and commodities, these social inequalities hindered the transportation and sale of cotton on a national scale. British traders faced botanical problems too. New World cottons, *G. hirsutum* and *G. barbadense,* had a longer staple, or fiber, length that was better suited to mechanized weaving in England. South Asian cotton, *G. arboreum*, had a shorter staple that better suited household-scale Indian handlooms.

Irritated by competition from these industrially superior New World varieties, the East India Company invested in infrastructure and experimental farms, ultimately hiring American planters to teach Indian peasants to sow varieties for mass production in 1840 (S. Guha 2007). The going was slow. British-Indian cotton strains yielded 25 percent more, but only with a 200 percent higher cost in production capital. Few Indian farmers found this trade-off attractive. They themselves were not reaping higher wages, and the new system of production asked them to invest heavily in cotton at the expense of planting food crops or crops destined for side markets. Why devote such time and resources to enrich foreigners? American and British growers struggled to replicate an American plantation system built on enslaved labor, facing Indian smallholders who could not be easily coerced, unreliable roads, and a lack of storage necessary to maintain the kind of cotton monocultures seen in the United States.

Indian cotton would not retake the global market until a cotton drought brought on by the American Civil War (Beckert 2014). In the first months of the war, Northern naval blockades interrupted British access to the high-quality fiber. Thinking it might force British help, the American Confederacy decided to ban exports. This turned out to be a bad idea. By the time they realized that they had abandoned their best source of capital, the Northern blockade was so effective that Southern exports to Europe, totaling 3.8 million cotton bales in 1860, dropped to virtually zero in 1862 (Beckert 2014, 246). That same year, Indian cotton farmers provided 75 percent of the British cotton and 70 percent of the French cotton spun into clothing.

In the aftermath of the American Civil War, British farm administrators flooded the Indian market with new seeds, relaxing planting regulations and allowing farmers to plant new varieties where the climate suited them as part of a larger agricultural cropping pattern. British administrators pinned their hopes on local knowledge and agricultural improvisation, and they were not disappointed. Farmers mixed local varieties with foreign cultivars to hedge their bets on the new seeds (S. Guha 2007), developing a successful local variety of *G. hirsutum* by the late nineteenth century. Today, *G. hirsutum* accounts for 90 percent of our clothing (Oosterhuis and Jernstedt 1999). That local strain "flourished" under the name Dharwar-American (S. Guha 2007, 315), dominating the global market even after the United States reentered the global cotton trade. Later, this dominance helped make Mahatma Gandhi's Quit India and handloom campaigns so economically and politically successful in the struggle for independence.

POSTCOLONIAL COTTON

The political power of production was not lost on the framers of India's independence movement. In a conversation with a visiting Charlie Chaplin, Gandhi even argued that boycotting British mechanization and spinning cotton by hand was a patriotic duty (Weber 2015). The Quit India campaign made cotton a cornerstone of the independence movement, asking weavers to refuse to sell to British buyers and instead focus on becoming self-sufficient villages (S. Guha 2007). While initially successful in building a national identity and breaking from British economic power, Gandhi's vision of socialist-inspired, self-sufficient village republics ultimately lost out to capitalist-flavored central planning, the vision of India's first prime minister, Jawaharlal Nehru.

After independence, Nehru's vision of tempered capitalism and industrial growth superseded Gandhi's village India agricultural policy. By the late 1960s, India's five-year plans shifted decisively toward capital-intensive agriculture (Perkins 1997). The growth in manufacturing brought new factories that built farm equipment, synthesized nitrogen fertilizers, and pumped chemical pesticides. The sudden availability of chemical fertilizers, pesticides, and new water infrastructure allowed Indian crop breeders to focus on breeding high-yielding varieties and hybrids that would respond to these inputs, ensuring as well that the new seeds would produce longer fibers and more cotton bolls.

Political machinations fell into place too. Indian geopolitics in the 1950s pitted Soviet and American interests against each other through competitive large-scale development projects (Cullather 2013; Perkins 1997), using a non-aligned strategy as a means to secure food aid and infrastructure. Whether American capitalists or Soviet communists built them, India encouraged the construction of each dam, factory, and university partnership. Paranoid about the links between hunger and communism, and seeing an opportunity to woo India away from Soviet influence, the United States initiated a series of agricultural development projects that came to be known as the green revolution. The green revolution was multinational from the start. American crop scientists, working in Mexico on strains of wheat developed by Japanese farmers, bred cereal grains that could transform new excesses of industrially synthesized nitrogen fertilizer into hefty seed heads. The new crops fostered new international partnerships between the United States and India, which had been previously much friendlier to the Soviet Union. Crop scientists linked up with state and university extension services to work with farmers and local breeders, Indian and American companies doubled their efforts to produce machinery and agrochemicals, and the American government subsidized grain exports to India through a food for peace (PL-480) program that allowed farmers to focus on unfamiliar grain varieties (Kloppenburg 2004; Perkins 1997).

Indian wheat and rice yields climbed as farmers made the technology relevant on their own local terms, although the yield gains continued a strikingly linear trend in Indian grain production that preceded and followed the green revolution, and yield growth actually slowed during the green revolution years (Stone 2019). Farmers incorporated chemical inputs into their extant views of healthy field ecology and came to terms with a farm budget that saw fertilizer as a commodity distinct from animal production. Yet there were some unintended consequences. Gupta (1998) and Vasavi (1999) show how farmers saw green revolution crops as "weak," in need of pesticide and fertilizer protection. Wealthier farmers disproportionately benefitted from purchasable inputs and new forms of irrigation (Shiva 1993), an inequality that the Indian state was willing to accept if it ended grain imports and famine scares (Perkins 1997; Ross 1998; Yapa 1993). The changing logics of Indian agriculture had rippling effects, even for Indian scientists at public institutions working on noncereal crops. Soon, teams breeding cotton hybrids also turned their focus to crops that would respond to the system of pesticides, fertilizers, irrigation, and state subsidies that farmers adopted throughout the country after the 1960s.

In 1970, a public research collaboration between a cotton research station in Gujarat state, the All India Coordinated Cotton Improvement Project, and the Indian Council of Agricultural Research released commercially viable hybrids. Farmer interest in these hybrids grew, but only gradually. Although hybrid seed production tripled from 1970 to 1993, hybrids accounted for just a third of cotton acreage by the mid-1990s. Nor was this market dominated by the private sector, which distributed just over half of those hybrid seeds in 1995. While somewhat popular, these seeds were hardly overwhelming or even normal in fields across the country.

To spark widespread interest, the seed sector had to reorganize. Over the next ten years, the cotton sector redirected public research, building efficient seed distributors in public and private sectors, incentivizing cheap rural labor, lobbying for guaranteed maximum retail prices on seeds, subsidizing fertilizers and pesticides, and partnering with the textile industry to use more cotton in the ever-faster global fashion industry (A. K. Basu and Paroda 1995). For Indian agribusiness, interested in selling seeds, fertilizers, pesticides, and machines, and the Indian government, interested in increasing cotton production and moving farmers from rural to urban areas, these gains were good news. With only a third of farmers planting hybrids, and nearly half of them buying public sector seeds, Indian agribusiness saw an enormous potential for growth.

Far more significant were the larger changes in cotton agriculture and the opportunities for farmer learning that swept across India. While hybrid seeds remained rarer, the associated inputs of fertilizers and pesticides exploded. Long-staple hybrids encouraged some cotton growers to steadily increase production from 1970 to 1995, but fertilizer and pesticide applications rose even for farmers not planting the hybrids. By 1998, Indian cotton farmers were applying between 30,000 and 35,000 metric tons of pesticide (Kranthi 2012), representing as much as 45 percent of the total pesticide applications in India. At this time cotton was cultivated on only 5 percent of India's agricultural land (Shetty 2004). Despite growing cotton for centuries, Indian farmers found their knowledge base undermined and exploited first by colonial and then by capitalist markets. Farmer uncertainty and the new need for outside expertise were not inevitable but set in motion by this chain of historical and political events.

GENERATIONAL VULNERABILITY ON TELANGANA COTTON FARMS

G. hirsutum lacks coevolutionary resistance to Asian pests, and its root is shallower and more sprawling than *G. arboreum*'s deep tap root. To grow this crop to its full potential, farmers had to defend it with pesticide sprays and dole out more regular and gentle water than the monsoon rains usually provided. With increasing sprays came increasing insect resistance, a pesticide treadmill (Brookfield 2001; Nicholls and Altieri 1997; Lansing 2006) in which farmers had to spray ever more to combat insects' evolving tolerance to those poisons.

From the perspective of political ecology, this ecological disaster is not completely the cotton's fault. *G. hirsutum* was especially vulnerable because farmers grew it in monocultures, an artificial and tempting landscape for the numerous pests and crop diseases that feast on cotton. The rise in fertilizers and pesticides brought new debts and insecurities, including a wave of farmer suicides that peaked in the late 1990s and has not receded (Galab, Revathi, and Reddy 2009; Gruère and Sengupta 2011; Pandian 2011; Scoones 2006). As rural Telangana and India broadly enacted neoliberal policies, farmers used to seasonal loans with local landlords and ecological relationships with homemade inputs (Ludden 1999; Gupta 1998; Vasavi 1999) learned to navigate an unfamiliar landscape of credit, labor, seeds, and inputs as citizen consumers. Farmers could get rich by selling commodity cotton but weighed these new aspirations against rising costs in rural life, what anthropologist K. C. Suri (2006) contextualizes as the political economy of agrarian distress. As in neoliberal states around the world, Indian policies increased the costs of agricultural inputs, proposed new fees for social services like schools or medical visits, and facilitated the rise of a fabulously wealthy upper class (Mohanty 2005; Parthasarathy and Shameem 1998).

The Telangana region has historically received less industrial and infrastructural development than the coastal and southern areas of Andhra Pradesh. This structural underdevelopment and agrarian-focused economy are the outcome of centuries of socioeconomic domination by political and economic elites. Some of these elites were born and raised within the local hierarchy of class and caste. Local zamindar landlords formed the upper class of this society along with the civil service of the Muslim nizam. These rulers oversaw the Deccan plateau region encompassing parts of modern-day Telangana, Karnataka, and Maharashtra as a principality of the Mughal empire from the eighteenth century until India's independence. To other elites, caste was a foreign system that provided an opportunity to exercise local authority from afar. British and French colonial officers who collected cotton and the American and Soviet development officials who tried to woo India toward capitalist and socialist state building all recognized this established hierarchy. Telangana's smallholding farmers, especially those belonging to scheduled tribe or scheduled caste communities, have been historically excluded from the best opportunities offered by these local and foreign powers. From the agrarian countryside, cotton and rivers were diverted to value-added industrial and manufacturing centers outside Telangana. For the vast majority who did not own land or saw most of their profits go to landlords and lenders, this economy did not provide many opportunities to build wealth. Telangana cotton farmers, impoverished by colonialism and actively agitating for their own state, were among those hardest hit by this combination of debt, pesticide use, and suicide after 1990. Telangana's rural poverty is in this sense generational.

Hyderabad, independent India's largest princely state, defied efforts at unification for over a year as modern India coalesced in 1947. Threatened by a Muslim-dominated, potentially hostile nation bisecting the new country, Indian troops stormed the nizam's palace in the city of Hyderabad, claiming it for the new state of India on September 17, 1948. On that day, the Deccan plateau, a majority Hindu agricultural area dominated by Muslim and British influence for nearly seven hundred years, suddenly became part of a Hindu-led secular democracy. In the rural areas outside Hyderabad, much of Telangana's politically active citizenry supported the rising Indian communist party, which called on peasants to overthrow their oppressive landlords and various systems of exploitative bonded labor (Lalita et al. 1989). In the riots that followed, the people of the new state killed thousands of former Muslim and Hindu landlords. Historically dominant castes and historically subjugated tenant farmers and Adivasi peoples in the interior of the Deccan plateau achieved an uneasy peace by making Hyderabad the capital of the new state of Andhra Pradesh (Zubrzycki 2007; R. Guha 2008; Ram 2007). While the state itself was unified on linguistic grounds, a sizable minority in Telangana continually agitated for a separate state. On July 30, 2013, the central government and the ruling Congress party began plans to bifurcate the state. By the following February, the legislative assembly passed the Andhra Pradesh Reorganization Bill to officially split the state on June 2, 2014 (B. M. Reddy 2014; Joshua and Reddy 2014).

As Hyderabad has become a hub for India's information technology (IT) boom, the surrounding area of the Telangana region has remained comparatively underdeveloped with a largely agrarian base, poor irrigation (Vakulabharanam 2004), and a disproportionate number of farmer suicides (Galab, Revathi, and Reddy 2009). This agricultural-industrial divide pervades the cotton sector as well: the Telangana region supports the majority of cotton producers while the Andhra Rayalaseema region is home to the majority of the cotton mills (K. V. Kurmanath 2013; Mitra and Somasekhar 2013). To maintain control of a state

founded by courting rural voting blocs, Telangana politicians support policies
that please cotton farmers as they incentivize links between industry and agriculture in line with India's larger vision of national development. Subsidies on
agricultural chemicals, like fertilizers and pesticides, benefit farmers as they spur
the construction of new chemical plants. Meanwhile, a continued undermarket
maximum retail price for cottonseed, a high minimum support price for cotton
lint, and subsidies on electricity and irrigation (Mukherji 2014) continue to
incentivize urban industrialization as they ease some concerns for farmers. As
if a microcosm of India's larger tensions, the bifurcation of the state sought to
rectify the damage felt by rural farmers excluded from the larger technocratic
development of coastal Andhra Pradesh, while simultaneously keeping the economic engine of high-tech and scientific development running in Hyderabad.
In Telangana cotton fields, state support, scientific progress, environmental sustainability, socioeconomic uplifting, and since the 1990s, suicide, are all intertwined with the mutually exclusive visions for the future offered by GM and
organic agriculture.

NEOLIBERAL COTTON AND SUICIDE

In the 1990s, the Indian state began loosening government regulations over the
economy and pulling back rural extension services. Simultaneously, new public
and private organizations, ranging from environmentalist NGOs to corporate
seed distributors, began courting farmers with new opportunities to invest in
new products and chase higher profits. This neoliberal reorganization has had
several effects on Telangana cotton farms.

As pesticide applications ticked up after 1990, so too did farmer expenditures
and seasonal debts. When market controls loosened, private buyers offered to
pay lower prices for cotton on the spot. This undercut government buyers who
took weeks to pay, while the same private sellers flooded the market with new
agricultural products. As India's rural population migrated toward urban opportunities, the underpaid, landless laborers, mostly female, began charging more
for their services as cotton pickers and *kuli* (day labor) weeders (Kothari 2005;
Stone and Flachs 2017). Irrigation spread across India, but the richest farmers
were able to secure the earliest and deepest tube wells, ensuring that the rich
got richer as communal groundwater diminished (Gupta 2017; Taylor 2013).
While investments rose, payoffs shrank, and credit, labor, and water each crept

further out of reach of the poorest farmers. The most vulnerable farmers grew increasingly anxious and resource stressed, and some turned to suicide.

The difficulties in counting farmer suicides allow them to be contested in statistical terms by skeptics who question their severity (Plewis 2014) as well as by skeptics who say that the issue is systematically underreported (Sainath 2015). These are important conversations, but I worry that they shift the conversation away from the farm field. While national-level analyses are correct to note that farmers as a whole are not more susceptible to suicide than anyone else, poorer, nonirrigated, more marginal farmers *are* at greater risk for socioeconomic ruin and suicide (Gutierrez et al. 2015; Gupta 2017). This conclusion, while true, should be apparent to anyone considering agrarian distress in context. I argue that the larger problems of suicide and distress are much more about generational poverty and global inequity than any inherent failings of cottonseed biology. Each of the minor economic and agricultural changes above has made farmers, especially marginal cotton farmers with relatively small land holdings, increasingly vulnerable to fluctuations in global commodity prices or unpredictable weather patterns that flooded and scorched plants. Farmers found their costs more expensive and their final sales less lucrative, and so, squeezed on all sides, they gambled.

As droughts struck in 1998 and 2004, farmer suicides spiked. Farmers realized they did not have enough money to repay lenders or take on new loans (Sridhar 2006), a structural violence brought on by this cumulatively slashed rural safety net. We are left with an analysis that is as sad as it is obvious. The poorest and most indebted cotton farmers, those with small holdings who lack irrigation and economic opportunities outside of cash cropping, remain the most at risk for suicide today because they remain the most vulnerable population (Gupta 2017; Gutierrez et al. 2015). It is complicated but correct to note that (1) farmers as a whole are not at a greater risk for suicide than others in India, (2) more marginal farmers are at greater risk for suicide than others, and (3) that the GM and organic cotton solutions to this crisis can only address some aspects of this economic and ecological insecurity. To really help rural communities, interventions must go beyond technological fixes and address political and social insecurities of neoliberal life.

Suicide is not the only possible response to agrarian crisis. In the past, agrarian crisis and extreme indebtedness led to riots and demonstrations against zamindar landlords who controlled rural wealth (Lalita et al. 1989; Rao and Suri 2006). Yet the new framings of neoliberal life seemed to lead farmers to internalize this failure as personal and desperate. This crisis was deemed to be worthy of suicide but not collective political action (Sridhar 2006; Suri 2006) because the precariousness of rural life has been recast as an individual, not systemic, failure. Such individuals find themselves in what anthropologist A. R. Vasavi (2012) calls shadow spaces, shameful and neglected rural places marring India's ideal path to modernity. While debt and the uncertainty of agrarian life in neoliberal India are clearly important to this story, Vasavi along with anthropologist Daniel Münster (2012) caution that we must understand suicide and agrarian crisis as complex lived experiences. Identifying indebtedness and drought as proximate causes suggests certain kinds of policy answers to agrarian crisis. Yet these can take neoliberal forms, as seen in the attempts to introduce microfinancing and innovative irrigation tools (Taylor 2013, 2011) to curb suicide. These solutions are unsatisfying to the political ecology approach I take in this book. They continue to centralize wealth and opportunity among those with access to new opportunities, and they can recast agrarian crisis as an ecological or financial issue of technology or climate rather than a socioeconomic and political issue of justice. By understanding how neoliberalism redefines farmers' relationships to the state and encourages them to see agrarian distress not only as their fault but as a shameful public defeat, Vasavi and Münster encourage us to understand how suicide haunts rural communities.

The Indian government itself collects and distributes data on suicides, thereby creating categories of need and crisis by producing data about citizens. In response to the crisis data, state governments like Kerala and Andhra Pradesh identified suicide-prone districts and households and began paying families up to fifty thousand rupees (approximately eight hundred dollars) to mitigate the agriculture debts underlying the crisis. At first, given a new opportunity for legibility and compensation, households and officials began recording deaths as farmer suicides. Soon, this squeezed state budgets and led to changes in the National Crime Records Bureau, as state officials faced pressure either to quietly omit agricultural suicides or to record them in an "other" category (Menon and Uzramma 2018; Münster 2012; Sainath 2015). Activist-journalist P. Sainath, who aggressively pursued agrarian suicide stories across India and has helped keep attention on the issue of agrarian suicide in books and national newspapers, notes that these changes led twelve states and six territories to declare zero farmer suicides in 2014 (Sainath 2015). This startling turnaround from the previous years' data denies farmers the state recognition that Münster (2012, 205) calls posthumous citizenship.

Through these state tools, suicide becomes a category produced by the state, not just an individual or community response to debt, anxiety, and neoliberal modernity. Ethnographically, Münster notes that suicides in Kerala share many similarities to those in Telangana—a boom crop, pepper or ginger in Kerala and cotton in Telangana, provided new opportunities for an agrarian population left out of the neoliberal narrative of modern India seeking success defined by agricultural capitalism. This is the cost of India's capitalist and socialist rural development in the first fifty years since independence, which sought to shift surplus to industrial cores, scale up production, and incentivize peasants to move to cities (Cullather 2013; Suri 2006). Living well as a farmer is outside the scope of this national development. Farmers' debt, growing disparities between rural and urban economies, and exclusion from former socioeconomic guarantees fed a sense of rural desperation and farmer suicide (Rao and Suri 2006; Vaidyanathan 2006).

Despite arguments over how to count suicides, the crisis narrative became an inescapable force in public discourse about agrarian development and the nature of public or private response. The story resonated in India, a nation with an agrarian identity neglected during the ascension of planned industrial modernity, neoliberal market reforms, urban development, IT infrastructure, and special economic zones free from India's socialist-flavored labor and trade regulations (Münster 2012). The timing was just right for GM and organic crops to make a difference in this tragedy—by 2000, GM and anti-GM institutions were already claiming that cotton farmers could be saved or destroyed by Bt cotton technology (Stone 2002b).

GM AND ORGANIC SOLUTIONS TO COTTON CRISIS

The crisis, both biologically and sociopolitically, was complex and multifaceted, the result of systemic policies and hard choices made by India's central government. Different stakeholders sounded different alarms: policymakers stared down the crisis of farmer suicide, the loss of India's most vulnerable population and the core of its agrarian identity (Sainath 2013; Vaidyanathan 2006); environmentalists cited the alarming rise in pesticide use (Shetty 2004); and public health advocates noted that pesticides put not only poor farmers but cotton pickers, weeders, and other agricultural laborers at risk (Mancini and van Bruggen 2005). India was not necessarily unique in this combination of rural socioecological disasters. Farmers in the United States (Stallones 1990), the United Kingdom (Malmberg, Simkin, and Hawton 1999; Stark et al. 2006), Australia (L. Bryant and Garnham 2015; Judd et al. 2006), and Brazil (Faria et al. 2006) have committed suicide in response to a mix of higher input prices, greater exposure to global market price fluctuations, individualistic profit seeking, and conspicuous consumption associated with neoliberal reforms of the last forty years. In each case, agricultural workers face a broader socioeconomic distress in rural areas that perpetuates desperation and, in some cases, suicide.

In India, agrarian distress, cotton, and suicide became inextricably linked because these farmer suicides coincided with the pending release of the highly controversial GM cotton (Stone 2002b). Cotton modified to express the insecticidal Bt gene achieved commercial success in the United States with little fanfare but was protested in India on the grounds of criminal biosecurity risk and neocolonialism (Shiva 1997). Cotton faced special scrutiny because of its association with the famously impolitic multinational corporation Monsanto (Charles 2001; Schurman and Munro 2010) and the erroneous but widely circulated belief that the seeds contained a "terminator" gene that would shut down natural seed reproduction (Herring 2006). Social scientists (Stone 2002a; Herring 2007) watched as defenders and detractors rushed to link GM seeds with suicide, either to claim it as a cure for (Paarlberg 2001; Prakash 1999; Qaim 2003) or a cause of (Shiva et al. 2002; Perrière and Seuret 2000) the larger crisis. Despite its complexity, the macabre poetry of farmers overspraying crops and then committing suicide with those same chemicals became a rallying cry for those demanding answers to agrarian distress. The race to solve the crisis would be run by cotton: on one hand, a GM hybrid seed that would work within the existing system of chemicals, debts, shops, and plant scientists; on the other, a non-Bt seed that would call upon international green marketing and farmer education. The regulatory frameworks of these solutions would determine the marketing structure and diffusion of these technologies and thus have a profound impact on the knowledge and performances that farmers would produce in their fields.

REGULATORY LEGACIES IN TELANGANA BT COTTON

Much maligned and praised, Bt cotton represents many of India's agroenvironmental paradoxes: the promise of high-tech modernity as well as the threat of eroded past values (Paarlberg 2001; Pearson 2006; Scoones 2008; Shiva 1997; Stone 2002a); the influx of new capital and technology amid the danger of increased corporate control (Bagla and Stone 2012; Jasanoff 2005; Newell 2003; Schurman and Munro 2010; Scoones 2006); and the acquisition of new farming methods at the risk of interrupting the farming learning process (Kloppenburg 2004; Pollan 2002; Stone 2007).

The 1980s witnessed an explosion in the research and development of GMOs, largely because American patent laws classified GMOs as significantly different, novel creations. This allowed private citizens or organizations to patent discoveries or inventions funded by public tax dollars in university laboratories (Charles 2001; Jasanoff 2005). China was the first nation to plant a GM crop, virus-resistant tobacco, on a commercial scale, but GM crops were not adopted globally until 1996 with the release of insect-resistant and herbicide-tolerant crops developed largely by teams based at Monsanto and Washington University in St. Louis. Since 1996, biotech crop plantings have increased from 1.7 million hectares to 185.1 million hectares in 2016, planted by eighteen million farmers in twenty-six countries (C. James 2015; ISAAA 2016). Because agribusiness and biotechnology firms provide the startup capital and facilities required to create GM crops, these traits are typically traits amenable to agribusiness. Overwhelmingly, most crops grown on a commercial scale are agricultural commodity crops modified to express resistance to agricultural pests, to be resistant to herbicides, to express both traits, or to express virus resistance. While many other GM traits exist for a variety of commercial and subsistence or specialty crops, and commercial food crops have been released with proconsumer traits like extended shelf life (Martineau 2001), the most widely planted crops globally continue to be soybean, maize, cotton, and rapeseed. More than three quarters of these crops are grown by large-scale producers in the United States, Brazil, and Argentina. With 10.8 million hectares in production, India, where the only commercial GM crop is cotton, is by far the largest producer of GM crops by smallholders in the developing world.

The mechanisms of genetic modification are subject to constant change. The newest development has been CRISPR, a much cheaper, easier, and more precise tool for so-called gene editing. In this tool, biotechnologists use nucleases to cut DNA in any organism at a particular place, ensuring that when the DNA repairs itself, it will also add the new gene in precisely the correct place. This is a major shift from previous methods that included more uncertainty into where and how fully a gene could be added to a target piece of DNA. Furthermore, CRISPR editing can include small changes in a gene rather than the introduction of fully new genes. It can also delete gene sequences, forcing us to consider in what sense a genome with no new DNA is "modified." While philosophical, such questions are also regulatory: Should an organism with no new genes be subject to biosafety protocols designed to prevent modified genes from escaping into wild populations? As these issues are debated, much GM crop breeding is done using older tools—namely, gene guns that fire particles coated with desirable DNA into the cell or the exploitation of the natural gene introgression mechanisms of bacteria like *Agrobacterium tumefaciens*, capable of changing the genomes of other species.

Once modified, GM crops are grown like any other commercial crop. Plant cells proven to express the target gene are cultivated and developed, and then bred with plant lines suited to a particular area and set of conditions. In India, GM traits are bred into hybrids that produce exceptionally high yields when given water and fertilizers. If saved and replanted, the plants lose this hybrid vigor and so farmers are better off buying seeds new each year. While it is illegal to save and replant GM seeds, the agricultural disincentive is a far better deterrent for small Indian farmers. American cotton growers, who lack this long tradition of seed saving and manage much larger farms, plant GM varieties and not hybrids.

The use of American GM technology required a regulatory policy that would satisfy countries in the textile commodity chain, international businesses, green activists, foreign investors, and a poorly educated but democratically active rural population. In the late 1980s, only the USA possessed a working regulatory framework regarding gene patenting and GM safety, and so those legal decisions were largely adapted to service Indian needs (Heinemann 2012; Newell 2003). Cognizant of the risks of upsetting rural voting blocs, and India's green NGO sector, Indian policymakers began adapting American GM regulation in 1989 to obviate potential objections, thirteen years before it would be approved for farmer use.*

---

* Knowing that they would face considerable resistance from environmental and farmers' rights groups, Indian biotechnology regulators established the Rules for the Manufacture/Use/Import/Export and Storage of Hazardous Microorganisms, Genetically Engineered Organisms or Cells through the Notification No. G.S.R.1037(E) in 1989, six years before transgenic material would be imported to India and thirteen years before the first GM crop's commercial release in 2002. This set of rules was a precedent and a promise for a decade of transparent legislation and a growing bureaucracy. The Department of Biotechnology wrote the Recombinant DNA Safety Guidelines in 1990 as a preemptive measure anticipating genetic modification and then updated these rules in 1998 to respond to activist concerns regarding the security of field tests. Additionally, GM crops must be approved by the Genetic Engineering Approval Committee (GEAC), and any rulings made by the GEAC can be appealed by pro- or anti-GM parties.

This cautious bureaucracy was designed to address the concerns of both global agribusiness and wary citizens. Regulators hoped that the density and complexity of this framework would lend a sense of security to farmers and environmentalists while promoting economic growth in the biotech industry (Scoones 2006). Ever cognizant of India's colonial history, regulations restrict foreign multinational companies from direct investment or management in Indian companies. This forces major agricultural producers like Pioneer Hi-Bred, Monsanto, and Syngenta to buy noncontrolling shares in subsidiary Indian companies. By the mid-1990s, the government's authority to restrict field trials and GM seed sales had frustrated biotechnology stakeholders used to quicker development cycles. In response, they formed lobbying groups to clarify the industry's needs to the regulators. This in turn has led to sprawling networks linking foreign biotechnology companies, domestic companies, foreign and domestic labs, regulators, importers, lawmakers, and public advocacy groups. Companies with GM technology, particularly Monsanto, have found it more profitable to lease the rights to their patented genes rather than breed hybrid seeds themselves in India (although they continue to produce seeds in India). A steady seed market provides a steady reason to continually license GM technology to domestic breeders.

While GM regulatory frameworks are drawn from the United States, the actual seed breeding and business of agriculture is a domestic industry. For example, Monsanto India, not Monsanto, sells GM crops in India. Domestic companies like Nuziveedu and Kaveri Seeds have the best connection to state agricultural extension services and local cotton germplasm, and thus the best-suited hybrids for local markets. As such, they dominate Indian seed sales. Indeed, Indian law is sensitive to a history of peasant exploitation that can frustrate foreign companies used to stronger intellectual property protections. Under lax regulation, Indian seed breeders have seen some spectacular theft of patented GM seed technology (Jayaraman 2001). Monsanto, which owned the rights to the first Bt technology, began negotiating commercial approval for Bt cotton in 1995. Subsequently they purchased a 26 percent share in the Indian company Mayhco to create the Mayhco-Monsanto Biotech India Ltd. company in 1998, acquiring shares in an established Indian company and a company executive with key government connections (Newell 2003, 4). India's shifting regulatory landscape means that although foreign companies like Monsanto collect royalties no matter which company sells the seeds, those royalties are constantly under assault in the court system.

ORGANIC REGULATORY POLICY

Where GM regulation preceded GM production, India's organic regulation did not coalesce until 2000, sixteen years after the first NGO-sponsored organic conference (Narayanan 2005). As with GM seeds, organic proponents tout organic agriculture's potential to cure India's chemical overuse, reverse nutritional deficiencies, stop poverty, and bring Indian products to new markets (Altenbuchner, Vogel, and Larcher 2017; Panneerselvam et al. 2012). Seeing that environmental organizations received groundswells of support during GM debates in the 1990s (Schmid 2007), environmentalist policymakers in the United States positioned themselves as an alternative to genetic modification and the kind of agriculture it represented (Jasanoff 2005). This opportunistic alliance would lead American regulators to outlaw GMOs from organic production, thus banning them in all subsequent national and international legislation in the name of global consistency. To maintain equivalency with these standards, India's organic guidelines have been adopted directly from USDA protocols, themselves the legal coalescence of more than thirty years of minor regulation by international networks of organic farmers (Conford 2011). All such standards deny certification "when use of [GM] products is detected at any stage" (Department of Commerce 2005, 92).

In aligning themselves with extant American regulation, India effectively gained equivalency with all worldwide organic markets. This has allowed India's organic market to boom, providing 74 percent of all the organic cotton sold across the world in 2015. India exports $380 million worth of organic products, grown by more than three times as many certified organic producers as any other nation (Willer and Lernoud 2016). Because organic cotton is not ingested, much Telangana organic cotton marketing takes place within a specific ethical development context, supporting rural empowerment or environmental health for producers rather than consumers. This framework is supported by regulation, images, labeling, and ethical consumption.

Indian organic regulation has been built through the concerted efforts of domestic NGOs working to comply with established international regulatory frameworks. The government endeavors to promote organic agriculture via the Agricultural and Processed Food Products Export Development Authority (APEDA) and the National Programme on Organic Production (NPOP). NPOP, run through APEDA, defines organic standards, criteria for accreditation, and certification procedures (APEDA 2012). These standards focus largely on production practices, including chemical inputs, crop rotation, and humane treatment of animals, but also specifically ban the use of genetically modified plants (Department of Commerce 2005). Organic certification can be revoked if GM contamination occurs at any point in the production chain, including shipping, packing, and transportation. Organic cotton farmers therefore rely on non-Bt seeds and buffer areas to prevent neighbors' seeds from drifting into their land, while organic distributors must buy time to clean industrial cotton gins of errant GM lint before their product can be deseeded and packed into bales. Without the authority conferred by international consensus and clearly defined standards for organic certification, Indian organic exports would lose their added value in foreign markets. Thus is organic agriculture heavily audited (Galvin 2011) to ensure trust. For national certification and access to foreign organic markets, inspectors of farms and processing facilities are accredited by APEDA, which oversees certification in compliance with the regulations established by NPOP's steering committee. One of APEDA's major selling points for foreign markets is TraceNet, an electronic database of quality assurance data collected by operators and producers within India's organic supply chain.

All this oversight can be expensive, discouraging organic certification. The guidelines are largely modeled after European and American standards (Narayanan 2005; APEDA 2012), a decision necessary to gain equivalence with foreign organic markets, but one that creates significant barriers for many farmers. To become certified and label their products as organic, farmers must contact certifiers accredited by the National Accreditation Body, a committee of APEDA. Farmers apply to government or accredited private certifiers for a crucial one-year license that permits use of the organic label, are judged on their adherence to NPOP standards, and can appeal inspector decisions. In practice, farmers are usually recruited by larger organizations who have established these necessary regulatory connections. Because of this complexity and the differing demands of farmers and international buyers, farmers often work in cooperatives or groups at the village level to clarify their needs to organic buyers and learn about required practices.

With regulation in place after 2000, both GM and organic cotton production have continued in India, each receiving billions in public and private support (*Economic Times* 2010, 2012). Because of laws decided in the United States and Europe, cotton farmers choose between a high-tech, neoliberal, GM market and a low-tech, bureaucratic, organic supply chain.

DEFENDERS OF GM AND ORGANIC COTTON AGRICULTURE

Pro- and anti-GM voices often talk past each other, seeking politically expedient arguments. V. G. Ramesh, director of a Secunderabad NGO that sponsors organic agriculture, regularly speaks out against GMOs and their introduction in Indian development. Despite more than 95 percent adoption of GM cottonseeds, he told me during an interview that he remains convinced that

> RAMESH: GM at this point and time is not a viable technology. There are biosafety issues with it. So, [other development agencies and I] don't agree on that. It's not about whether [organic groups] are certified or they don't certify. If somebody wants to put [GM technology] in organic agriculture, it doesn't matter for us, as long as the biosafety issues associated with GMOs are resolved, that's all. That's what I would say.
>
> ANDREW: You have concerns about gene escape, cross contamination, these things?
>
> RAMESH: Gene escape is one problem. You look at the impacts on soil health, impacts on people's health, it's huge. The process of gene transfer itself is not yet precise. . . . Obviously it will have biosafety implications. This is one part of the story. The second problem is [GM seeds] have patents already. They have legal controls on them, so obviously that gives monopoly rights for some. We are opposed to that as well.

Ramesh knows that his specific concerns about biosafety cannot be truly resolved. In practice, Ramesh has no interest in working with GM developers, not only because GMOs are incompatible with organic regulatory structures but also because he disagrees with the heavily corporatized kind of agriculture that genetic modification represents. Such development is, for him, inherently dangerous and unjust.

On the other side of this divide, G. Shankar, an executive with Monsanto India, has grown frustrated with what he sees as an "unscientific" criticism of his industry. Indeed, rumors of animals dying from eating GM crops persist despite any conclusive evidence of Bt's harm and despite Bt-derived products' long-standing use as organic pesticides. Most irritating, however, is organic agriculture's refusal to use chemical fertilizers and pesticides on principle. This opposition frustrates Shankar when I ask him about organic agriculture's potential:

I'll tell you, I think we have to be a little more real in life. I think that people confuse organic and inorganic in many ways. To me, field crops have to be looked at from a different perspective. As I said, soil is important. First you have to understand whether soil is good in organic content or not. Right? And in fact I believe in integrating [some organic methods]. . . . I would say that organic methods can work with us in a nicer way and say we will work on integrated pest management, integrated useful management. I would be very open to those ideas. . . . My feeling is that the hardcore organic lobby believes farmers are fooled, which I think they are not. If anything works on their farm, they will adopt it. . . . If you have to think of improving only organic cotton, you need twenty tons of farmyard manure per year. They have to be, you know, a little more practical about such things.

High-level managers fashion themselves as happy to work with the other side, but in the next breath cast their opponent as unwilling to listen to reason, whether it be biosafety concerns or the practical realities of farming. Despite, or perhaps because of, Bt cotton's massive adoption, GM and organic farming systems must present themselves as alternative visions of India's agriculture.

Even as more than nine out of ten farmers sowed GM seed, protests across five states heralded the tenth anniversary of Bt cotton's commercialization in India (Parsai 2012). Protestors have marched continuously since 2002 and continued to march in 2014, as Monsanto finished field tests for herbicide-tolerant (HT) cotton. GM and organic cotton remain in the balance in India for all of the reasons that this crisis story was so compelling in the first place: the existential threat of farmer suicide to India's agrarian identity, the conflicting perspectives on GMOs and biosecurity, and the suspicion of multinational interference given India's history with biopiracy. Although statisticians like Plewis (2014) convincingly show that farmer suicides are no better or worse than other suicides, the Indian press (*Deccan Chronicle* 2018; Sarma 2017; U. Sudhir 2017) produces a steady outflow of farmer crisis headlines and macabre photographs each cotton season. Farmers, the press, and the Indian public are not swayed by statistical reports that suicides have plateaued. Collectively, they have decided that one farmer suicide is too many.

Social scientists observe a different, equally distressing disjuncture. The same general rural distress, whether we analyze it as indebtedness, insecurity, anxiety, or volatility, remains in India. In the larger context of economic uncertainty and neoliberal development, technological approaches alone are not mitigating the generational poverty of places like Telangana. Farmers seek private credit to drill wells, an indication of the unreliability of public irrigation and a threat to the rapidly decreasing aquifers under India's Deccan plateau (Taylor 2013). Meanwhile, microfinance institutions fill the gap between reliable services and credit, profiting from the desperation of small farmers who go to great lengths to pursue elusive agricultural success (Srinivasan 2010; Taylor 2011). Political scientist James Scott's *The Moral Economy of the Peasant*, a classic work in agrarian political economy, showed how well-meaning development programs can undermine local safety nets with market reforms. In the Southeast Asian villages where Scott worked, many villagers made more money most of the time by focusing on cash crops, a gamble that reaped higher profits from greater initial investments. Yet when the harvest failed, as it inevitably does because of variations in rainfall, prices, the availability of labor, and coexistence with a larger ecology, the market had no mechanisms to see rural communities through to the next season.

Agriculture, as theorists of neoliberal India like Daniel Münster (2015a) and Akhil Gupta (2017) write, is inherently speculative. These vulnerabilities add up. We should not be surprised to learn that small farmers who lack reliable irrigation or depend more on informal predatory creditors to recoup last season's losses are more prone to suicide (Gutierrez et al. 2015). Nor should we be surprised to find that the poorest and smallest farmers most engaged in commodity production and most beleaguered by debt have the highest rates of reported suicides (Kennedy and King 2014; Merriott 2016). This is not because GM crops are foreign and poorly regulated, or because cotton agriculture is new and unfamiliar to Indian farmers. The socioecological factors above tell us that agrarian distress is a function of hopelessness, of being left behind by India's profound technological and economic development. The proscriptions of organic agriculture and the Bt genes in GM cotton do not solve these problems because they target pest attacks, not politics. If one purpose of socioecological innovation is to improve agrarian life, solutions must begin to address these underlying vulnerabilities. In the next chapter, I argue that the current GM cotton market is uniquely unsuited to do this.

4

FALSE CHOICES

The Problem with Learning on GM Cotton Farms

N THE eve of GM Bt cotton's commercial release in 2001, farmers and multinational agribusiness waited with bated breath. As regulators scrutinized Bt cotton test plots, Indian cotton farmers faced a sweeping bollworm infestation—the very problem that GM cotton promised to solve. Although no GM cotton was yet available, one hybrid brand, Navbharat-151, mysteriously resisted the bollworms and saved harvests for farmers in the northern state of Gujarat. Farmers were overjoyed; regulators, environmentalists, and seed companies, less so. Ensuing investigations revealed that the Navbharat company had stolen, bred, and illegally sold seeds containing Monsanto's bollworm-poisoning Bt gene for at least three years (Jayaraman 2001) in Gujarat. By the end of the 2001 season, the illegal seeds were so widespread that the central government conceded that further GM approval delays would have been "pointless" (Roy, Herring, and Geisler 2007, 160). In March 2002, India opened its doors to three provisionally approved hybrid Bt cottonseeds. Twelve years later, more than 95 percent of cotton planted across India contained Bt genes (Cotton Corporation of India 2016).

By the time that I began ethnographic fieldwork in 2012, non-Bt cotton was no longer sold in the input shops where farmers buy seeds. Observing nationwide adoption and rising yields, Bt cotton proponents embraced the promise of pesticide decrease, socioeconomic improvement for farmers and laborers, and suicide reduction as India became a net cotton exporter in the late 2000s (Herring 2015; Plewis 2014; Qaim 2010). Addressing India's Lok Sabha parliament in 2013, agriculture minister Sharad Pawar argued that farmers were choosing the best technology available to them. "I honestly feel that the farmer of this country is wiser than me," he said, adding that farmers preferred GM cotton as it gave higher yields, was more disease resistant, and provided more profit (V. Mohan 2013). Pawar and others (Herring and Rao 2012; Kathage and Qaim 2012) have interpreted this rapid and overwhelming adoption as proof of Bt cotton's inherent superiority. However, this interpretation divorces GM cotton management from the quotidian performance of agriculture—it implies that sustainability rests in the seed technology, not the farmers. I argue in this chapter that this is the wrong focus. We need to understand if, why, and when farmers are able to engage in sustainable agricultural practices and live their lives as they want to live them. Sustainability and knowledge are performances and daily practices. To ask about the impact of GM seeds and sustainable farming, I argue that we need to look at the learning process that makes it all possible.

Farmers and local knowledge are central to the question of global sustainable agriculture, even though they can be sidelined in larger discussions. Policymakers like Pawar speak in abstractions of seeds, preferences, yields, and profits, and this can be a problem for anthropologists who are concerned with how individuals and communities make decisions on the ground. At the heart of this problem is choice. Do farmers make rational choices when they select their seeds? Rational in what context? Rational to whom? Do increases in seeds planted or cotton produced really indicate that GM seeds are a long term, even sustainable, solution to agrarian distress? What sorts of choices and daily performances are possible in the rural villages where Telangana cotton farmers live and work? All of these questions revolve around the ways that farmers make decisions about the seeds that they plant. If the decision about a cottonseed was truly a free choice, one made rationally on the basis of price, expected returns, satisfaction with the technology, and the ability to differentiate it between other similar seeds, then we might be able to answer each of these questions with a resounding yes. If seed choice is not this kind of free and calculated decision, and, as I argue here, the choices offered in the context of Telangana's neoliberal seed market actually destabilize farmer knowledge, then we need to ask a different set of questions. In this chapter I discuss what farmers are learning in their fields and how the complex performance of Telangana agriculture sits within local and global changes in the political economy.

A focus on how farmers learn allows me to move beyond the question of free economic choice in cottonseeds, the implicit assumption of policy and techno-scientific voices arguing that Indian farmers adopt Bt cotton because it is better. Throughout this chapter I will show that the field trial language of choices and evaluations applies poorly to the lived experience of cotton farmers. My unit of measurement is the same used by farmers: evaluations and subsequent plantings of individual seed brands. The results are ambiguous to farmers and social scientists alike, an inability to find clear connections between agricultural variables and seed choices. My data shows that even as farmers go to great lengths to plant particular seeds, no seeds yield demonstrably more cotton than others do. Neither do richer, more experienced, or older farmers have an edge over the rest of the village when it comes to cotton agriculture (Flachs 2016a). Importantly, this is not because farmers are not capable of making choices or evaluating results. Many farmers, especially larger farmers with more land available for conducting trials, plant multiple seeds and compare their yields and profits. However, none of this seems to provide dividends during the harvest, and farmers start each new season by largely disregarding what they know about the previous years' seeds.

These are false choices in a confusing market that is good at producing cotton and selling seeds, but bad at fostering stable socioecological relation-ships on farms. While almost all cotton farmers are now planting GM seeds, deciding which particular seed to plant is a far more difficult decision. Farmers have learned to plant the newest, most popular seeds, but this knowledge is effectively not subject to iterative correction. Lacking firsthand environmental knowledge about their seeds, farmers are learning to seek out new brands and chase profits—leaving the concerns of seed breeding, pest control, or agroeco-logical management to agribusiness. Farmers are not learning which seeds are best. They are learning that they should not trust their own results.

SEED FADS AND THE SEARCH FOR GOOD YIELDS

Bt cotton's market share is due in part to a tremendous advertising push and investment by a multinational private sector in this previously public and heavily subsidized market. Thanks to early reports of success in a crop plagued by a decade of crisis alongside a state regulatory network that privileged yields and techno-scientific approaches to agriculture (Herring 2015; Stone and Flachs 2014), it has become virtually impossible to find non-Bt seeds in Telangana seed shops. Bt is

here to stay in India. Yet Bt is not a brand but the generic name for GM Bt cotton.
This highly successful technology is branded and sold by dozens of companies.
GM seeds' national appeal misses an important part of this story as it relates to
the experiences of farmers. Since 2002, private companies have released more
than 1,200 new seed brands into commercial cultivation (USDA Foreign Agricultural Service 2015). Examining how farmers chose those seeds, anthropologist
Glenn Stone (2007) found an unexpected pattern, one that we (Stone, Flachs, and
Diepenbrock 2014) saw intensify by 2013. Despite this diversity of possible seed
choices, farmers overwhelmingly planted particular seed brands only to abandon
them after a few years. Figure 3 shows the transient, faddish popularity of seed
brands in the Warangal district. As we show in a 2014 analysis, lucky brands enjoy,
on average, a year of ascension, a year of popularity, and a year of decline (Stone,
Flachs, and Diepenbrock 2014). This graph shows the severity of the fads and the
depth of their reach—in 2011, for example, more than 60 percent of cotton farmers
bought either *Dr. Brent* or *Neeraja*, two seeds marketed as a pair by the Mahyco
seed company, only to abandon those seeds in droves by 2013. Why?

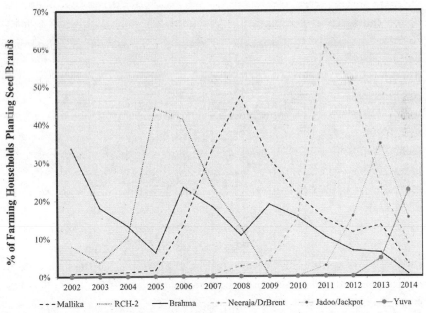

FIGURE 3. Cottonseeds by percentage of households buying a particularly popular brand.
Cottonseed trends for the most popular seeds 2002–14. Figure adapted from Stone,
Flachs, and Diepenbrock 2014.

There is nothing inherently wrong with quickly switching seeds, explains Warangal agricultural extension scientist Ramarao:

> If it performs well, they'll keep going with that hybrid. Otherwise they'll throw it in the dustbin. . . . Suppose, based on his previous knowledge [a farmer] may choose three varieties. We're all farmers and we have chosen three varieties, because in our discussion you might have told me about other new varieties which have performed very well this year. That's your feedback. I will additionally choose those two hybrids: I will take those five seeds and I will raise them in five acres. Different acres, one hybrid, one acre only. . . . Due to our training programs, due to paper reading and by watching TV, now they have become more knowledgeable. Based on all this knowledge, they are choosing the hybrids and they are going for different hybrids in five acres or three acres or two acres.

Ramarao describes an ideal learning scenario: farmers learn from their own handiwork, consult with friends and neighbors on their experience, and listen to government training programs that advise them to plant only one seed in one farm plot to ensure comparability. It all seems plausible as we drink tea in the air-conditioned office at the plant science station where Ramarao conducts research and teaches graduate students about the scientific aspects of cotton agriculture. Here in the office, we can draw columns listing seed qualities and make predictions about which seeds we would sow in our own, hypothetical, cotton fields.

Yet this is not the reality for most farmers. Ramarao's example of five seed trials in five acres is inadequate to test 1,200 possible windfalls, to say nothing of the problems with unlabeled, mislabeled, deceptively labeled, or aggressively promoted seeds procured from black-market brokers (more on these later). To consult others, farmers would have to know exactly what their neighbors planted and how many times they fertilized, plowed, weeded, or sprayed pesticides. To work well with the extension services, farmers would have to trust that their problems will be heard and that help will arrive in a timely fashion. "They come trying to solve our problems," snarled one cotton farmer from Srigonda, "but they don't listen to the farmers. They don't know our problems here, especially when compared to people like us who have been doing this all our lives." Anyway, if farmers could learn from those trials and coordinate with one another to test the wide spread of available seeds for the agronomically "best" seed, then the fads should have greater staying power. Instead, farmers go for a new seed each year. The whole concept of free, informed choices and calculating evaluations breaks down in this field-level analysis of agriculture.

To many anthropologists, the rational economic actor theory is a straw man argument. Very few of our choices in practice are cold, calculated rational acts. After one long day of household surveys in which we asked farmers to justify their seed choices, I sat with my research assistant, Arun, as we waited for a bus back to his family's house. He began fiddling with my GPS device, a tool I used to model seed choices across the village geography. "Why'd you choose this kind?" he asked, smirking. "I don't know," I stammered in response. "I heard it was good from a friend and I like that it's small, but really I just saw it in the shop and I bought it." "See!" Arun laughed. "You're choosing things for no good reason, just like the farmers." My choice of clothing, the toothpaste and shampoo I buy, the crackers I eat—all of these are choices that I don't think about too hard as a consumer. They are certainly not choices that I make as a rational actor who weighs all the costs and benefits. Yet seeds are not toothpaste, shampoo, or crackers. My uninformed consumer decisions do not have the power to make or break my livelihood. When seeds are treated as flippantly as shampoo, farmers may have a problem.

Because agriculture is such an important sphere of economic life, scientific publications in agronomy, agricultural policy, agricultural economics, and global development consistently argue that farmers choose seeds because they know that they will deliver superior yields (Herring and Rao 2012; Herring 2015; Kathage and Qaim 2012). This story is retold and contested in reports of Indian farmers' experiences with cottonseeds, embodied by policymakers like Sharad Pawar who claim that Bt cotton's spread is the result of millions of free, rational, wise choices. This is the neoliberal present, where seeds are not enmeshed in historical and material conditions but simply consumer choices made by individuals. And so, I take this claim seriously as well, investigating what people learn, how they learn it, and what sorts of practices are possible. The relationship between seed choices and cotton yields for the Telangana farmers who plant GM cotton is a testable question, one that I can unpack through a triangulation of surveys, interviews, participant observation, and spatial analysis.

Rising costs in rural life, including agricultural labor and inputs, but also school fees, weddings, and consumer goods further drive the farmer imperative to accumulate wealth or pay off debts (Mohanty 2005). The refrain of *manci digubadi* (Telugu: "good yields"), farmers' preferred justification, can get tiresome for an interviewer, but it underscores how farmers relegate seed decisions and pest management to seed shops when they chase the great cotton harvests

FIGURE 4. Farmer cotton field comparison. Photo by Andrew Flachs.

that they've seen in newspapers or on television. In figure 4, a farmer showed me two fields side by side. I asked the farmer on the right which seed was better, and he laughed, saying, "What, can't you see? Look how much thicker, fuller, greener my seed is than my neighbor's seed." He was gleeful in the moment, content that he had chosen well. The following year he had switched to a new seed. This is not because his yield was inadequate. The hope for *manci digubadi* as expressed is really a hope for limitless growth and improvement. This is a very good rural calculus for selling seeds and inputs, but not for combating agrarian distress. Unaddressed in this statement is the hope to send children to school, to live without spraying poison, or to steward land and eventually distribute it among family. Cotton may be a vehicle for these aspirations, but the highly commodified seed market is an especially uncertain way to pursue them.

EVALUATING GM COTTON IN THE FIELD

I am critical of yields as the end-all-be-all metric of success in cotton farms because I worry that it obscures other important factors in smallholder

agriculture like stability, predictability, and flexibility in agroecological management. Still, yield and profit are the benchmarks by which GM cotton's success
have been measured, and so an analysis of yield response could at least clarify
how farmers pick seeds. One explanation of this unusual spiky seed-fad pattern
is that each year, one of these brands is truly superior. The spikes therefore
represent farmers successively finding the best technology. This is an aspect of
decision-making that I investigated with agricultural surveys that asked farmers
about their yields, labor, expenses, and seed choices (Flachs 2019). In Kavrupad,
the main bus stop has a large banyan tree encircled by a stone wall. In May
and June, farmers share newspapers and argue with each other about weather,
fertilizers, price hikes, and new technology under the shade of the banyan's
twisted branches. Who talks with whom and who feels comfortable approaching whom to discuss farming are matters mediated by social distance, caste, and
wealth, but rumors fly about new and old seeds. No matter who is talking, the
conversations are all the same—what will be the high-yielding seed this year?
For all the anxiety and uncertainty about making the right decision, cottonseed
decisions are, in this way, a fundamentally hopeful act.

   In practice, yield is a poor explanatory factor for shifts in seed choice from
year to year. Measuring reported farmer yields of the most popular, fad-like
seeds in 2013, a year in which six fad seeds were planted in the sample villages,
I found that any yield advantage for a particular seed was well within the range
of variation for cotton as a whole (figure 5). As shown above, farmers conduct
experiments and track the differences between their seeds, keeping a watchful
eye on their neighbors to compare their productivity. But farmers ultimately
cannot be finding these seed trials all that effective if these data reveal no yield
differentiation between these very popular seeds. The yield analysis contradicts
a simplistic economic rationalism in which farmers simply test samples of seeds
and hone in on the best options.

Descriptive Statistics Table

	DR. BRENT	NEERAJA	JACKPOT	JADOO	YUVA	ATM
n	64	43	51	74	20	23
Mean	7.43	6.57	6.98	6.66	7.5	8.17
SD	2.75	2.65	2.84	2.4	2.94	3.09
Minimum	1.5	.17	1.7	1.7	2.86	2.6
Maximum	15	15	15	12	15	15

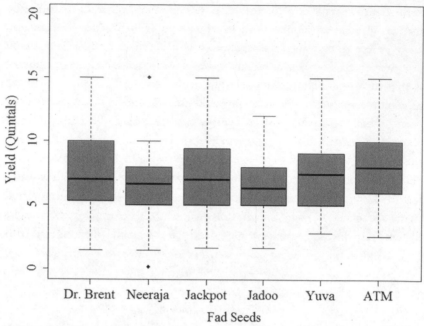

FIGURE 5. Boxplots for 2013 fad seed yields. Source: Flachs farmer survey 2012–14. Figure adapted from Flachs, Stone, and Shaffer 2017.

As I discussed in chapter 2, iterative learning is an important component in the sustainability of agricultural systems. Yet the farms where Telangana famers grow cotton are inauspicious places to conduct trials. Cotton farmers rarely keep detailed records of their seed choices and inputs, and the landscape is littered with seed packets that crunch underfoot, discarded and half-forgotten soon after planting. Management strategies including pesticide sprays, plowing, and fertilizer application vary between fields depending on who can afford what or who has reliable access to water and electricity. Not only does cotton agriculture involve multiple pickings over several months, but farmers rarely plant seeds long enough to gather much firsthand environmental knowledge about particular brands (figure 6). One Kavrupad farmer, Ranjith, who had planted Mahyco's *Neeraja* seed for nine years, abandoned that seed in favor of Kaveri's *Jaadoo* seed, which he had never planted but heard was successful in neighboring Srigonda. "Everyone was planting this seed this year," he explained, and it would have been foolish of him to miss out on this potential windfall. Certainly, there is a logic to this choice in his situation, but it is hardly an informed or calculated choice. Figure 6 shows that most farmers do not plant their seeds for more than one season before they switch to something new. Who can say if differences come from weather, insects, seeds, or bad luck? The hope for high yields is paramount, and the fear of missing a widespread trend takes precedence over firsthand experience. If farmers are supposed to be choosing seeds because they know best, then what can they learn under these circumstances?

One might assume that farmers would know more about the popular fad seeds, but this too breaks down under ethnographic scrutiny. I measured farmers' knowledge of individual seed brands through a consensus analysis, a tool to measure agreement. While agreement does not necessarily mean that the farmers were "correct" in describing a particular seed's attributes, it does indicate that farmers have a widespread agreement that some quality, such as the predicted boll size of a cotton plant, is true. For each cottonseed choice, I asked farmers to predict boll size and growth habit, a cotton plant's tendency to grow with

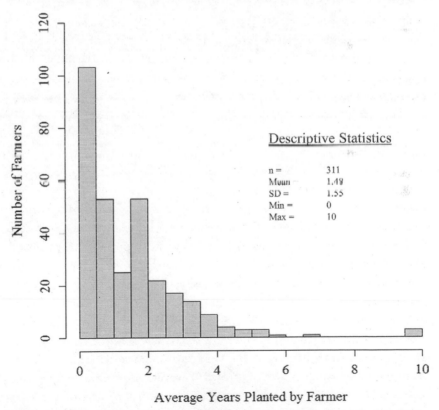

FIGURE 6. Average number of years farmers planted cottonseeds 2012–14. Source: Flachs farmer survey 2012–14. Figure adapted from Flachs, Stone, and Shaffer 2017.

multiple branches or to grow tall. These are easy to observe and crucial factors for cotton agriculture because they reflect yield, fertilizer response, and susceptibility to pest damage. While dependent on a number of variables, including inputs, weather, and soil conditions, these phenotypic factors govern farmer seed decisions. Yet, as I describe in other work (Flachs and Stone 2018), the spread of this data shows a consistent divergence of farmer opinions. Farmers planting a given seed rarely agreed on boll size or growth habit, while "I do not know" was often as likely an answer about a seed choice as anything else. It was rare for more than half the farmers who planted given seeds to agree on those seeds' attributes. Linguistically, farmers often couched their descriptions by placing the suffix *–ta* at the end of their verbs, indicating that their descriptions were based on secondhand knowledge—an aspiration, but not a guarantee.

Warangal farmers in general have been herding toward certain choices over the last ten years (Stone 2007; Stone, Flachs, and Diepenbrock 2014), even though the fad seeds do not provide better yields. Given the exhaustive array of seed choices and the uninformed way in which they are purchased, seed choices are often more a social choice than an environmental choice. If this approach suggests that these farmer seed trials have broken down, then we need to start measuring social learning. Farmers are still making decisions, and so I ask, How does that knowledge move around?

UNEVEN GEOGRAPHIES OF KNOWLEDGE

Kavrupad farmer Rajaiah wasn't sure which cottonseed to plant in 2013, and so he did what many small, low-caste farmers do in this situation. A *kuli* worker on the field of a rich farmer, Rajaiah saw that his wealthy neighbor planted seeds that grew tall and yielded well. For the smallest landowners and day laborers, cotton agriculture is an aspirational act. To farm is to work for oneself, capture a piece of the socioeconomic capital held by former landlords and zamindars, or assert one's family in a sector from which lower castes and tribes were historically excluded (Ramamurthy 2011; Vasavi 2012). Farming claims this upward mobility, although as Ramamurthy (2011) and Vasavi (2012) show, these historically marginalized new farmers have few of the social or economic resources available to the previous landlords who struck it rich growing cash crops. Rajaiah assumed that his employer had a good reason to purchase the seeds that he planted and copied that choice in his own field. He wasn't sure exactly what seed he had purchased, but after I asked him to bring the seed packet, he nodded with recognition. "It's *Jackpot*. All are taking *Jackpot* this year, so I am too." In some years, this high-caste neighbor even buys the seed for Rajaiah. "I ask him to bring back some of whatever he thinks is good for my own fields," Rajaiah explains. When farmers can't know that a trusted seed will be a better choice than a dozen new varieties, why not turn to local high-caste, wealthy farmers? The irony is that despite having better access to seed shops and more money to buy fertilizers or pay labor, those farmers with the greatest social prominence are just as caught up in the seed fads as everyone else. Effectively, their daily practice of agricultural knowledge is not much different from that of their poorer neighbors.

In a cottonseed market with hundreds of choices, there is a logic to social learning, where farmers copy neighbors when making seed decisions. The question "Why did you choose this seed this year" is often answered with "Because it is popular," a circular argument that speaks to general uncertainty in seed choices. Farmers often have no satisfactory answer to that question because of the overwhelming combination of rumors, advertisements, and unclear environmental feedback from their own fields. Standing amid the branches, flowers, and white bolls of a field of cotton, it is difficult to say if and how different one's yields and profits are from those of the farms around you. There is no way for a single farmer to trial all the possible seeds on their own farm, so peering over hedgerows to see how neighbors fare adds breadth to their knowledge base. Farmers know that their neighbors are also testing seeds, and so their decisions are based in a calculus of what they themselves know, what shops or intervention programs have told them, what they've seen on neighbor fields, and the presumably well-informed decisions of others that they seek to copy—this was agricultural scientist Ramarao's argument. A Kavrupad farmer focus-group member offered the following advice: "When you're planting for the first time you should ask all of your neighbors about seed choices to find what is best. They'll let you know about their yields, and you can make a decision based on the way in which the harvest comes." Another farmer added, "You'll ask ten neighbors, and based on their suggestions you should plant the best one." What goes unsaid in such comments are the dynamics of who asks whom about planting and how variable the inputs on a farm can be.

Social emulation reveals hidden vulnerabilities, anxieties, and missed opportunities to build knowledge. As farmers claim to be following neighbors, the rise and fall of fad seeds across this landscape can be measured spatially through a geographic information system (GIS). In Kavrupad and Ralledapalle, the two villages where I spent the most time with farmers, I conducted a bivariate regression analysis. This statistical test measures the relationship between two factors to see if one, like yield, caste, or a farmer's experience with a seed, might predict another: seed choice. The analysis that I conducted with my colleagues Stone and Shaffer (2017) showed that yield was not a significant predictor of seed choices, while farmers who planted a given seed were significantly less likely to plant it in the future. But when we tested a spatial variable, the influence of the nearest farm neighbor, we found that the mere presence of that seed in a neighbor's field was the most reliable predictor of seed choices. This GIS provides another way of visualizing the seed fads, showing spatial trends over time (figure 7).

These results are another way of confirming some of the general uncertainty surrounding cotton knowledge, a pattern that results in what theorists of social learning call *conformist* bias (Henrich 2001). Over time, people are increasingly

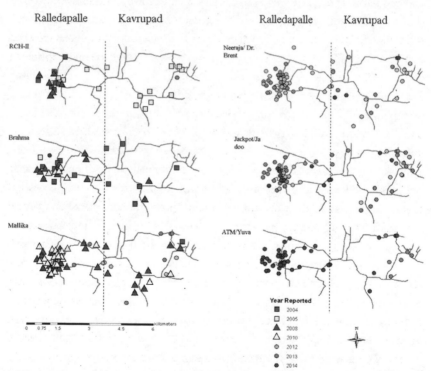

FIGURE 7. Spatial patterns of seed fads in Kavrupad and Ralledapalle over time. Figure adapted from Flachs, Stone, and Shaffer 2017.

likely to choose what farmers nearby are choosing in the hopes that the group as a whole has the right choice—even when those same neighbors are abandoning those seeds! Importantly, no single person is consistently predicting the popular seeds, because the pattern would then show ripples out from central points. Instead the spatial distribution shows that a farmer's own experience with a seed is less important in determining whether they continue to use that seed than its sheer presence in their neighbor's field.

Although farmers do not tend to copy people without some evidence that they are worthy of copying, this emulation is more prone to social biases. Rajaiah copies the choices of Ganesh, the large farmer that he works for. Ganesh does not ask Rajaiah for advice, nor would he think to ask Rajaiah to bring back "whatever he thinks is good." Within the patterns revealed by space, it is important to recognize that rural India is also socially divided across geographies of caste, landholdings, and gender. Although men are the main people making decisions about what to buy, hired female labor more often does the weeding and the picking, telling male landowners when and where there are problems. That is, the men buying seeds are often one step removed from the daily work of managing cottonseeds, feeling root structures, touching and observing each plant to build environmental knowledge. The women who have that knowledge are not usually making seed decisions in the shops.

"YOU HAVE TO PAY ATTENTION TO WHAT THE LARGE FARMERS DO"

In these villages, landholding *size* is often intersectional with caste, wealth, and status. Social stratification within small villages in Telangana is readily apparent through competitive conspicuous consumption, as in much of rural India (Linssen, Kempen, and Kraaykamp 2010). Manifesting in tractors, satellite dishes, livestock, or fresh paint, farming and rural life often have a competitive bent to them. This competition is part of the process of cultivating a virtuous, modern, or otherwise correct way of living (Pandian 2009). As Srigonda farmer Malothu explains, agriculture is a way of performing your virtues on a public stage to the rest of the village: "You should always seek to produce more than your neighbors. If they spray four times, you have to spray five. That way, you'll always have the best yield." It does not matter what the pest populations are, because Malothu wants to be seen spraying and caretaking. If he does not spray, he may be accused of creating a safe haven for predatory insects and blamed for crop damage. The sprays are as much about social performance as they are about pest control.

In a day of interviewing it is common to speak with both large and small farmers and to hear divergent narratives from each. One large Ralledapalle farmer showed me how he compares his yields with *Neeraja* to his brother's *Jaadoo* seeds, judging as well the many neighbors whose fields line the path to his own. "I am a good farmer," he bragged, "because I have educated sons who help me read and keep track of prices and seeds. Also, I have many friends in the shops and in the agricultural offices. Between all of these insiders I can continue to do well." Although these advantages do not pay dividends in cotton yields, they help to build influence in the village social learning pool.

"Any time I have a new problem, I ask Deva," explained one Kavrupad small farmer. I was asking him to outline a series of possible problems and solutions, a flowchart of farmer decisions. No matter how many different ways I phrased this question, the answer was the same. "You have to pay attention to what the large farmers (*pedda raytulu*) do. Deva is the closest large farmer to our field, so I ask him." Larger farmers have access to more land and therefore have a greater ability to plant more different kinds of seeds. While it is unlikely that a handful of different seeds is a good trial of all the possible options, they cast an influence over seed choices through what theorists of social learning call a *prestige* bias (Henrich 2001). The Telugu phrase *pedda raytu* literally means "large farmer," but it connotes that he or she enjoys higher status and importance in the village. In South India generally, caste and power are historically linked to holdings and relationships of labor whereby poorer farmers in the village work for richer farmers with more land (R. Guha 2008; Mines 2005; Vasavi 1999). These historical relationships ripple into the present. To be a large farmer is to be well respected, to be relatively wealthy, to have the potential to make your land productive, to be trusted by creditors, to hire others to work for you rather than vice versa, and to have influence over others in the village as a function of these historical and material advantages. Large farmers press their edge by talking with shop and university experts to get the latest gossip and the most encouraging advice.

"We're the same caste," explained one *pedda* farmer when I asked if he could trust the advice of a local shop owner. "He wouldn't lie to me." This trust in vendors is important. When comparing farmers' cottonseed vendors from 2012 to 2014, smaller farmers, lower-caste farmers, and tribal farmers were more likely to buy seeds from traveling brokers or to ask larger farmers to bring seeds back with them during trips to regional cities like Warangal. Some of the reasons for this disparity are obvious, historical, and structural: large, rich, high-caste farmers hire poor, low-caste farmers as agricultural laborers, while the reverse is unthinkable within the village hierarchy; traveling brokers more often visit tribal *thandas* because those farmers are less mobile due to a combination of poor roads, greater distances from public bus routes, and ethnic differences from shop owners, and because these *thandas* lack agricultural input shops; wealthier farmers are more likely to have working business relationships with shop owners who are, like them, native Telugu speakers and members of higher castes. In combination, these factors give *pedda* farmers a negligible edge in agricultural capabilities but a large advantage in socially mediated access to knowledge and resources. Unsurprisingly, one recent study (Maertens 2017) found that such better-educated and larger farmers continue to influence the seed choices of others in their village above and beyond the rest of the village social network.

Despite having greater income and assets available to care for their plants, larger farmers enjoy no yield advantages. When I conducted a statistical test of the difference between the yields of the largest 20 percent of landholders and the yields of the rest of the farmers, I received a p value of .780, far above the conventional scientific cutoff to determine significance, $p = .05$ (Flachs 2016a). Even though yields are not statistically related to farmers' holding size, smaller farmers nonetheless emulate the seed choices of their *pedda* neighbors. Ironically, when these influential people hear about faddishly popular seeds, they go plant them, not realizing that they are part of the reason that the seed is popular in the first place! In addition to the conformist bias of space, the prestige bias of high-status people, the lack of information flowing from female workers to male seed buyers, and a lack of environmental feedback, this general sense of anxiety and confusion can be traced to the market itself.

AGGRESSIVE BRANDING AND ANXIOUS CHOICES

A Telangana cotton farm is a poor place to conduct a seed trial. Despite clear and dramatic patterns in seed choices, farmers' yields are no better or worse with the popular seeds than with the others. Yield response does not explain seed choices. Farmers often look closely to the fields of their neighbors to determine which seed to plant, and they are clearly influenced by the presence of seeds in nearby fields, but they do not seem to be learning much about their neighbors' yields or inputs. Farmers rarely replant seeds for more than one season, meaning that they have little firsthand knowledge about the differences between seeds and that their knowledge does not account for variability in weather or pest attacks. In sum, these are problematic choices. With hundreds of new seeds each year, farmers simply do not have enough information to make the kinds of informed calculations celebrated by people like agricultural scientist Ramarao or policymaker Sharad Pawar above. Many farmers find this situation frustrating. For every peak of seed certainty in these villages, there is a valley wherein the farmers are collectively adrift, unsure what is best because there's no good way to discern between the 1,200 potential cotton brands available to choose from.

The branding for GM Bt cottonseeds is aggressive and intense. Advertisements hang from trees, fly over fields, blare over the radio, fill newspaper pages, and sound from small vans hired to play jingles in the city. Each summer cotton season, I travel from Telangana villages to the regional capital, Warangal, watching rice paddies and dusty red clay cotton fields give way to the beige concrete of suburbs and midsize towns. Finally, we enter the bustle of Telangana's second-largest city. Between the post office and the main bus station lies a strip of several dozen agricultural input shops. For a few weeks each year this is the busiest street in Warangal, as farmers from around the district listen to vendors

FIGURE 8. Seed shop in Warangal, Telangana. Photo by Andrew Flachs.

hawk seeds, herbicides, pesticides, and fertilizers. In any given shop, farmers will see between fifty and one hundred brands, and between shops, farmers will find over a thousand possible options (figure 8).

On the bus ride up to Warangal, I ask Shiva, the Ralledapalle farmer from the first chapter, if he knew what seed he was going to buy. "Maybe *Dr. Brent*, maybe *ATM*," he answers noncommittally, providing names that he has seen advertised in the village. This time of year, even the bus we ride is painted with seed advertisements. When we get to the shop, Shiva, who is a member of a historically marginalized scheduled tribe (ST) and is thus ethnically distinct from the Telugu caste majority, grows quieter. He stands in the back, waiting for other farmers to finish their business before cutting in, an unusual act in a setting where people commonly elbow one another to be served. "What do you want?" asks the shop clerk. Shiva replies, "Give me what is good this year." "All my seeds are good," answers the clerk. The clerk's eyes travel to me and to the customers outside. "Many people have been buying *ATM* this year. Buy that." Shiva nods his head in assent. The clerk continues to offer pesticides and fertilizers, but Shiva refuses these, as he doesn't need them yet. "Okay, are you finished then?" the clerk asks, looking again at potential customers walking by. Shiva leaves, but I stay for a moment to watch the next interaction. The clerk shakes his head at me, "It's always the same with these ST people. They don't know what they're buying and they only buy cheap seeds, they never buy the quality fertilizers or pesticides that go with them."

Even for farmers not facing ethnic discrimination at shops, this is a difficult and important decision that goes by in an instant. Shiva's concerns and anxieties are brushed aside in a brief, careless suggestion—buy *ATM*, many people are. English names like *ATM* or *Jackpot*, and Telugu brands like *Jaadoo* ("magic"), make promises that farmers do not know if they can trust. Shiva could refuse an offered brand out of righteous indignation or an independent streak, but what would be the point? Like many other farmers, he has little firsthand information on which to judge the seeds. Shiva had spent the previous year learning how *Neeraja* responded to different fertilizers and fought off pests, listening to his neighbors and the labor he hired to see how the plant fared against weeds and how deep the root stretched to collect rainwater on his unirrigated field. But that was only one season, and who knows if one of the hundred seeds behind the clerk holds a greater potential? Shiva can never know for certain if *ATM* is an objectively better seed choice this year, in his own field.

As the season progresses, farmers return to Warangal with cuttings from their plants to ask for fertilizers and pesticides, all sold by the same shops that sold them seeds. While these costs mount, their management knowledge is largely unchanged. Who could say if one solution for an old seed will be the same as a solution for a new seed? "If you're sick, you go to the hospital," explained Shiva. "If you get an injection from the doctor and you don't heal, it's not the doctor's fault. You can't blame the shops for an ineffective pesticide. They did not force you to buy it." Yet, in a sense, Shiva is forced to buy the pesticide. To keep his crop alive, to continue being a good farmer, to support his family and pay school fees and wedding costs, and to keep up with the farmers profiled in the news programs he watches, he must buy the pesticide. This is Shiva's neoliberal paradox—surrounded by choices, he finds little control over what he plants or how he manages it. And if he fails, he fails alone.

GAMBLING ON BLACK-MARKET SEEDS

From early November until January, farmers like Shiva obsessively scan televisions, radios, and newspapers for reports of the day's minimum support price, the price at which the government will buy cotton. When the price is high or when farmers run low on cash, they stuff this cotton into burlap sacks and bring it to regional open markets where it is weighed, argued over, and sold. While the government offers the best price of the day, many farmers have found that the government payments are too slow to arrive. Instead, most farmers that I met sell to third-party brokers who will pay that very day. Buyers may downgrade cotton because it is discolored, because the fibers are short, because it has too many seeds or leaves, if it smells, or if too many insects crawl across it as the buyer inspects the load. Buyers tear the cotton and shake their heads sadly at farmers, scolding them for its low quality and weak tensile strength. Farmers fire back, pointing to the bright white colors and rubbing the threads together to form long, tight strings. Eventually, though, farmers in collared shirts, jeans, and dhotis reach an agreement with buyers in trousers, white collared shirts, and gold jewelry, and cotton piles up on loading docks. Most farmers will bring in cotton within a few days of picking it, as they do not have adequate facilities to store it in their homes or near their fields, a rush to the open market that depresses prices. Like sowing seeds, storing cotton is a gamble—wait too long for a good price, and you risk insect infestation, mold, or fire.

Cotton agriculture has a relatively high investment, mostly because of labor and chemical inputs, and so there's a strong imperative to chase whatever has the highest yield, even if farmers haven't seen firsthand proof. Most often, the same shop clerks who sell farmers seeds will sell them pesticides and fertilizers as well, on credit that is paid back at the end of the harvest season. While few urban shops in Warangal will buy the cotton itself, smaller rural shops, like Vikram Rao's shop in Kavrupad, will take a percentage of farmers' cotton harvest as a lean against their debts. A GM cotton farmer will commonly spend close to ten thousand rupees ($153) per acre to grow cotton (Stone and Flachs 2017), a gamble that may only pay off one year in four in Telangana (A. A. Reddy 2017). My surveys showed that most households had roughly equal debts and incomes each year. The margin of error is thin. Choosing the seed is only a tenth of this acre-wise budget, but the seed is the first decision farmers make, one that sets in motion everything else. Farmers have no reliable source of environmental information—no consistent answer revealed by yields, experience with seeds, or consensus on which seeds are best. Given the stakes of this gamble, not knowing which seed to plant compounds this agricultural risk. Indeed, the justification that "everyone was planting these seeds" makes as much sense as anything else!

Some years, the fads get so intense that there are statewide seed shortages. In 2012, a spike in demand for three seeds[*] from Mahyco and one seed[†] from the Nuziveedu seed company led to shortages across Telangana. The seed companies that serviced Telangana, and particularly the Warangal district where Shiva lives, had failed to allot enough seeds to meet projected demand. The maximum retail price assigned by the state prevented shops from legally raising prices in response, so farmers who could afford to do so rushed to Warangal city shops to preorder seeds. To control demand and temper high market prices during this period of seed scarcity, the state government distributed permits that guaranteed a given seed's price and availability based on shop preorders. Permits (figure 9), distributed to farmers from their local government office through a lottery system, specified a particular shop, seed brand, price, and the number of packets an individual could purchase. In this way, one farmer got one permit for one package at one shop. This solution is, at best, naïve. As the collective spikes in seed-buying show, farmers were not necessarily acting rationally based on prices or yields—they wanted the popular seeds! In practice, by capping the cost for these seeds far below what farmers were willing to pay, the state government unintentionally created a black market to serve those farmers without seed permits.

---

[*] *Neeraja* (MRC 7201-BGII), *Dr. Brent* (MRC 7347-BGII), *Kanak* (MRC 7351-BGII). The trade name of the seed brand is listed first with the hybrid number given in parentheses.
[†] *Mallika* (Bt-NCS 207).

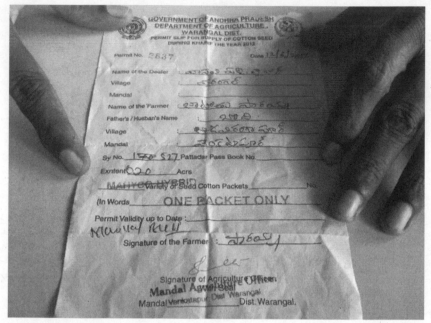

FIGURE 9. Government seed permit distributed to guarantee seed packets to farmers. Photo by Andrew Flachs.

Black-market brokers provided 12 percent of cottonseed choices I recorded between 2012 and 2014. Prices varied, but farmers could expect to pay at least twice the shop rate (two thousand rupees or forty dollars) for black-market seed packets that should cost ₹930 ($18.60).* Selling seeds covered under the permit system in 2012 was expensive and required shop owners to take out loans with high interest rates—the "more we invest in [subsidized brand] *Mahyco*, the more we lose," scoffed a Warangal shop owner in an interview. To mitigate this loss, some shop owners charged farmers extra "transportation costs" that mysteriously disappeared from receipts. Most of the black-market seeds, however, came from entrepreneurial smugglers. Gongapalle, one of the sample Warangal villages with wealthier farmers who had family connections to the state of Maharashtra, sent a delegate with pockets full of cash and an order to bring back *Neeraja*, 2012's popular seed. Prakash, a cotton farmer who received these seeds, leaned forward

---

* One seed packet is sufficient to plant one acre of cotton at a "double lining," in which plants and rows are equally spaced, usually about 90 cm × 90 cm. Since 2013, many farmers have begun "single lining," in which the spacing is tighter and two packets are required to plant an acre. Spacing will be discussed later in this chapter.

on his cloth cot conspiratorially to tell me how the smuggler crossed the border. "He bought the seeds in Maharashtra and then smuggled them back in his bag, in his coat, even under his turban!" "What happens if he had been caught?" I asked. "He would've been sent to jail, of course," Prakash answered. "Haven't you heard about shop owners being sent to jail?" Such stories were rampant in the press in 2012 (*New Indian Express* 2012; *Hindu* 2012). Grinning, Prakash concluded, "It is worth the risk. He who does not get caught will be king!"

In addition to the necessarily higher investment cost of purchasing their favorite seeds in the black market, farmers stressed two risks when buying seeds from brokers: seed resellers give no bill of sale, and they sometimes sell *nakkali* (Telugu: "fake" or "duplicate") seeds. *Nakkali* is a broad category and can refer to seeds labeled as the wrong brand, seeds containing no Bt gene that are supposed to be sown in a non-Bt refuge border around the field, or seeds that fail to germinate. In one instance, an angry farmer showed me *nakkali* seeds from a packet that turned out to contain pigeon pea, not cottonseed. The problem of receipts is significant, as receipts give cotton farmers a path to recourse. Should the seeds fail to germinate, as is especially likely in times of drought or unpredictable weather, they can present their bill of sale to agricultural officers, who may then compensate farmers for lost revenue. When farmers buy at extra cost in the black market, they waive their right to this compensation. This places farmers with the least access to desirable seeds at the most risk for being cheated. In a spatial comparison of Ralledapalle and Kavrupad farms, we (Flachs, Stone, and Shaffer 2017) have shown that the relatively poorer, tribal farmers of Ralledapalle followed the seed fads more intensely during the first ten years of GM cotton planting. When shops run out of fad seeds, it is these farmers who are most likely to turn to unscrupulous brokers. All this for a seed with no discernable benefit over the others!

LEARNING AMID CHOICE OVERLOAD COTTON AGRICULTURE

In 2002, Indian farmers had the option of buying three legal GM seeds alongside a cottage industry of illegal Bt seeds based in Gujarat. By 2012, the illegally produced Gujarati Navbharat-151 had disappeared, and farmers in the Warangal district were choosing among 1,200 legally available seeds. Facing seed shortages, Warangal cotton growers in 2012 turned to riskier, smuggled, unlabeled seeds sold by brokers only after they failed to obtain those seeds legally and always with the hope that the seed they purchased was the brand it claimed to be. Troublesome though the black market is, farmers are perplexed enough by the explosion of legal seed brands purchased at seed shops, many of which are duplicitously labeled and contain the same hybrid constructs. The unrecognizability, fast-paced change, and inconsistency of labeling in the Indian cotton sector led Stone (2007) to argue that the market had "deskilled" farmers. As of 2018, legally planted GM seeds contain one of seven gene constructs, but the vast majority (table 1) of these seeds contain the gene construct MON 15985 since 2013, a second generation, Bt-expressing Cry gene construct licensed by Monsanto under the trade name Bollgard II. MON 15985 contains two different versions of the insecticidal Cry proteins found in *Bacillus thuringiensis*. Although I spoke with some Maharastran farmers in 2014 who planted illegally obtained F1 research hybrids of the as-yet unreleased next generation of GM cotton, which stacks traits for Bt and resistance to Monsanto's herbicide Roundup, the corporate market has little to fear from spurious and viciously hated *nakkali* seeds.

TABLE 1. Gene constructs in Indian GM cottonseeds, 2002–11.

GENE CONSTRUCT	2002	2004	2005	2007	2008	2009	2010	2011	GRAND TOTAL
(Cry 1Ab -Cry 1Ac) "FM Cry 1A" G				3	10	32	12	7	64
Cry 1 Ab+Cry 1 Ac			1						1
Cry 1 Ab+Cry 1C			1						1
Cry1C (Event S9124)					2				2
Fusion-Bt/GFM Cry 1A								3	3
MON 15985			7	10	53	130	142	256	598
Mon 531	3	1	38	50	43	53	34	8	230
Grand total	3	1	47	63	108	215	188	274	899

Source: GEAC 2012.

Note: Numbers reflect the number of seeds approved by GEAC per specific genetic modification, representing fifty-four companies. By 2011, most new seeds contained Monsanto's 15985 event, the second-generation Bt technology Bollgard II. No new constructs have been approved since 2012.

Farmers in Warangal encounter hundreds of seeds between different shops. Such brand diversity and heavy competition should be a boon for farmers, cutting costs and raising the quality of the seed products. As illustrated by the seed fads, however, this is not the case (Stone, Flachs, and Diepenbrock 2014). One barrier to this behavior is a lack of price differential. State governments across India have subsidized agricultural inputs, including seeds, and the Telangana seed market is capped by a maximum retail price. Individual seed brands cannot distinguish themselves on the basis of price points, and companies have few incentives to develop and sell superior products. Because no GM cottonseeds could be sold for more than Rs 930 when I was conducting this research, all seeds with Bollgard II technology were sold for Rs 930. Furthermore, farmers have no guarantee that differently labeled seeds are, in fact, different. As Monsanto India supply-chain lead C. Rajesh explains:

> It is possible in India to market the same hybrid code, same basic thing, under different brand names. . . . You may want to do it partly because the Indian farmer is looking for diversification. You know, even if your product is very, very good. The theory at least doing the rounds is that the Indian farmer never wants to put [just] one hybrid, all their eggs into one basket. Even if he's got a tiny farm of under five acres, you take that and you split it up between two, three, or four hybrids. That is one part of the equation. The other part of the equation is the retailers. . . . In the same road there can be twenty, thirty shops all selling the same product. As the demand of a particular product becomes high, people start to compete with each other.

Rajesh was quick to note that this is not Monsanto India's strategy, as his company makes money more from GM licensing than seed sales. Observing multiple hybrids marketed under different trade names, Stone (2007) argues that the destabilization of the local farmer knowledge base may have begun with the introduction of hybrid seeds but has intensified with GM hybrid marketing. Available seed brands jumped from four to fifty-one in 2005 and continued to grow every year since (table 1). What manifested first as village-wide fads had become more intense, district-wide fads by 2012, manifesting as a distinct herding phenomenon (Stone, Flachs, and Diepenbrock 2014).

In part, cotton knowledge is so surprising because the exact same farmers make completely different kinds of decisions about the rice and vegetables that they grow alongside their cotton (Flachs and Stone 2018; Flachs 2015). While cotton grows from July until January, farmers also plant two crops of rice, many plant maize, and nearly all plant small vegetables and flowers in the gaps where cotton fails to germinate. Yet because farmers often save those seeds, have more experience planting them, and change them more slowly, they can build and use rice knowledge far more effectively than they use cotton knowledge. The daily practices associated with rice seeds, for example, allow farmers to build very different kinds of socioecological relationships in the field. Local taxonomies distinguish rice by grain thickness and taste, distinctions that farmers create by running their hands through rice seeds, noting variation and damage. This is not possible with packaged neon-pink cottonseed. Rice cultivation is a nuanced process of change and becoming, sometimes literally, as in the Telugu word *annum*, which signifies both rice and food. The labor relationships are also different. While hired labor is certainly present in rice agriculture, the labor is often more communal and managed by relatives and neighbors. Rice fields must be shaped, flooded in coordination with neighbors, transplanted, and harvested within short time frames. Rather than seeking the most expedient way to transform commodities into profits, farmers choose rice or vegetable seeds based on known aesthetic qualities or because of a personal connection to the grower. Farmers calculate risk completely differently in rice and field-gap vegetables because these seeds are hardly ever gambles that the unknown will produce for them. Yet, farmers can make much more money from cotton. Overwhelmingly, it is older farmers with relatively small landholdings who grow rice and don't grow cotton—people with little interest in risk and for whom even a small gain is worthwhile.

I do not want readers to come away with the idea that farmers are stupid and incapable of making important decisions, or that this phenomenon of uncertainty exists only in agriculture. When seeds become a commodity produced off farm, and when that commodity becomes difficult to distinguish, farmers encounter a space social psychologists and behavioral economists call *choice overload* (Chernev, Böckenholt, and Goodman 2015; Scheibehenne, Greifeneder, and Todd 2010). It is hard to pin down exactly how many choices are overwhelming, but choice overload describes the tendency for more options to lead to fewer actual purchases and less satisfaction with them. Studies of choice overload question if more is actually better. In one influential study, Iyengar and Lepper (2000) asked grocery store shoppers, Stanford undergraduates, and Columbia undergraduates to choose between a wide or narrow field of jams, essay topics, and chocolates respectively. The results were surprising: 30 percent of the jam shoppers bought jam when presented with six choices, compared to 3 percent presented with an array of twenty-four jams; Stanford psychology undergraduates scored better and were more likely to complete an essay assignment when given fewer options; and the Columbia students were four times more likely to take chocolate rather than a comparable cash prize when presented with six rather than thirty chocolate options. Unlike cottonseed choices, food and essays are low-stakes decisions, but Iyengar, Huberman, and Jang (2004) also examined choice overload in American 401(k) plans. Even though a 401(k) can make or break an employee's retirement, participation dropped as employees were offered more plan options. Among those who had invested with the management company Vanguard, employees were less likely to contribute as the list of funds grew: every ten funds added was associated with a 1.5 percent to 2 percent drop in participation.

Choice overload does not happen in all cases of large and confusing markets—the supermarket where Iyengar and Lepper conducted their initial study offered 250 different varieties of mustard, seventy-five different varieties of olive oil, and over 300 varieties of jam. Rather, meta-analyses indicate that choice overload is prevalent when the decision is high stakes, when consumers have problems differentiating between products, when a clearly superior product does not exist, when the intended use for the product is difficult and complex, and when it is difficult to clearly compare, or experiment with, similar products (Chernev, Böckenholt, and Goodman 2015; Scheibehenne, Greifeneder, and Todd 2010). All of these factors hold true in the Telangana cottonseed market. Iyengar and Lepper suggest that the anxieties of choice are exacerbated when truly informed decisions are difficult and the costs of making the wrong choice, or believing that one has made the wrong choice, are higher (Iyengar and Lepper 2000, 1004). Like the farmers who shrug and ask shops or *pedda* farmers what they think is best, the authors note that "the more choosers perceive their choice-making task to necessitate expert information, the more they may be inclined not to choose, and further, they may even surrender the choice to someone else—presumably more expert" (Iyengar and Lepper 2000, 1004). In the parlance of choice overload theorists, more seed product options lead to more poorly informed and anxiety-ridden decisions.

MAKING GMOS WORK THROUGH COOPERATIVES

When Kavrupad farmers like Ranjith above discuss great yields that seem attainable, they often refer to newspaper stories that profile Srigonda farmers. The village of Srigonda is just as far from Warangal as Kavrupad, but it is dominated by a large OC population of ethnic Kamma caste people who migrated to this region from comparatively better developed and richer coastal Andhra. Srigonda's soils include large swaths of fertile dark earth in addition to the red clay soils found throughout Telangana. These richer soils hold organic matter and water better than red clay, both of which help cotton grow. Yet more important to the success of the village than the soil quality or caste is Srigonda's cooperative shop. As I have argued, one of the key problems with GM cotton is the confusing market in which farmers plant their seeds and the unreliability of much firsthand information in their iterative learning process. I have described several typical shops so far, including the busy and stressful streets of Warangal and a Kavrupad shop that sells dubious products. Srigonda's cooperative is different.

To begin with, it is welcoming. Unlike many rural shops, the cooperative's cement foundation extends for several feet beyond the storefront, creating a porch. Most days, Naniram, the cooperative's manager, sets out chairs and extends a cloth awning over the space. As soon as the shop opens, farmers linger on the porch, drinking tea and debating newspaper and television reports with Naniram. The cooperative is the first place that I go when I arrive in Srigonda because it is a central node in this local social network. Like me, research scientists and corporate brokers also work through it, giving Naniram and the cooperative members access to a wide range of centralized expertise and resources.

The cooperative was steadily growing when I first visited in 2012, attracting forty-five members by 2013 and offering discounted prices to the region at large. Established in partnership with Umesh, a prominent crop scientist based at the Warangal plant science research station, the shop lowers prices through wholesale buying and reduces farmers' exposure to spurious seeds, expired pesticides, and corrupt shop owners. Like any cooperative, it collects shares from members and uses the money to buy in bulk or invest in larger projects. Through this financing, the cooperative has arranged for interest-free loans and purchased collective equipment. Because he is a trusted intermediary between farmers and the networks of scientists, companies, state extension, and NGOs that would work with them, Naniram frequently hosts crop management workshops or negotiates lower prices for new inputs. These interactions allow the cooperative to pass on expert knowledge rather than profiting from uncertainty in the cotton market, explains Gopaiah, Naniram's uncle and a high-caste, wealthy older farmer. "Not only do they only sell high-quality chemicals and give you what you ask for," he continues, "they help you even when you don't know what to ask for." Seeds, workshops, interventions, or management programs may come and go, but Naniram and the cooperative stay. This stability and local accountability help to maintain the shop's comparatively relaxed atmosphere.

Rather than scanning for other customers or selling substandard products, Naniram encourages a friendly atmosphere where farmers feel comfortable asking follow-up questions or returning to the shop with grievances. As rumors flew during the 2012 seed shortage, Naniram called a meeting to explain why some popular seeds were unavailable. He suggested, and participating farmers agreed, to democratically distribute the seed packets that their shop had been allotted. Farmers wanted to know the best alternative seeds, so Naniram called Umesh, who in turn consulted with his colleagues at the extension service and at corporate breeders. This lengthy and collective discussion on seeds and their alternatives would be unfeasible for any normal village shop. It is unthinkable in the melee of the Warangal seed and input sellers, who have their own problems with inventory, thin profit margins, and stiff competition. Naniram grimaces when I tell him about Shiva's experience in the Warangal shop. "We're all part of the cooperative," he explains, gesturing to fellow farmers on the porch. "There wouldn't be any point in cheating them." This grain of trust in an anarchic GM cotton market may explain why he sold fully half of the Srigonda farmers' cottonseeds that I documented from 2012 to 2014, dwarfing the market share of any other individual vendor in this area. Farmers from around the district, whether they are members of the cooperative or simply browsing, know and trust the shop. "The cooperative gives us good prices and advice," offered a Kavrupad farmer, highlighting its expert connections. "It has both businessmen and scientists there to help the farmers."

Naniram's pesticides and fertilizers are between twenty and one hundred rupees (one to two dollars) cheaper than those of other Telangana shops, and he sells seeds at a hundred-rupee (two-dollar) discount from the maximum retail price. But more important than this minor cost saving is the peace of mind that the cooperative provides in assuring local high-quality products and in providing trustworthy management advice. "There in Warangal they'll try to link a good seed with a fake one," explained Srigonda farmer Karthik during a focus-group discussion on the porch by the shop. "Warangal shops sell fake seeds?" I asked. It is not unheard of for urban shops to sell black-market seeds, but this is rare, and shop owners often face public sentencing (Wadke 2012). I suspected that Karthik was exaggerating here. He continued, conceding,

Not fake seeds, necessarily, but old stock. Here, Naniram is giving only what farmers are asking for. But in Warangal they are giving another unknown seed along with the best one. They are marketing people! They are marketing these fake seeds. They'll give us last year's stock this year.

At these words, the assembled farmers grumbled and nodded in assent. One farmer who had come to buy seeds and stayed to listen to our discussion pointed his finger at Karthik, saying, "It shouldn't happen like that, they shouldn't just cancel their license. Instead, they should seize the owner's property." Naniram, sitting next to Karthik, agreed, adding, "He shouldn't be eligible to issue seeds again for the rest of the season." Karthik mulled this over for a second before yelling, "Or we should throw him in jail!" We all erupted into laughter. Black-market seed brokers and shop owners did indeed see jail time in 2012 and again in 2017 for smuggling seeds (*New Indian Express* 2012; *Hindu* 2017).

The cooperative is not a perfect social institution. Naniram belongs to the village's most prominent high-caste family. Some lower-caste and Adivasi farmers complained during household interviews that Naniram's family continues to control access to agricultural resources and the flows of information from the university extension offices. Because the cooperative demands monetary shareholder investments, some poorer farmers do not participate. As wealthier and predominantly high-caste farmers invest more money in the cooperative, they have a greater say in how money is spent than the poorer lower-caste and Adivasi farmers. Naniram's friends and social circle are often the first to participate in new and subsidized development schemes including IPM or field trials of new seeds, where scientists fully compensate farmers for any lost revenue. Two of Naniram's family friends were selected for cost-saving agriculture schemes including drip irrigation systems, bird perches, and subsidized seeds. The rice sorting machine that cleans grains and filters away dust is housed at Naniram's uncle's house, meaning that anyone who wants to clean their grains must go to him to use it. Even Umesh, the Warangal extension scientist who helps to connect Srigonda to state resources, is a distant relative. In the cooperative, as in many public universities, state services, and corporate offices in South India, many of the best positions or places of power are occupied by the class of people who have held power historically. Even here, status is a generational issue.

And yet the institution as a whole strengthens farmers' ability to learn about their seeds and apply local management knowledge. Farmers can trial new methods or seeds in their fields and then work with Naniram and the extension service to correct mistakes. When the cooperative makes demands, these experts listen and help. Kavrupad and Ralledapalle farmers look to Srigonda with a mixture of jealousy and aspiration, noting their higher yields and better connectivity. This does not mean that the farmers here are necessarily wiser or better resourced. Instead, they lean on a social institution that centralizes expert knowledge and administers it collaboratively with farmers through meetings and shop consultations. The cooperative has returned trust and iterative learning to cotton agriculture in Srigonda. In the absence of this kind of social institution and iterative daily practice, Kavrupad and Ralledapalle farmers turn to rumors, social emulation, and marketing. In the confusing, unreliable world of Telangana cotton farming, Naniram's cooperative provides some much-needed stability.

POSSIBLE FUTURES ON GM COTTON FARMS

Cotton, with its high investment and potentially high payoff, is a gamble for farmers. If it pays off, farmers revel in the income and social recognition that accompanies high yields. If it fails, farmers speak of suicides, abandoning their fields for urban slums, and cutting costs like school fees, weddings, or transportation. "Why is this seed popular this year?" asked one farmer in response to my survey question. Exasperated, she delivered the Telugu proverb "*oka gorra bavilo padatha, anni gorralu bavilo padatha*": "If one goat jumps down a well, they all jump down a well." If agriculture involves improvised performance, then experience, *métis*, and personality all play a role in what sorts of decisions get made and what knowledge gets built. But in this world of uncertainty, anxiety, intense commodification, and goat-based gallows humor, what is ultimately being performed? Why is consumer science so helpful in exploring this pattern? Given this stage, farmers are performing the role of confused, frustrated, yet fundamentally hopeful consumers. And as consumers, their knowledge shifts to keeping up with the latest potential return on investment, leaving the concerns of seed choice, plant management, or field ecology to agribusiness.

As Ralledapalle farmer Shiva laments above, no one is being forced to buy pesticides or buy seeds. Furthermore, I hope I have made it clear here that there is nothing about GM seeds per se that is damaging to farmers' knowledge or environmental management. However, these are seeds introduced amid a neoliberal reorganization in rural India, one where farmer knowledge is systemically devalued in favor of commodified knowledge coming from off the farm. A cash crop, they are designed to grow in monocultures, and success is defined as only one thing—a large yield of white, fluffy cotton. This narrow framing of success closes off other possible visions of fulfillment and well-being as a cotton farmer. As a consumer, Shiva chooses seeds and inputs, learning to see his successes and failures in light of these individual choices. It does not matter that these choices are overwhelming, the result of a private market let loose in a singularly poor environment for trialing seeds. If Shiva fails to produce a high yield, perform for his community on the farm stage, or learn much about his seeds, he fails alone. Bt cottonseeds offer no change to this course.

If the question of agricultural sustainability rests as much in the knowledge of farmer-practitioners as in the technology itself, more attention must be paid to how GM farmers learn. The ability to trial various technologies in your own field and respond to the results is a necessary precondition for GM cotton knowledge among farmers adrift in a confusing market and hierarchical social geography. All farming is speculative to some extent (Gupta 2017), requiring investments of money, land, seeds, and social relationships. But farmers don't know much about the gambles they take with GM seeds, leaving few options to learn what one did wrong or manage the field better next season. As debts rise and farmers see new seeds on the shelves, they have few reliable options to improve their odds.

To call GM seed technologies sustainable, either because GM seeds raised yields or decreased sprays on a national level (Qaim 2010; Kouser and Qaim 2011; Kranthi 2012), sidesteps this anthropological question: Can farmers use this technology to learn and cultivate rural well-being? The externalization of knowledge from the farm field to the managerial office is compounded by economic factors associated with caste and social status in rural Telangana. Often, opportunistic brokers or large farmers simply sell the seeds they bought to small and marginalized farmers who desire them only because they are "popular." The original marketing thrust of GM seeds assumed that farmers would not need to do anything different to successfully grow cotton (*Thaindian News* 2008). Instead, most farmers do not trial or assess new seeds in the time required to use environmental learning to make seed decisions. Given that intimate local ecological knowledge has been shown to be crucial for sustainable endeavors, the GM seed market erodes rather than builds local efforts at sustainability. That the farmers driving village-level social learning appear to be the wealthiest, highest-status farmers rebuts claims that GM crops are a "pro-poor" technology (Qaim 2010).

The risks of GM cotton monoculture are not equally distributed across society. Women make up the vast majority of *kuli* labor because women are typically paid less than men, but landless rural men will also take jobs as weeders and pickers. Sometimes, male or female members of the household will join laborers in the field as a way to keep an eye on their workers. "If I weren't here, they wouldn't be doing anything," complained one farmer from Kavrupad. "I have to come out on days when it's very important [such as when a storm may come and promote more weed growth] so that the work gets done on time." While economic studies underscore how important underpaid women's labor is for this agrarian economy (Deb et al. 2014), in-depth qualitative work is lacking—my own included. This is especially problematic because the predominately female and poorer laborers working to weed and pick cotton experience extra risk for pesticide exposure. Even when pests are within normal parameters, farmers anxious to produce as much cotton as possible will spray their crops. After all, as Malothu argued above, if one's neighbor sprays, then you must also spray. After a long day of spraying, the smell of diesel and pesticide is thick in the air. Although men do most of the spraying, the largely young and largely female labor force of weeders and pickers are exposed to these persistent pesticides during crop management. These chemicals blow into groundwater and well systems, and those same sprays will persist on their foods. Exposure to these pesticides can cause DNA damage, hair loss, and neurological harm (Venkata et al. 2016). After a day of spraying, field workers are dizzy, nauseous, and fatigued. Even though sprays targeting sucking pests are less toxic than those targeting bollworms, this exposure is still dangerous because of the way that cotton is managed in practice (Flachs 2017a).

A GM seed cannot solve all these problems at once. The moving parts of Telangana's agrarian distress are connected through the complex socioecological relationships of the farm field. I have argued that, rather than providing a purely technological fix to solve a purely agricultural problem of pest attacks, GM seeds have compounded a social problem of uncertainty in the seed-choosing process. These seeds make cotton farming less sustainable on Telangana cotton farms because they have created a system in which farmers can't learn much about their seeds or apply that knowledge when they're at the market buying seeds next year. By examining performance, I argue that we can move beyond agriculture as a rational choice in a free market and look to stages and roles in one's daily practice. These trends aren't evidence of an inevitable market but a situation in which environmental learning is devalued. This leaves farmers still aspiring to live well as cotton farmers subject to the whims of the larger seed cycle of boom and bust. To find different assumptions about what farming is and why people should do it, we should look at an alternative system of cotton agriculture—organic production.

5

OPPORTUNISM, PERFORMANCE, AND UNDERWRITING VULNERABILITY ON ORGANIC COTTON FARMS

IKE THE other organic farmers in his hamlet, Korianna planted non-Bt cotton-seeds in 2013 and 2014. He obtained these seeds, free of charge, from Prakruti, a certified organic agriculture company that connects farmers and buyers in his part of the Adilabad district. In accordance with the trainings and guidelines set by Prakruti, Korianna fertilizes his land with cow manure and vermicom-post, and sprays his fields with a homemade mixture of cow urine, neem leaves, chilies, and garlic. "If we use [the common chemical fertilizers] DAP [diam-monium phosphate] and urea, or spray pesticides, we'll incur a loss and need to take on debt. We don't want that," explains Korianna. He was drawn to organic agriculture by the promise of higher incomes from lower costs, a chance to relieve his concerns over growing agricultural debts. Each year he found himself paying more for fertilizers and pesticides, while the yields on his unirrigated land stayed stubbornly low. This is common across Telangana because the hybrid cottonseeds that farmers plant respond best to irrigated, heavily fertilized con-ditions. Over the past several years, he read with morbid curiosity the stories of farmers who killed themselves when harvests failed and debts grew too high. Suicides peaked first a few hours north, in Vidarbha, Maharashtra, and then a few hours south, in Warangal. "You don't worry about your body or see a doctor until you're hurt," he says, justifying his recent interest in organic cotton.

I am not talking with Korianna by happenstance. Prakruti often asks him to speak with visiting scientists, donors, investors, certifiers, or interested farmers. For his time, and for conforming to Prakruti's certificatory guidelines, Korianna has received interest-free loans, seeds, and equipment. Some of his neighbors have formal part-time jobs with the company. Above all, his village has been offered a new way to succeed in low-input cotton farming that sidesteps the competitive nature of spraying and chasing yields that defines GM cotton agriculture in the Warangal district. Korianna is putting on a bit of a show when he points out the vermicompost pits and neem oil preparations stationed around his organic farm, but that effort has a cumulative effect in what Korianna knows and does. By engaging with a version of environmental development that appeals to consumers of organic clothing around the world, Korianna has changed the way he farms day to day. In building a relationship with Prakruti, he and other cotton farmers have redefined the way they calculate agricultural success.

Learning looks different on this kind of farm because the institutions that support organic cotton agriculture are fundamentally different. Korianna can conduct experiments with his seeds to seek out the best yields, but those seed choices and other management strategies are proscribed by the rules of organic agriculture. Many farmers like him develop special relationships with organic program coordinators, adapting program recommendations to local conditions as they and their households collect the lion's share of program incentives. Others participate from the margins, unwilling to completely commit to this new form of production. Any time I buy organic cotton, I support all of them through a series of interrelated assumptions: farmers do not plant GM cotton, they live better lives, and the organic clothing supply chain allows consumers like me to support this improvement.

Organic programs sell cotton by telling consumers about farmers who are isolated, poor, and in crisis. This is not a misleading description. By and large, the Telangana farmers who work with organic development groups are indeed isolated, poor, and navigating levels of agrarian distress. Yet, the story is complicated. I show in the next chapter that these labels are elements of larger and historical development narratives about crisis and isolation. Telling their story without contextualizing this crisis in India's neoliberal rural development, generational poverty, and the inequalities of global agricultural trading can lead to problematic, overly simplistic understandings of these systemic issues. Organic agriculture is not a panacea, even though it can help some farmers in some cases. Alternative development projects do not work because they are inherently better or more just. If they work in Telangana, they work because they provide an alternative way to live well as a cotton farmer.

To understand why and how organic agriculture works on these Telangana farms, I argue that we must view it as both a strategic choice to follow didactic instructions and a performance on a new kind of agricultural stage. In this chapter, I examine how farmers and NGO managers mutually develop strategies to keep donors and cotton growers engaged in organic projects even as the rest of the country is dominated by Bt cotton cultivation. On GM cotton farms, the markets and dynamics of learning prevent farmers from learning much about their seed choices. On organic farms, choices are actively, institutionally taken out of farmers' hands. Is it possible for such proscribed learning to be sustainable when NGOs mediate the production process and elite foreign consumers are the primary market? I argue that organic agriculture can help farmers pursue well-being, but only when farmers adapt agricultural knowledge to their fields and benefit from new forms of social capital.

TRUST AND REGULATION IN INDIAN ORGANIC AGRICULTURE

The global organic industry is built on trust. International brands with names like Synergy, PACT, Shift to Nature, and Bhumi (Sanskrit and Telugu for "earth") emphasize that their extra costs are paid forward to the workers and environments where cotton is grown. Unlike organic food, consumers gain few direct benefits from organic cotton clothing (an exception being infants and those especially sensitive to pesticide residues). Rather, many consumers buy certified organic clothes because they trust that the label guarantees a better life or environment for the people who grow the cotton (Seufert, Ramankutty, and Mayerhofer 2017; Franz and Hassler 2010). In contemporary global capitalism, where goods are produced around the world, many of us construct identities through the brands we consume, to showcase our trendiness in a classic case of conspicuous consumption (Guthman 2009; Linssen, Kempen, and Kraaykamp 2010; Veblen 1899) or to seek solidarity with poor producers (R. L. Bryant and Goodman 2004). I might buy an organic cotton shirt to wear my environmentalist politics or because I hope that my purchase benefits small farmers in India.[*]

India's access to these global ethical markets depends on regulatory consistency and the compelling "commodity biographies" (Franz and Hassler 2010) that attach stories and sentiments to clothing across this ethical supply chain (Ramamurthy 2000; West 2012). Expanding access to international markets has allowed Indian organic agriculture to flourish, cotton included—by 2014, India boasted far more organic farmers than any other nation. Sustaining trust and providing stories of development and improvement are crucial to this growth.

Even if a GM seed is grown under organic conditions, without chemical fertilizers or pesticides, it cannot be certified as organic under any national or international label. American consumers of organic goods didn't like the kind of agriculture that GMOs represented when the USDA began drafting organic regulations (Guthman 2004), and, in the name of global consistency, the GM ban has become part of certification standards around the world. This has had a special impact on organic cotton agriculture in India. Although seeds are a relatively small part of the farmer budget, the swift and massive adoption of GM seeds has caused the alternative agriculture sector to scramble to address a non-GM seed shortage for India's organic cotton farmers and marketers (Desmond 2017; Kumbamu 2009). So far, they have been wildly successful. Although more than 95 percent of the cottonseeds planted in India are genetically modified and prohibited from organic markets, Indian organic agriculture provides a whopping 74 percent of the organic cotton in the market today (Willer and Lernoud 2016)! Most of this cotton is destined for an international export market that dwarfs domestic consumption.

Telangana organic cotton farmers tend crops in a historically underdeveloped region known for the aggressive adoption of GM crops and farmer distress (Stone 2007; Galab, Revathi, and Reddy 2009), a narrative that organic cotton producers have embraced to rally support for their alternative (Desmond 2013; Flachs 2016b). To justify organic clothing's added costs, farmers and merchants must convince consumers that they're buying ethical or environmentally sound clothes. This means that organic agriculture relies on a kind of audit culture

---

[*]   This benefit does not always come to fruition. Anthropologists like Paige West (2012) and Sarah Besky (2014) have noted that ethical trading premiums do not translate to increased farmer incomes in their studies of coffee and tea, respectively. The cotton farmers that I met received only a modest (6–10 percent) price premium for their efforts. As I discuss below, there are other reasons beyond the price premium that motivate farmers to grow organic cotton.

(Strathern 2000), in which bureaucratic institutions ask communities to perform accountability: trust is maintained through certification forms, auditing field-coordinators, fact-finding visits from investors and scientists, and internal inspections that ask farmers to regulate themselves and make sure that their neighbors maintain transnational standards (D. Sen and Majumder 2011; Galvin 2018). Organic companies then brand this trust through labels, legible to consumers and backed up by international regulations. Labels differentiate commodities in the store, emphasizing the people and places hidden by mass textile marketing across cotton's long and complicated supply chain.

Unlike organic farms in countries like the USA, where organic markets are well established and consumers trust regulatory apparatuses, Telangana farmers hoping to sell organic cotton cannot simply declare themselves to be organic and sell to foreign buyers or urban elites. This again is a matter of trust. Cotton must be grown, spun, dyed, woven, and exported, and each of these steps requires oversight and infrastructure to challenge the environmental and socioeconomic injustices of the clothing industry (Brooks 2015). Rather than face this as individual smallholders, organic cotton farmers join forces with development programs, including NGOs and corporations who bridge gaps in marketing, regulation, quality control, and transportation between farms and buyers. International regulatory consistency allows European, Japanese, and American accreditation bodies to accept Indian products without recertifying them, while growing domestic demand has fueled a rise in third-party NGO or corporate certifiers preferred by smaller operations in India (Fouilleux and Loconto 2017). These partnerships are built on a shared vision of agricultural development, but both parties have reason to be wary: farmers have learned to be skeptical of agricultural interventions promising change but producing few practical results, while organizations watch for farmers who break rules and compromise their certification status (Altenbuchner, Vogel, and Larcher 2017; Prashanth, Reddy, and Rao 2013).

Just as unenthusiastic development workers can frustrate farmers, rule-breaking farmers can cause major problems later in the supply chain. In one well-publicized scandal, Swedish clothing manufacturer H&M sold fraudulent organic clothing revealed to contain Bt cotton. The resulting inquiry, led by Germany's *Financial Times*, found that as much as 30 percent of certified organic cotton from India contained Bt genes and thus could not have been grown by organic farmers (Ecouterre Staff 2010; V. Deshpande 2010; Illge and Preuss 2012; Graß 2013). The different strategies by which these farms and programs make organic agriculture effective reveal both their promise for long-term sustainability and the danger in assuming that these strategies are generalizable to the larger phenomenon of organic agriculture in India or worldwide. As ever, the devil is in these farm-level details.

LOCAL ENFORCEMENT, LOCAL STORIES

Organic agriculture does not look the same across India. Despite the early promise of organic certification in states like Kerala, Sikkim, and Uttarakhand, which aggressively pursued policies of 100 percent organic production to curb socioecological distress, farmers and organizations faced difficulty enforcing regulation and finding competitive markets (Nazeer 2015; Tewari 2017). Since 2002, certification bodies have diversified throughout India, easing logistical and pricing problems faced by some early Indian organic groups (Eyhorn 2007). These platforms incentivize different kinds of farmer and institutional relationships. Although any organic cotton programs will be concerned with producing ethical textiles in a broad sense, NGO-based development programs may be more focused on farmers' socioeconomic or environmental uplifting, while private companies may be more concerned with producing competitively priced clothes that consumers desire. During my fieldwork, I met with farmers engaged with both NGO and corporate organic agriculture programs.

PANTA is a third-party NGO certifier that connects noncertified organic farmers with environmentally conscious consumers in urban Hyderabad and Secunderabad. One of PANTA's key partner villages is Ennepad, where a relative lack of infrastructure and predominately low-caste population made this community all the more appealing when PANTA began promoting IPM and later uncertified organic agriculture. Residents (and visiting anthropologists) rely on passing trucks, tractors, or bullock-carts to get to this village because it lacks bus or autorickshaw stands. In addition to cotton, Ennepad farmers grow vegetables and rice under organic conditions, including experimental water-saving rice cultivation through the system of rice intensification (SRI), a popular agricultural method for groups promoting adaptations to climate change or water scarcity (S. Basu and Leeuwis 2012; Glover 2011).

PANTA's executive director holds a PhD in agricultural extension and has worked for more than a decade to build organic agriculture networks in Telangana that circumvent state regulation in favor of internal checks and self-certifications. To add value to organic cotton, PANTA will subsidize inputs, consultations, and seeds, and help arrange trips to the buyers' markets, although the organization does not buy cotton directly. However, they do help to connect participating farmers with organic rice and vegetable buyers. Engaged urban residents can even buy organic fruits and vegetables from a store under PANTA's Hyderabad office, reassured not by a state certification but by PANTA's guarantee that the food is up to their standard. Skeptical consumers are invited to visit the farm and see for themselves, which has led to thousands of annual visits to this small village of about forty farming households. This openness is an attractive policy for me as an anthropologist seeking access to farmers, and it underscores how PANTA relies on farmers to make themselves available to visitors.

Prakruti, an internationally certified corporation also based in Secunderabad, works with farmers in Telangana, Odisha, and Maharashtra. Prakruti functions as a two-tier program. As a development NGO, Prakruti secures international funding, applies for grants, partners with national and international development initiatives, and promotes education and local entrepreneurship through community workshops. As a corporation and cooperative, they organize farmers into village, district, and state buying and selling groups that partner with other cooperatives and companies to buy and sell certified organic cotton. These commercial and development motivations are often synergistic, as international organic cotton retailers benefit by publicizing the ways in which their products contribute to socioeconomic growth, education, modernization, and village livelihoods (broadly defined). In Telangana, Prakruti certifies, inspects, and provides non-GM seeds for several ethnic Gond Adivasi villages that I call Addabad and Japur in the Adilabad district. As in Ennepad, these farmers grow cotton as part of a larger system of crops. Because they do not have access to irrigation, some Prakruti farmers will grow varieties of rice suited to dryland conditions, but most grow sorghum, purposively saved and replanted each year as a subsistence grain, along with a wide variety of vegetables, maize, and soya for market sales.

The farmers who work with Prakruti and PANTA are recruited because they belong to historically marginalized castes or tribes, they are relatively poor, they have poor relationships with agricultural extension, and they farm marginal land. Their poverty and marginality help create a story that justifies extra costs to urban or foreign consumers, adding value through a commodity biography built on environmental and socioeconomic development. Prakruti connects buyers and farmers, hiring trucks to transport cotton, building storage sites to hold the cotton until prices rise, and funneling payments back to each village's cooperative group. These arrangements can be a risk for organic buyers, as when price spikes or the need for faster cash lead farmers to sell their harvest in the open market in spite of promising it to Prakruti. Although Prakruti does not yet buy noncotton crops, they promote agricultural biodiversity by providing trainings and seeds for other crops as a cushion against total reliance on the fickle cotton market. Certified Indian organic agriculture is overseen by NPOP, which ensures that local, state, federal, or international certifiers are qualified to inspect farms and stamp the organic label. Certification involves farm-level inspections to ensure compliance, although Prakruti also receives regular audits and visits from potential investors and representatives from fair-trade certifiers who assess compliance, personally meet potential business partners, and tour farms.

Because Prakruti allowed me to sleep in their regional office when speaking with their farmers in Adilabad, I was able to accompany several official tours. Each room in the office is lined with shelves where stacks of binders house farm diaries of planting dates, field maps, landholdings, purchase records, and other details. These records are then digitized as Microsoft Excel files, comprising a paper trail and digital backups for any potential auditor or skeptical buyer. As a soft backup, many field coordinators are now entering farmer data through a smartphone and tablet app that updates to a cloud-based server. Finally, each Prakruti farm is registered with TraceNet, an online government database of producers and processors. Through TraceNet, organic exports can be tracked with a barcode that links them to export facilities, processing plants, certifiers, and the farms themselves. Registered producers can check a farm's organic conversion status, date of registry, which products and tonnage are certified for export, and even the farmer's name (APEDA 2012, 2011), entered from the handwritten records like those that teetered over the Adilabad cot where I slept. A certificate from TraceNet declaring that the product is registered in the national database has become an essential step in selling to foreign markets.

This combination of regulatory, electronic, and firsthand assurance is important to ethical cotton buyers. About once a month, visitors from foreign companies or campaigns visit Prakruti facilities on fact-finding trips to meet many of the same organic farmers I interview. The narratives, stories, experiences, photographs, and videos that they gather while on the ground in India inform the conspicuous consumption or awareness promoted by international development groups ranging from the World Bank to high-end clothing companies. When possible, I joined these tours. This is how I met Greg, the cofounder of an organic clothing company based in the United States, when his tour of Adilabad district farms intersected with my organic farmer surveys. By the time we met, Greg had already seen the corporate office in Hyderabad, met with farmers, seen Prakruti's model farm, and visited a school where some of the profits from Prakruti's value-added cotton helped to build a science lab. This was Greg's third visit to India, including stops at mills, farms, and ginning facilities. His company's website features the stories of cotton farmers, which he has personally collected during his travels. "We demand transparency," he explains, referring both to his business philosophy and his consumer base. "I always go through the whole supply chain." After lunch with Prakruti representatives at the school, we returned to the regional office where Greg's team pored over binders that lined the office. Everyone in the group was still wearing their flower garland and dot of red turmeric powder, gifts customary for guests and special occasions.

Like high-end coffee blogs that promote the exotic and aesthetic qualities consumers crave (West 2012), organic fashion blogs (Coexist Campaign 2016; Upasana 2017) highlight the transformative power of ethical consumption in the lives of cotton producers and factory workers. The stories Greg has collected are equally important in this market, and these development narratives build trust above and beyond state certification. A picture of Greg wearing a flower garland in the science lab is just as important to organic cotton sales as a certificate from TraceNet. Noting production schedules and occasionally questioning purchases of cows or chicken coops, the visitors pored over Prakruti's records and collected notes on crops sown, animals purchased, and hand-drawn field maps. The certification standards and traceability offered by APEDA and TraceNet allow Greg to use the USDA organic label that makes his products legible to American consumers like me.

PANTA and Prakruti build farmer narratives that accompany these products to sell cotton as a symbol of sustainable development. At each step in cotton's supply chain, ethical consumers face social and environmental woes: GM seeds, pesticide exposure, child labor, factory collapses, sweatshops, chemical dumping, and clothing waste. Farmers are only one node in this dizzying network of cotton's injustices and consequences, but they kick off the whole process. Their willingness to plant seeds scorned by 95 percent of the country demands special attention. Further, these farmers, and the stories they create, are the first stop of fact-finding tours by media and interested buyers seeking proof that their purchases will have a real and meaningful impact on the environment and rural life in the developing world.

"SELLING POVERTY": THE ORGANIC COTTON DEVELOPMENT NARRATIVE

"Every brand wants a story." Ceiling fans spin furiously in the conference room of a Secunderabad office, where Chender, executive director of Prakruti Organic, is explaining how he balances the demands of farmers, regulators, retailers, consumers, and his own socioenvironmental agenda through Prakruti's production chain. It is May, Telangana's hottest month, and I am sweating in my office chair next to Gulgoth, a representative of Fair Trade UK. We listen as Chender describes the time, money, and logistical difficulty he faces ensuring that brands track their spending and develop media around organic textiles. The correct balance between adding value through the commodity biography and providing a viable product can be difficult to reach, even at the highest levels of cotton corporations. "What is the advantage of tracing it back to them? What value does it add?" countered Gulgoth. She had traveled to Secunderabad to meet with representatives from Prakruti and to collect narratives from producing farmers. Like many ethical supply-chain companies, Prakruti leans on the authority of the fair-trade label in addition to the organic label, which affirms that Prakruti products are produced at higher wages, avoid child labor, return profits to villages through education and infrastructure projects, and encourage environmental conservation practices. Important for Indian cotton, fair trade bans the intentional use of GMO products. Thus, to get non-GM seeds, most Telangana fair-trade farmers would have to be part of organic programs anyway.

As a cotton marketer, Gulgoth's main responsibility is in justifying costs and campaigns to buyers. "It's a story for a product, that's what I'm saying," answered Chender. "[Our product] actually addresses poverty issues on the farm. And this is what I do, and so I think people buy it for that. But the same set of people, if they go to [British supermarket] Marks & Spencer, they may not buy that. They may not be interested because they are looking for a five-pound shirt." This is a difficult but common discussion among the staff of ethical clothing organizations. How do we make consumers and retailers used to cheap fashion care about the lives of producers? Well aware that development rhetoric can oversimplify complex socioecological issues, Indian NGOs and companies also recognize that this development story can sell cotton that improves the lives of Telangana cotton farmers. Organic cotton companies, who cannot compete with the low prices of the conventional fashion industry, shape and sell the commodity biography as a story of development and agricultural education.

Many researchers have questioned if the elite consumption of organic agricultural products is really the best way to address long-standing political and economic injustice in rural areas (Besky 2014; Jaffee 2012; Raynolds 2004), especially when most of the value generated by these supply chains remains off the farms. Practically speaking, these organizations must make the case to funders and consumers that the places where they work are the most worthy, a justification of dollars well spent. "We choose only the rainfed [unirrigated] areas," explains Prakruti program manager Sama when I asked why all the farmers that I met lived on marginal land or belonged to historically marginalized social groups. Sama continued:

> We work with cotton farmers mainly where there are high suicide rates, and we mainly focus on rainfed areas. . . . These people don't have access to resources. So, in a way they're resource-poor farmers, compared to other farmers where they have access to marketing and all. These people face a lot of exploitation, and we want to address the issues related to these problems.

Similarly, PANTA's program in Ennepad began after a pest infestation and drew on the narrative of suicide and agrarian crisis widely reported in India (Galab, Revathi, and Reddy 2009; Sainath 2013; Parsai 2012). These and other NGOs position organic agriculture as an alternative to agricultural production that favors privatized seed brands and intensive chemical inputs (Pearson 2006). By selecting marginalized people and marketing textile consumption as a development tool, these organic cotton programs make agricultural education central to consumption.

Although numerous studies have shown that cotton farmers in rainfed areas are at greater risk for suicide and chronic indebtedness (Gupta 2017; Gutierrez et al. 2015), organic development managers can feel conflicted about their role in commodifying this precarity. "I don't want to be selling poverty," admitted Prakruti finance manager Ravi as we rode between farms on a donor fact-finding trip, "but in India it happens everywhere." He reflected for a moment and continued, "I want to sell opportunity." Ravi, Sama, and almost every organic program staff member that I met struggled with this duality, balancing the clear needs of farmers facing structural difficulties in neoliberal rural India with their unease in creating a market for poverty through the very neoliberal markets that created this instability in the first place. "Selling opportunity" is the most concise way that I heard this conflict resolved, but each of these managers, from Chender and Gulgoth to Ravi and Sama, makes peace with this struggle by focusing on getting funds to local smallholder groups.

This method of reframing charity as opportunity becomes clearer as our tour continues. Ravi and I sat in a rented car at the back of a small convoy of American investors, like Greg, who were considering buying cotton from Prakruti farmers. We parked near the front of a village under a banner that welcomed our visit and thanked the visiting group of American cotton retailers for financing a small poultry breeding facility. Like Greg's impact at the science lab, these side projects inform the commodity biography of organic cotton: buy these farmers' cotton, and the premiums will be invested in entrepreneurial and social-justice initiatives.

The investors toured the mud-brick chicken coop, noting its corrugated steel roof, light fixtures, plastic water feeders, and several dozen chickens. How much did this cost? asked one. Arjuna, a Prakruti field coordinator, answered that the coop cost forty-five thousand rupees (approximately seven hundred dollars). This seemed excessive to me, and I raised an eyebrow at Ravi. "Don't ask me, ask them," Ravi suggested when I voiced my suspicions. And so, I asked the farmers directly, in Telugu, who answered that it had cost fifteen thousand rupees. Ravi explained that the forty-five thousand rupees referred to the total amount given for the small project. That amount would be good enough to fund other projects and subsidize low cotton yields, with money left over to repair and maintain the coop.

Superficially, this is fraud—retailers donated money and were misled about the use of their funds. But I argue it would be wrong to understand this financial alchemy as theft. Prakruti farmers and managers, far more than foreign retailers, recognized the need for extra funds and the uses to which they could be put. Everyone involved recognized the narrative of crisis and charity, and rather than accept it uncritically, used it to their advantage: the foreign retailers used the story to help brand their textiles; Prakruti staged this tour to satisfy the buyers and provide a legible example of the rippling benefits of organic, fair-trade cotton; farmers and regional Prakruti coordinators worked together to stretch that money as far as possible and subsidize agricultural work for the next season so that farmers would not have to take on more debt. This escape valve from the seasonal debts of cotton farming has made organic agriculture attractive and stable for farmers like Korianna. Given that indebtedness is a major factor for farmer suicides, organic agriculture's potential to reduce debts on these and other Telangana cotton farms

(Desmond 2016) is promising. Importantly, this is not because organic agriculture is inherently more profitable or better for farmers, but because organic institutions like Prakruti work with farmers and donors to create socioeconomic safety nets. If the goal of this kind of agricultural development is to reduce rural precarity and make it easier to be a cotton farmer, this isn't fraud—this is the social work by which alternative cotton agriculture is sustained.

In adapting the donation to the local needs of the village, Prakruti helped to make this well-meaning project far more sustainable and useful to the overall mission of organic cotton and socioeconomic development in Japur. Prakruti and the foreign retailers have a great deal invested in making organic agriculture work here. When farmers and program managers fail to maintain organic management through the cotton supply chain, the resulting miscommunications can cause serious problems for clothing retailers, as H&M discovered. The question is thus one of long-term sales: How to maintain regulation that appeals to consumers, farmers, funders, and managers?

INCENTIVE AND PERFORMANCE: UNDERWRITING VULNERABILITY IN ORGANIC AGRICULTURE

In published literature (Forster et al. 2013; Kathage and Qaim 2012) and in my own study, the average differences in yield between organic and Bt cotton agriculture are stark (figure 10). Because organic agriculture in many countries is tied to land remediation or the socioeconomic development of marginal farmers, yields can be highly variable (Seufert and Ramankutty 2017). Still, they tend to be 10–25 percent lower than comparable nonorganic production (Meemken and Qaim 2018).

Descriptive Statistics Table

	2012 GM	2012 ORGANIC	2013 GM	2013 ORGANIC (ONLY PRAKRUTI FARMERS)
n	293	98	226	94
Mean	7.64	2.00	7.06	2.45
SD	3.66	2.38	2.78	3.90
Minimum	0.50	0.00	0.17	0.02
Maximum	27.5	13	18	40

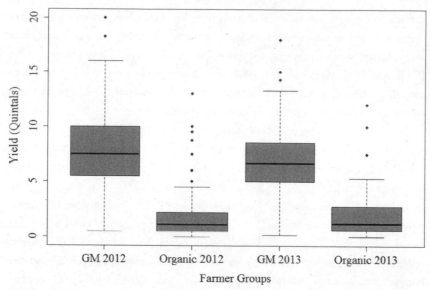

FIGURE 10. Boxplot of cotton yields per acre per household of organic and GM farmers. In each year, these differences were statistically significant at $p < .001$. Source: Flachs farmer survey 2012–14. Figure adapted from Flachs 2016b.

There are several problems directly comparing Adilabad organic farmer cotton yields with the GM Warangal district farmers. These organic farmers were recruited because they are more marginal and live on more marginal land, so one should expect them to have lower yields anyway; I did not survey GM-planting farmers in the Adilabad district, so while the agronomic conditions are similar to Warangal farmers, they are not exactly comparable; the seeds organic farmers plant are most often fertilizer- and water-intensive hybrids bred for non-Bt refuge areas by GM hybrid seed breeders and so underproduce on fertilizer-free, rain-fed organic farms.

Caveats aside, these cotton yields are poor. Recall from the previous chapter that Warangal GM cotton farmers are obsessed with yields, and the hope for good yields, *manci digubadi*, is paramount on those farms. Organic farmers in the Adilabad district and Ennepad are well aware that their yields are below those enjoyed by their pesticide-spraying, Bt-cotton-planting neighbors. During one interview with a Prakruti farmer, a neighbor driving a motorcycle stopped to tease us. "Why are you asking about their farms?" he asked me. "With [Bt cottonseed] Ajeet-155 I am getting much better yields than these people. Besides, with this organic production you have to spend time at many meetings!" Stung, the farmer I was speaking with countered, "Those with money can afford to use GM seeds and make large investments." The neighbor rode away, but not before bragging about his recent impressive harvest with Bt cotton and pesticides. Program instructions may help farmers feel better about their planting choices or convince them that these choices are correct, but that active instruction can only last so long in the face of economic failure or this social jousting. This begs an interesting question that strikes at the heart of economic rationalism, farmer decision-making, and the spread of technological innovations. With such low yields, why do farmers not leave the programs that I studied?

By this point in the book, I hope that readers are convinced that Telangana cotton agriculture can be a difficult livelihood. Pesticide exposure, rising agricultural costs, and the specter of suicide haunts the margins of agricultural life. Yet while India's neoliberal success story privileges urban development and the conspicuous wealth of open markets, farmland has signaled wealth for centuries in India (Ludden 1999), an aspiration only recently available to historically marginalized Dalit and Adivasi farmers throughout Telangana and elsewhere in South India. For farmers open to a vision of agriculture larger than the *manci digubadi* future offered by GM seeds, organic development programs provide an alternative reward structure. Prakruti and PANTA succeed insofar as they offer (1) structural incentives that reduce socioeconomic vulnerability in organic agriculture and (2) various forms of affective value through celebrity and living well in rural India.

Like Korianna in the opening vignette, organic farmers argue that agrichemical inputs damage the land or create debt. "Urea and DAP stop working after fifteen days, while cow manure gives energy to the soil for three years," explained a Prakruti participant during an interview. His neighbor added, "By using outside methods like chemical fertilizers, we spend too much. We used these fertilizers with Bt cotton, which yielded somewhat more, but it was not worth it. With organic farming we need only cow dung. The organic yield is less, but the investment is zero—all we get is profit." The material incentives are crucial for the long-term success of Indian organic agriculture, a move I have discussed elsewhere as redefining success in the cotton sector (Flachs 2016b). However, understanding the ways in which organic agriculture allows farmers to see themselves as soil builders (Galvin 2014) or stewards of an alternative future (Thottathil 2014) is also crucial to learning why organic agriculture succeeds or fails. In each case, farmers learn how and what to be. As in Debarati

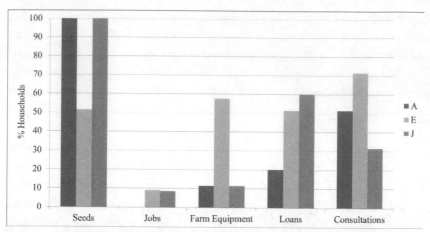

FIGURE 11. Percentage of households receiving material benefits from organic programs 2012–13 (*n* = 101) for Addabad (A), Ennepad (E), and Japur (J) villages. Source: Flachs farmer survey 2013. Figure adapted from Flachs 2016b.

Sen's (2017) study of organic tea farmers in Darjeeling, new organic identities are performed and reinforced through the daily practice of agriculture. Through agriculture, farmers fulfill obligations and responsibilities to audiences including households, visitors, and their own farms.

Ultimately, these organic development programs replace the high-stakes quest for yields with a subsidized quest for stability and security. Many farmers in these villages benefit from equipment, seeds, and access to government schemes (figure 11). In 2012 and 2013, organic programs provided access to a huge percentage of the seeds that farmers planted. One hundred percent of Prakruti farmers in Addabad and Japur receive free seeds, for example. Given that more than 95 percent of the cotton planted in India is genetically modified, many programs find it best to provide the seeds they want farmers to plant (Altenbuchner, Vogel, and Larcher 2017). Providing the seeds also saves time and stress. Comparatively isolated, poor villages like Addabad and Japur are at least an hour and a fifty- to one-hundred-rupee round trip transport fare from the nearest store. This is a lot of time and a not insignificant expense. As with Shiva in chapter 4, many shop owners will treat Adivasi farmers with contempt or brusqueness. Why spend time and money to be brushed off? Kranthi, an older Japur farmer, grimaced when asked to recount a recent, preorganic interaction in an agricultural input shop. "I ask for cotton, he gives me what he thinks is best, he doesn't ask my name, I don't ask his name, I don't say my name, and he doesn't say his—he just takes the money and I take the seeds and no one knows anything else!" This interaction is much funnier in Telugu, as Kranthi could escalate the volume of the story with each negation, *emi ledu*. In this context *emi ledu* negates all of the asking and knowing of his name (*emi ledu*), the shop owner's name (*emi ledu*), and the seed name (*emi ledu*), before bellowing (*EMI LEDU!*) that no one learned anything from the interaction and dissolving into bitter laughter.

Like all Telangana seed shops, the organic distributors will give seeds on credit. Unlike those shops, they provide credit at low or often zero interest rates and allow more wiggle room during repayment. Unlike, for example, the shop where Kranthi would buy seeds, the organic project directors made a point to personally know the farmers and discuss buying and selling options with them at length. In addition to seeds, many farmers also secure equipment or loans through these programs. While the government has a number of schemes designed to appeal to farmers, the inefficient and sometimes inept bureaucracy can be difficult to navigate for individual marginal farmers. Organic intervention programs step in to connect farmers with money or infrastructure for which they are eligible. Through these programs, farmers have received seed-cleaning machines and water infrastructure, and some are even directly employed to lead workshops or report rule breakers.

ENFORCING SUSTAINABILITY THROUGH EARLY ADOPTERS

In organic and nonpesticide management (NPM) training programs throughout South India (Eyhorn, Ramakrishnan, and Mäder 2007; Mancini, Van Bruggen, and Jiggins 2007), development programs working in a new area first recruit influential farmers. Their backing helps to build rapport in villages chosen because they are poor, isolated, or otherwise in need of development in the first place. Prakruti farmer Jenaram seized on the opportunity to try organic agriculture as a way to stop spraying pesticides. Like other early adopters of new technology, including hybrid maize seeds in the United States and Bt cottonseeds in India, Jenaram was wealthier and better educated than the other farmers in Japur. His bachelor of science degree gave him social clout, and when he spoke about the risks of pesticide sprays for the village's long-term ecology, fellow farmers listened. As a child, he helped his family grow cotton, but "now we're the computer generation," he said, sheepishly. Educating children and going to school are obviously good opportunities, he explained, but India is a nation of farmers. "I want my children to have good land." This ambivalence about the kinds of rural well-being offered by speculative agriculture and educa- tion is common among GM and organic farmers alike. While celebrating their achievements, many older farmers lament that educated young people have left the village for opportunities in Hyderabad and Bangalore that impel them to sell off family land.

For their part, educated farmers in their thirties like Jenaram are frustrated that they are losing some of the ecological knowledge of their parents and that they did not see a good way to make a living as farmers. "How are your yields?" I asked Jenaram, and he waved this question aside. "They're lower than my neighbors, especially in the first few years of organic farming," he answered, "but that's not what this is about. More important are the benefits that we get for our health and to *this* health." He gestured to a farm containing dozens of plant species. "When you are not using any chemicals, there is no risk of poisoning yourself, or the animals, or other people who work in the fields. It's poison, it's dangerous! Look at the soil—cow manure gives it lasting strength through all sorts of micronutrients. This is just good science." The reference to manure and soil health has special resonance for religious Hindu farmers like Jenaram who regard cows as sacred. As anthropologist Akhil Gupta (1998) observed, many Hindu farmers value cow manure over chemical fertilizers because it provides a broader, incalculable, holistic benefit to the land itself.* Initially recruited farm- ers like Jenaram are called upon to help enforce organic methods and demon- strate new techniques. These are the farmers who must learn to create organic pesticides and build vermicompost pits, whether they ultimately use them in their fields or not. Rather than learn to produce organic fertilizers and pesticides themselves, others in the village rely on these zealous early adopters to distribute them. Jenaram alone in Japur creates and shares the organic pesticide mixture of neem leaves, chili, garlic, and cow urine, which burned in my nose for an hour after I smelled it.

The demands of village meetings, self-help groups, and cooperative planning sessions fall to the most enthusiastic farmers. Others are happy to avoid this time-consuming work. "I'm not educated, how can I go?" complains Prakruti farmer Mankarao. "In group meetings, everyone else explains what to do,

---

* This has been a major concern outside of India as well, where farmers in Europe and the USA con- cerned about soil health have chafed against the reductionist logic of nitrogen-phosphorous-potassium fertilizers (Foster and Magdoff 2000; Kloppenburg 2004; Stoll 2002).

especially the *sarpanch* and the educated farmers.'" "We don't go to meetings, they're far away—others go and report back to us," agreed his neighbor. Such farmers are, as a rule, uninterested in going to meetings and participating in tours or lengthy training sessions organized by the organic groups. In turn, these programs recognize that many of their farmers are happy to participate but not proselytize for them.

This has complex consequences for firsthand environmental learning and the ultimate staying power of these interventions. Where GM farmers have too many choices to parse through, many organic farmers have no real choice in what they plant. Organic farmers must buy from their sponsoring programs, which provide Telangana's only source of reliable non-Bt seed. These seeds are sometimes sold to farmers at favorable prices, but more often they are provided for free due to various state and NGO subsidies. In 2013, 2014, and 2018, farmers I met only had access to two seed brands through organic vendors: non-Bt *Mallika* and non-Bt *Bunny*, purchased from the non-GM refugia stock of commercial Bt seed breeders. What would be the use of firsthand knowledge about these seeds? Farmers have no choice in their seeds and no need to trial methods because their sponsors have an active interest troubleshooting these problems to keep the program attractive.

Prakruti farmer Anil planted non-Bt *Mallika* in 2013 but remembered that *Bunny* had been good in the past. "Last year my neighbor did well with this seed," he noted—a direct observation of yield payoffs. In 2014 he planted both to see which would be better in his field. According to his observations, *Bunny's* plants are smaller and produce fewer bolls than *Mallika*. His neighbor, Allaram, is copying those choices because Anil is an experienced organic farmer and a Patel, meaning that his family owned many acres and was socially important in the past—an example of a prestige bias influencing social emulation. Fourteen of the Prakruti farmers followed suit, planting both of the organic seeds offered in 2013 and 2014. Others, like Ponam, who lives on the other side of the village, sought out *Mallika* on the recommendation of their neighbors. These dynamics are not dissimilar from those on GM farms. Except here, the stakes have been removed. Ponam could not plant *Mallika* because that seed had sold out by the time he was ready to sow. Unconcerned, he planted *Bunny*. "So far, it's growing fine," he offered. "We have to wait for the harvest." If the harvest flounders, Ponam can take solace in knowing that other aspects of his farmwork

---

* The local elected village leader and liaison to other municipal authorities.

will be subsidized, or that proceeds from the broader community's profits will go toward school programs and infrastructure. Certainly, he has no reason to pay extra or seek out a black-market broker! Rather than careen from seed to seed, anxiously chasing rumors of high yields, organic farmers consider only two seeds and receive explicit instructions about how to manage them. Organic agriculture takes the gambling out of farmwork.

THE SOCIAL BENEFITS OF BEING AN ORGANIC SHOW FARMER

Cotton breeding is difficult work. Cotton flowers usually self-pollinate, leading to drop-offs in yield if hybrids cross-pollinate and reproduce from this limited stock. Commercial and village breeders must painstakingly collect pollen from cotton's male stamens and brush it onto other plants, while emasculating those flowers to prevent self-pollination. In Ennepad and on a demonstration farm in Japur, some farmers rise to these challenges. Mahesh, a respected *pedda raytu* in Ennepad, has been making his own cottonseeds for several years: "We are the farmers," he explains. "We should not depend on others to get seeds." How's it going? I asked. "Terrible! The seeds are not coming up, it didn't work this year," he answers with a grin. This casual rejoinder is the response of a farmer for whom the stakes of environmental learning have been removed. These seeds and knowledge about them are, in effect, inconsequential to Mahesh's livelihood. Instead, he pursues this knowledge for its own sake and to secure his position as a trusted PANTA intermediary. Mahesh showed me how he identifies the best candidates for seed saving by their thick leaves and large fruiting bolls. He surveys the field for uniformity in height and stem thickness, carefully checking his seeds for *beriki*, a term referring to a light or cracked husk that would suggest that the seeds are of poor quality. He tells me how one must time pollination carefully to spread desirable pollen while preventing unwanted male stamens from dropping their own genetic material. He explains that if you replant seeds too many times in a row, the production will drop and (he says with a wizened grin) "they will perform like an old man like me." When new infrastructure is available or when the media wants to feature a farmer, farmers like Mahesh step up to reap their social and material rewards.

For these few, organic farming is not merely a subsidized form of agricultural production. It provides a way to live well as a good farmer and a responsible, caring member of the larger community. Following Stone (2014), I have called these people "show farmers" (Flachs 2017b) to highlight the affective, performative nature of their agricultural work. Show farmers are often early adopters who develop relationships with the organic programs over time. Those closest to the program learn how to make and use organic pesticides, taking into account local variations in neem leaf toxicity or cow urine potency. These farmers are often, although not always, better educated, wealthier, and have greater landholdings than the rest of the village (Flachs 2016a), meaning that they not only have greater flexibility in trying new methods but are also better candidates for the rest of the village to emulate. This is a complex argument—I argue that is possible to be both a show farmer and a sincere agricultural manager engaged with an objectively beneficial institution for socioeconomic uplifting. I use the term here to call attention to the performative nature of agriculture, not to imply that these farmers are merely hamming it up for visitors.

Where the GM farmers I described in the previous chapter perform the role of hopeful consumers, Mahesh designs crop rotations, breeds seeds, and disseminates plant-based pesticides. An older farmer eager to share his experiences with visitors like myself, Mahesh performs the role of a highly skilled farmer. Like all such performances, it has shaped his sense of what it means to farm well and helped him build a nuanced local environmental knowledge. "We can't depend on the companies, because if their seeds fail or they mislead you, you have no recourse and no one to blame but yourself. If you go down that road, you just have to keep buying things until you can force success out of the plant. With your own seeds you can be sure of what you're planting and better predict how it will work." The rest of the village is less convinced. Mahesh's saved seeds account for only 16 percent of Ennepad cottonseed choices from 2012 to 2013, belonging to Mahesh and his closest friends. It is much easier to buy seeds, especially when PANTA subsidizes them. Mahesh doesn't have to breed seeds or perfect pesticide recipes, yet he does so to keep up this performance. "People aren't that interested in my seeds," he admits with a sigh. "They're happy to take from others but that's not correct." Performing this role and knowing these agricultural skills makes farming fun and worthwhile for Mahesh, who has by now given away most of his land to his sons.

Rather than encourage individual farmers to breed seeds, Prakruti has built a show farm landscape near Japur. Frustrated with the non-Bt refugia hybrids available to organic farmers, Prakruti CEO Chender procured germplasm from GM breeder Nuziveedu Seeds, as well as from university breeders. From a potential forty-two varieties, he has chosen twelve that may be viable for his farmers and is in the process of growing them on the demonstration farm. The show farmers who manage this space—namely Prakruti employee Tulanna, a farmer and organic village leader in Japur—look for desirable traits and use their experience with the different varieties to make suggestions for the rest of the farmers in the program. Tulanna has used his influence to test fruit tree and vegetable intercropping and in 2014 managed an experimental turkey and chicken coop. These provided extra fruit, vegetables, meat, and eggs, all subsidized by Prakruti. When showing me his field to demonstrate the range of useful plants he grows on his farm, Tulanna pointed out a row of fruit trees on the edge of his farm. "My mother loves these fruits," he said, grinning and pointing to custard apples (*Annona reticulata* L.). Show farming allows Tulanna to be both a dutiful son and a dutiful organic farmer. His success is a model to aspiring farmers and a warning to potential rule breakers. His own hamlet remains stalwart organic enthusiasts, while just a kilometer away, another hamlet lacking in-village supervision has dropped out of Prakruti's organic group.

Tulanna and Mahesh, among others who breed seeds or test complicated nonchemical field management methods, collect these benefits for the mutual improvement of the program and their own interests. They integrate that knowledge into a regular practice demonstrated to the rest of the village and to visitors. Over the years, these farmers have made minor improvements where necessary, working with the NGOs to adapt seeds, leaf sprays, and fertilizers to local conditions that they can distribute among the less invested majority of villagers. Because of their work, other farmers in the program can skip meetings and procure seeds or leaf sprays. In coordination with organic program directors, these engaged show farmers have learned and improvised in their fields. The success of these programs is as much theirs as it is Prakruti's and PANTA's.

Show farmers intersect with the learning process in interesting ways: they must prove themselves to be responsive enough to environmental feedback and prestigious enough to be followed with a degree of confidence; they must be amenable to the demands and risks placed upon them by intervention programs; and they must be personable enough to charm donors and media crews. These skills are just as important as the social and environmental learning practiced by other farmers when they evaluate seed choices. In many instances the confounding effect of institutional payments or farm equipment overshadows the risks of new technology, to say nothing of earning local renown. Show farmers provide idealized models for other farmers to follow and serve as resources or watchdogs for those farmers who are struggling. As with any social learning situation, farmers make an environmental calculus that these well-respected and successful growers must be on to something and are thus worthy of being emulated in the first place. As a rule, they are charismatic and opportunistic, and over the long term they by definition discover ways to shift the incentives of organic agriculture to the mutual benefit of themselves and the development program.

The most successful show farmers can create lucrative platforms that sideline farm management. Mahesh's work for PANTA has taken him and other farmers to cities and countries throughout South Asia, and he has received direct grants from the National Agriculture Bank for Rural Development as a result of his work with PANTA. It is these farmers who appear in compelling commodity biographies and blogs. However, they are not simply blank slates manipulated by foreign buyers. While farmers may not always realize the scope in which their images and stories will be used, they recognize that their cooperation can bring socioeconomic benefits over the short and long term.

Most importantly, show farmers learn to incorporate scheme opportunities into their improvisatory agricultural repertoire. The search for celebrity, socioeconomic security, and the earnest desire for alternatives to debts and chemicals have led these farmers to experiment with organic agriculture and leverage these new opportunities to improve their agricultural work, their households, and their communities on their terms. These performances bring seed-cleaning machines, water pipelines, premiums, and school fees, while empowering some farmers to experiment and enact their own vision of sustainable development. These performances also become part of the daily practice of agriculture, building *mêtis* by building social relationships, and here the clear differentiation between performer and performance becomes blurred. As with Mahesh, performances of transformation or fears of agribusiness dependency become part of a learning process in a socially embedded agriculture. Through quotidian performances of knowledge and self we see contests over larger expectations of development or modernity, not just a response to reward structures but a grappling with what it means to be a good farmer and live well. For these farmers, organic development has provided a new and appealing stage on which to practice sustainable agriculture.

IMAGINING DIFFERENT POSSIBLE FUTURES ON ORGANIC FARMS

After two months conducting household surveys and walking with farmers planting GM cotton monocultures in villages like Kavrupad, I learned to see and appreciate rural India's neoliberal capitalism in the landscape. There is a beauty in uninterrupted rows of cotton plants with yellow and pink flowers, occasionally dotted with household vegetables and flowers. I learned to live with the mingled smell of diesel and pesticides that lay over recently sprayed fields, and I grew accustomed to the bags of GM cottonseeds, fertilizer sacks, pesticide bottles, and plastic bags stamped with Warangal shop names that blow like tumbleweeds on Telangana farms. Cotton, maize, and rice dominate this landscape, sustained by farmers for whom the clearest marker of success is *manci digubadi*.

So I was immediately struck by the diversity of plant life when I stepped onto a Prakruti-affiliated farm in Addabad for the first time. I later found that organic cotton farmers here managed more than twice as many useful plants in their fields than the GM farmers of Kavrupad (Flachs 2016c). This is not an inherent feature of organic agriculture but an explicit design in Addabad—Prakruti CEO Chender feels that the added biodiversity helps to promote healthier soils while the extra crops feed household consumption and side-market sales. Farmers are required to plant more biodiverse fields, with special areas set aside for food crops and herbs. Rows of cotton are interspersed with lines of pigeon pea that fix nitrogen into the soil and provide food. Trap plants like castor (*Ricinus communis* L.) lure bollworms away from the cotton while ornamentals like marigolds (*Tagetes patula* L.) serve double duty as festive garlands that discourage nematodes. Farmers do not wash out fertilizer bags and pesticide bottles in the streams where children (and sweating anthropologists) swim and fish because they do not use them here. Scientific counts notwithstanding, these fields feel full of life in ways that made recently sprayed cotton fields seem sterile by comparison. Every home has a collection of vegetable and rice seeds, and farmers swell with pride when describing their fields to me and other visitors. They should be proud—their farms are beautiful.

Social scientists have a duty to measure and critique in our explanation of social and environmental systems. I am interested in how, why, and under what circumstances farmers can learn and have meaningful lives as cotton farmers. Thus, it is important to my line of research to ask about the relationship between incentives, yields, institutions, and regulations on these farms. All of this is part of the story. But let me be clear. While critically investigating the dynamics that guide learning on organic farms, I often support their ultimate outcome because they provide a future for rural well-being outside of *manci digubadi*.

Some organic agriculture programs provide a different set of ways to be successful in an agricultural sector where GM cotton farmers internalize their failures and commit suicide. In doing so, they address fundamental causes of agrarian distress where GM seeds only scratch the surface. I celebrate these changes while still caring exactly how they unfold and for whom they work best. My political ecology lens suggests that organic agriculture is not inherently better for farmers, debts, landscapes, or suicide rates than GM cotton, but will depend on local social institutions and the learning process of environmental managers. Organic farmers' occasional ambivalence toward adapting the technology given to them in the form of training sessions or seeds leads them to follow show farmers who stay engaged with the program and who do the iterative work of fitting that knowledge to local needs. This is a nuanced argument, but I still celebrate the efforts of show farmers like Mahesh and Tulanna. They are helping to make cotton agriculture sustainable by troubleshooting this proscribed development and showing that there is more than one way to succeed as a cotton farmer.

Amid varyingly successful development initiatives, these programs have managed to keep farmer interest and vest knowledge in local people rather than external experts in three ways. First, they capitalize on the social influence of early organic adopters, who convince the rest of the village of the program's benefits. This influence can stem from existing status, or it can be earned through their charisma and opportunism when they embrace organic project incentives. Organic programs encourage them to become show farmers, heavily incentivizing their agriculture, even when these early adopters are among the most socioeconomically advantaged in the village to begin with (Flachs 2017b). Seeing these influential farmers succeed then kicks off the social learning so important among all cotton farmers. Early negotiations with show farmers require some back-and-forth during which show farmers adapt program rules to local conditions. If successful, these adaptations then become standard practice for future interventions. This is a manifestation of environmental learning.

Second, organic programs incentivize organic production by compensating for the lost opportunity costs of planting a higher-yielding cotton and taking their chances in the open market. Organic cotton farmers in my sample produced much lower yields on average than did the GM cotton farmers. To some degree these lower yields might be expected because organic programs recruit poorer, marginal, low-caste, and tribal farmers. However, organic programs like Prakruti and PANTA provide a safety net wherein organic farmers do not need to chase yields and profit margins like their GM-planting counterparts. Where GM-planting farmers lack a widely agreed-upon knowledge base for seed brands due to a combination of choice overload, short-term trials, deskilling, and the undue influence of conformist bias, organic farmers receive loans, inputs, equipment, and social capital regardless of their seed knowledge. In exchange for coming under the socioeconomic safety net, some relinquish a material incentive to develop nuanced knowledge about their cottonseeds.

Third, these programs allow for a degree of flexibility in certification requirements that can manifest as fraud or rule-bending. In some instances, farmers are probably taking advantage of lax oversight to keep these incentives coming. In others, such as in famers' considerable stores of heirloom vegetables, sorghum, wheat, and rice, the organic program does not monitor or disrupt agricultural decisions outside of cotton. In Prakruti-affiliated villages from 2013 to 2014, 134 out of 157 (85 percent) of rice or sorghum choices came from saved seed. Further, 130 (83 percent) of those choices represented heirloom (*desi*) seeds specially adapted to the area and saved for an average of ten years. This diversity was evident in the fields where these crops grew, which stood out to this American researcher used to hybrid cornfields as strikingly nonuniform. As with rice, farmers purposively saved heirloom crops to find the best-tasting, most locally suited, or highest-yielding varieties. By asking farmers to devote land to heirloom sorghum and providing free vegetable seeds, Prakruti encourages organic farmers to cast a wide and biodiverse net in their agriculture. Through show farmers, underwriting vulnerability, and flexible agroecological management, organic programs structure a different kind of farmer learning process than that seen on GM farms.

I am skeptical that this approach will work on all farms. More so than Prakruti villages, Ennepad has emerged as a tantalizing model of organic agriculture for NGO promoters, journalists, and government representatives. Such proponents gain viewers and donors for celebrating Ennepad. But why academics should come to portray Ennepad as organic agriculture generally rather than a particular network of actors is less clear. With titles lauding "the road ahead" (Raghupati and Prasad 2009) and invoking Gandhi (Quartz 2010), academics threaten to take Ennepad out of context, away from the networks of capital and media that sustain it. In doing so, such studies provide, ironically, a poor explanation of how to move toward future development. The institutional incentives that make this village famous are just as important to its success as its innovative methods.

Reports stressing Ennepad's potential but downplaying the interaction between farmers and NGOs ignore the most important reason for its success.

After acknowledging that Ennepad is supported by numerous NGOs reducing cultivation risk, Desmond (2013) compares Ennepad cultivation "vulnerability" to two other villages, as though all three grew cotton under the same socioeconomic conditions. While claiming to show an analysis of differential material risks associated with three agronomic conditions, the study downplayed the safety net provided by aligning with an NGO. Another study, which interviewed thirty-six farmers in ten villages affiliated with an organic NGO, celebrated the agroecological benefits of in situ conservation for both poor farmers and for biodiversity (Bradburn 2014). While acknowledging that contacting only three or four farmers associated with a conservation-based NGO, may have influenced responses, the study concludes "that a large section of agrarian society in the Medak district is conserving many diverse landrace crops on their farms that hold important, and potentially important genetic resources" (Bradburn 2014, 79). Scientific studies that present organic and conservation development programs as if they are transplantable technologies rather than elements of a complicated agricultural and social system obscure how and why those initiatives really work. The data in this chapter shows how organic agriculture is performed and underwritten. As such, I caution against the suggestion that organic development is inevitably better than other kinds of agriculture.

Cultivating Knowledge asks how and when agricultural development improves rural well-being—underwriting vulnerability and promoting social capital are absolutely crucial to that goal on organic farms. Organic and conservation initiatives are successful because farmers learn to take advantage of program rewards, because farmers emulate particularly successful show farmers in their village, and because the programs provide enough flexibility to allow farmers to maintain a diverse agricultural skillset. Although some farmers benefit more than others and although this farming is often performative, organic agriculture has provided an alternative means of social and agricultural success in these villages. This alternative is desperately needed in Warangal cotton agriculture, where the safety net has disappeared, farmers clamber for ever-greater yields to combat input costs, and the only interventions come from predatory markets and brokers. Like GM trials conducted under unrealistic field conditions (Qaim 2003), studies that occlude the influence of social institutions (Bradburn 2014; Desmond 2013; Forster et al. 2013; Quartz 2010) disconnect agricultural methods from the people and programs that make them work. This is especially misleading for farmers affiliated with programs like Prakruti, where the social and economic benefits of participation in organic agriculture subsidize larger rural vulnerabilities. To work toward a more just and sustainable agriculture requires understanding why interventions work.

"They sucked my knowledge out with a straw," laughed Mahesh during one of our first interviews. He was not merely bragging—his adaptations to crop spacing, cow manure preparation, and pest trap management are now standard in the village. Similarly, Prakruti show farmer Tulanna kept program villages in line in exchange for preferential access to seeds, jobs, loans, and influence. Organic agriculture has provided these farmers with an alternative stage on which to perform agricultural development, and, in doing so, a different daily practice through which to build knowledge. It influences how they farm, how they frame their decisions about their work and their responsibilities to the larger village, and it shapes the kinds of *mêtis* knowledge they draw from when making agroecological decisions. Like all performances, it is contingent to the audiences and needs at hand. To investigate how these diverging visions of development address the underlying agrarian distress of neoliberal India, I turn to these contingent transformations in chapter 6.

6

PERFORMING DEVELOPMENT

Practice, Transformation, Suicide

ENNEPAD IS several kilometers from bus or autorickshaw transport. In November 2013, I walked to the crossroad to wait for a bus with Kanka, an Ennepad organic farmer on his way to a regional city—Kanka knew a shortcut. As we walked, he talked about the impact that PANTA, Ennepad's sponsoring NGO, had on his life and on the village at large. To begin with, they employ his brother part time. "They have been good to us," he says, explaining that they offer advice that has brought fame and expertise. Kanka speaks with a practiced certitude about his experiences, shaping them into a before-and-after narrative. He mentions how often he has been interviewed, that he's nearly as famous as charismatic show farmer Mahesh, championed on the NGO website and in numerous news reports. I tease him, asking if he uses any methods or materials outside of what PANTA recommends. He shrugs this off, saying, "If PANTA didn't tell us to do something, we don't do it. They're so good to us, why would we want to change that system?" "What about seeds?" I ask. Ennepad farmers are only offered two seed types, far fewer than the hundreds of choices they would find in a seed shop. "Before [PANTA] we spent all our money and we didn't know how to plant," he answered dismissively. "We used to be stupid and plant rice only for selling, we never planned according to the seasons. . . . PANTA only gives good seeds."

I was taken aback at the suggestion that farmers didn't know how to plant and plan according to the seasons—what farmer would know so little about the fundamental agricultural input, let alone admit it? Kanka, who has farmed all his life and knows quite a lot about agriculture, was performing a role: the transformed farmer subject. In the accompanying narrative, the village is a place of superstition, waste, and poor judgment. Since the intervention of the NGO, farmers have learned to save, eat their own rice, plan according to the seasons—to be, in essence, "good" farmers. While organic show farmers described in the previous chapter take the narrative of the transformed farmer subject to an extreme, all farmers participating in development projects must deal with new markets, new production methods, and new audiences. Engaged experts, visitors, and managers open the floodgates to farm equipment, seeds, loans, assistance programs, and ways to succeed and aspire in rural India. This chapter considers three kinds of performance in the agricultural development experienced by Telangana cotton farmers: the performance of everyday farmwork, the performance of transformation, and the performance of death through public suicides. These performances are interrelated, although I employ a subtly different meaning of performance in each, and each has a consequence for how and what farmers learn.

In everyday farmwork, performance recalls the improvisatory *mêtis* and repertory knowledge of practice—people doing what they know on the public stage of the farm field. Farmers perform each day for the audiences of their daily community, including fellow farmers, travelers-by, and the myriad animals and plants that demand some kind of response in the field, be it care (in the case of cotton or bullocks) or violence (in the case of insects and weeds). These agricultural performances signal to others that one is a virtuous or hardworking member of the community, the best kind of person in a small village, or that one is lazy or inept, the worst kind of community member. This is the performance of not just inspecting plants but being seen inspecting plants. As I've shown, these performances shape and are shaped by agroecological knowledge and practice over time.

Through these performances, some development proponents and opponents argue that farmer subjects become transformed—like Kanka, they claim to have passed from ignorance to a more conscientious understanding of their work. This transformative moment has a different audience: the newly attendant foreign visitors, neighbor farmers, scientists, and development workers who observe alternative agricultural development programs. Here farmers perform roles expected of them in part to secure access to new capital or agricultural resources that come with development programs, but also because they come to identify with those roles. It is not new to say that organizations use narratives from people on the ground to show how their products or services are changing lives. I want to know how this negotiation between farmers and intervention programs itself changes people's lives. Anthropologists have shown how Haitian refugees (E. C. James 2010) learn to shape the experiences of their trauma into legible narratives that smooth the path to international aid money, or how historically marginalized groups on South India's coast claim caste identities to gain rights to shorelines (Subramanian 2009). "Show farmers" (Stone 2014) and "superlative sufferers" (Heller 2018) learn to present themselves in legible ways to interested parties. Yet even as farmers perform these roles, those performances reflect the larger staged scenes, audiences, and scripts that farmers live with, a point I explore at length elsewhere (Flachs 2018).

Daily practice and development performances are informed by the lived experience of agrochemical overuse, debt, and suicide. Just as daily agricultural life is a performative act on the public stage of a Telangana farm field, so too is death. Farmer suicide is public, understood through a local cultural context whether it is a protest or a final desperate act by farmers overwhelmed by the changing nature of risk in rural India. Although each suicide has its own roots in individual troubles and injustices in the political economy, these suicides have gained an audience including family, neighbors, state officials, journalists, and concerned people around the world. By understanding daily agricultural practice, development transformations, and, finally, farmer suicide as kinds of performances, I argue that they are all in conversation with local knowledge, national aspirations, and the global political economy. On different stages and for different audiences, each is contingent and performative—shaping and shaped by daily life. These performances can change for better and worse when state, private, NGO, or village institutions provide different opportunities to live well as a cotton farmer. To call this agriculture performative is to assume that agricultural life is not a series of discrete choices. Rather, I call attention to the ways in which communities create value and make rural life, and death, meaningful.

PERFORMANCES AND DAILY PRACTICE

Agricultural performances illuminate the social work of adjustment and improvisation involved in managing an agrarian landscape (Flachs and Richards 2018): the "patch-and-mend" improvisations that manifest in a repertoire of adaptive strategies that farmers use to manage diverse socioecological problems (Brookfield 2001; Netting 1993; Leslie and McCabe 2013; Richards 1993, 1989); the stages built to inspire farmers ranging from model farms to the murals and cisterns found near organic agriculture projects (figure 12); and the way that these quotidian performances of knowledge and self reflect larger expectations of development and modernity in South India (Gupta 1998; Pandian 2009; Tsing 2005; Vasavi 1999). As a cumulative body of experiences and iterative course corrections, farmers' subjective and agricultural responses inform their *mêtis*. By viewing farmer decisions as performed and not merely rational economic acts, we begin to account for the hopes, fears, harsh realities, and small joys that drive decisions, practice, *mêtis*, and, ultimately, knowledge in the field.

Ennepad's agricultural products are not certified as organic, and so farmers recognize that their continued success with PANTA's organic marketing is determined in part by a positive working relationship with the more than ten thousand visitors who have come to visit Ennepad since 2006. As reported in national media and environmentalist magazines, Ennepad's origin story begins with a crisis of red hairy caterpillars (*Amsacta albistriga*) in the mid-1990s. As expensive pesticides stopped working and farmers looked down the barrel of crop failure, their desperation drove them to try experimental nonchemical approaches. These ultimately proved so successful that by 2006 the village had transitioned to become fully organic. Visitors come to see a place where farmers belonging to historically marginalized castes regulate one another, striking a balance between pests, people, and plants. News coverage has called Ennepad a beacon of hope amid Telangana's larger agrarian distress, and visitors include members of the legislative assembly and, more exciting, movie stars.

Development for this relatively isolated village of mostly low-caste farmers hinges on their education at the hands of high-caste scientific experts in the wake of a mid-1990s insect pest crisis. "Not only are they scientists and know everything," explains Ennepad farmer Siddalu, "but [program director] Laxman has fifty acres and is a farmer." Raju, sitting nearby, agrees: "What we had done [before 2003 when he switched to organic methods] was totally a waste, we didn't know how to use hen manure, lake soil, or vermicompost. We were using chemicals and thinking that if our neighbor used one spray, we should use two!" In the introduction and in chapter 4, I mention Malothu, a cotton farmer who employed that exact competitive logic to argue that if his neighbor sprayed four times, he must spray five. "We had a lower yield, more diseases, and we had to spend extra money on the chemicals," Siddalu continues. "Before we learned to use SRI, we were putting manure directly onto the land [rather than storing it or plowing with it] because we didn't know any better. Now we can use our own resources like manure and vermicompost." Evangelism for PANTA aside, Raju has gained a host of new skills and daily practices from the program. Some skills, especially labor-intensive SRI farming, may not ultimately impact daily agricultural practices. "It's a lot of work, and now that the children are going to school, I don't want to do it by myself," admitted one Ennepad farmer. Other skills, like Raju's new familiarity with intensive organic fertilizers including lake soil and concentrated cow manure, have helped him enrich soil fertility in ways that benefit cotton agriculture throughout the village. Although he initially stored manure merely as part of a PANTA training program, he has incorporated it into his daily farmwork and broadened his possibilities for responding to agricultural variables in the field.

GM cotton farmers by and large do not perform for or depend on international donors. Beholden to shops and agricultural extension officers, they perform good agriculture as they see it by extolling the virtues (or shortcomings) of GM seeds and their own prowess as seed consumers—this is what it means to chase success in neoliberal rural India. Farmers commonly plant two or more different cottonseed brands in their fields to gauge the differences between seeds, with the stated purpose of comparing their yields. Such comparisons are, in practice, very difficult to make, as I show in chapter 4. Indeed, I've shown elsewhere that farmers who plant a given seed are significantly less likely to plant it in the future even if they reap a high yield (Flachs, Stone, and Shaffer 2017). "You should change seeds every few years," one Kavrupad farmer told me. "The new seeds have the best *science.*" His use of the English word *science* in this Telugu conversation underscores how farmers have bought into the idea of new and modern seeds as a source of development, while his seed-switching logic shows the danger of applying this idea to Telangana's private seed market. He does not know what precisely this science is doing to improve the seeds, and this information does not help him navigate the seed market in any specific way. It does, however, ensure that he is continually buying new seeds and inputs. The path to good farming involves discerning purchases, not technical expertise, and so that is what these GM farmers learn to do each day.

Both GM and organic farmers hone their adaptive skillsets through daily practice, which includes social posturing. To gain an edge where knowledge is held by experts, some celebrate their close relationships with scientists, merchants, and educated children. "I always know which seed will be best," boasted Chandraiah of Kavrupad. "Both Vikram [the local shop owner] and I are well educated and wealthy, why would he mislead me?" This appeal to class and status is mirrored by the uneducated farmers who claim that they are better off listening to shops and large farmers because they have no such knowledge. "If you're sick, you go to the hospital, don't you?" explained Ralledapalle farmer Shiva, when I asked why he traveled to the seed shop for planting advice. The Telugu word for pesticide is *mandu*, or medicine, and so the comparison to hospitals is apt. Like the Ralledapalle farmer who sprayed an expired pesticide on his field in the introduction, many farmers have bought a small or cheap pesticide at a local store only to find insects on the plants the following morning. What can you do in this situation? I asked. "Go to a shop to get a new suggestion," he answered. "And if the local shops don't work, go to [nearby larger city] Nekonda for a *pedda mandu* (more powerful medicine)." Exhausted by a day of spraying and nursing a headache from hours of pesticide spraying, he leaned forward on his cot and pressed his palms into his eyes. When expertise is concentrated off the farm, farmers' options shrink in the face of a crisis.

This consumer perspective leads farmers to speculate about past and future Bt cotton brands. One common response held that Bt cotton had been good and very successful for the first several years that it was on the market. "I would have committed suicide if not for Bt seeds," recalls Venkateshwarlu, a large landowner renowned in Kavrupad as a hard worker. The cotton helped him reduce pesticide sprays and provided several years of consistently improved yields. "It made my life easier and is a big improvement," agrees Dasru. But Dasru's yields, and Telangana's cotton yields generally, have ticked downward since 2008 (Cotton Corporation of India 2018). What happened to the seeds? I asked. "The bitches are putting less [of a Bt dose] in it each year," he complained.

In the face of crop failure, farmers are largely unwilling to blame the shops, companies, or products themselves. Even if shop owners did not have their best interests at heart, farmers acknowledged that they still needed to buy their products. When that trust breaks, as with Dasru's bitter comments above, farmers continue growing cotton and seeking advice. The price for cotton is much higher than the price for the maize, soybean, pulses, or rice that conventional farmers would grow instead, while organic farmers hope that organic cotton will provide enough fringe benefits to uplift their communities more generally. This aspiration, whether to be celebrated in newspapers for a bumper crop or to continue paying for school fees and weddings, overpowers the anxieties of gambling on cotton. Through these daily acts of farmwork, navigating shops, or aligning themselves with experts, farmers hone a repertoire of socioecological skills (Richards 1993, 1989). When faced with unexpected agricultural problems, like severe rains or pest attacks, or political worries, like price hikes or labor strikes, farmers draw on this repertoire to improvise, plan, and otherwise play the roles of farmer, steward, caretaker, gambler, savvy consumer, or responsible patient that their practice has equipped them to perform.

GM AND ORGANIC INTERVENTIONS AS VEHICLES FOR TRANSFORMATION

The cistern in the center of Ennepad lists sixteen rules for organic production, while Prakruti erects signs and murals in partner villages celebrating the benefits of organic farming (figure 12). As visiting donors and journalists have found, these landmarks make excellent photographic backdrops for fact-finding reports. These displays list economic benefits, but they also remind farmers how much better organic agriculture is for their children, their health, and the stewardship of the land. Through such monuments, Prakruti and PANTA compete with Bt cotton brands and advertisements to transform and develop the countryside.

FIGURE 12. Organic cotton murals in Telangana. Organic signage, left to right, top to bottom: cistern with organic guidelines; welcoming sign for Ennepad village; Prakruti-affiliated sign with sponsors and organic requirements; Japur mandal sign proclaiming that Prakruti farm children are well cared for. Photos by Andrew Flachs.

Transformation is a pervasive and important performance in development. As postcolonial critics have argued (Pandian 2011; Gupta 1998), one must be underdeveloped to engage with development, and this development carries an obligation to show how change comes about. I am professionally suspicious of these narratives. Anthropologists revel in the gray, the messy social work of changing norms and changing practices. Simple, didactic stories about transformations from ignorance to sustainable agriculture may help to sell clothing, but I worry that they perpetuate a story where Indian farmers are inherently unwise and in need of enlightenment from development programs.

This is unfortunate for at least two reasons. First, these stories do not really help us understand how development works. If we simplify the back-and-forth process by which farmers learn, organizations adapt, and development occurs, we miss an opportunity to explore why programs seem to have lasting results at some times and places but not others. Technological solutions to complex problems like GMOs or organic regulations may be intuitively appealing because they seem to cut through this complexity to offer a simple solution. That these technologies do not always work as advertised speaks to the ways in which social factors muddy the waters. Indeed, many who promote both GMOs (Monsanto Company 2015) and organic agriculture (Panneerselvam et al. 2012) in India have become frustrated and blame farmers for their failure to use the technology correctly. If we are interested in figuring out ways to promote socioeconomic uplifting as it is experienced on the farm, this is clearly not a helpful approach.

Second, this logic that farmers are doing something wrong and that outside expertise is poised to help may be true in some cases. As I showed in chapter 4, pesticide overuse and seed uncertainty are problems. It is important to understand the history and political economy of why and how farmers engage with these potentially harmful practices in the first place. Within my academic framework of political ecology, I highlight the historical and political legacy of cotton inequality and agrarian distress in India. Simple narratives and technological solutions mask all this because they assert that the problem is in the use of sprays or the devastation of insects rather than in the inadequate infrastructure and limited possibilities of rural India. Technological innovations can provide alternative paths forward, but only as situated within the ways that development is tested and applied in the field.

Although most of my work involves speaking with farmers, I met Prakruti Organic's staff during field visits and returned to Secunderabad in May 2014 to accompany them on a village tour. As we left to meet farmers, Gulgoth, the

Fair Trade UK representative I introduced in the previous chapter, explained the way that fair trade connected farmers with consumers:

> How much you want to ignore that it's about money, it is still about that. So in a way we go over there try to create markets for [the farmers]. . . . Fair trade has got no value for the consumer as such. It's still the same product. So, it's the same banana or it's the same shirt, but if you tell people this is the impact it has, which is minimal [with respect to] what they have to pay, like five pence for one T-shirt. But for the farmer [five pence] is quite a bit. We sit there and we create markets and at the same time we campaign about it so that people are aware what fair trade does and what its impact is.

To find stories that encourage people to pay extra for a product that does not give them any extra benefit, Gulgoth spent three days touring Prakruti farms for experiences to take back to her office. Gulgoth, who holds a master's degree in development studies, knows that these narratives are carefully crafted to elicit a response from consumers. She herself is involved in the crafting and views it as a necessary part of fair trade's work. She is not alone: Monsanto India's website celebrates Pradeep Chivane and Daulat Raghoji Ghatod, small farmers who used GM seeds to save money for their daughters' marriages (Monsanto Company 2012); NGOs recruit charismatic villagers to stand in front of news cameras to extoll program benefits (Prabu 2013); seed and pesticide companies choose farmers living near roads for advertising campaigns, hoping that their signage will sway other farmers; and whole demonstration farms are raised to show visitors the potential, if not the reality, of agricultural technology. While some elite consumers wholeheartedly embrace these stories as a form of solidarity through consumption (R. L. Bryant and Goodman 2004), Paige West (2012) has shown through her study of specialty coffee that many young consumers are so inundated with this messaging that they have become cynical and dismissive of campaigns that bring farmer narratives to consumers.

Both Prakruti Organic and PANTA promote a transformation narrative through social media, marketing, fundraising, and promotion of their programs. "They're resource-poor farmers," explains Prakruti employee Sama. "These people face a lot of exploitation. We want to address the issues related to these problems. That's why we are working there." Ramesh, PANTA's executive manager, agrees: "We choose villages that are in deep crisis. That's the first target we have. All our projects are located in areas where there is a high use of chemicals. We don't go to villages or regions which are already low in pesticide use."

Prakruti's Facebook page offers hundreds of photos lauding education programs and the donation dollars that make those programs possible. Visiting donors are offered the chance to dedicate mango trees or science labs that will help to bring those communities out of poverty. In a promotional pamphlet entitled *Fashion to Field*, Prakruti stresses both that their products are of a high quality and that farmers involved have learned through "the unique concept of conducting Farmer Field Schools (FFS) trainings, where a technical expert is accompanied by the farmers of a village to their fields. Knowledge from the FFS then spreads amongst the others in the village through regular meetings of the self help groups." A farmer testimonial on the cover shows that "over these years with Prakruti we have realized the significance of quality . . . complying to the standards of certification are no more a burden, rather a customary practice of our lives." Surely, before working with Prakruti, the farmers understood that quality was an important factor in their cotton production. But the farmer testimonial underscores the importance of transformative sentiment. Solely thanks to your help, the farmers seem to say, we have changed our methods and mindset. This is unfortunate because it obscures all of the important negotiations between farmers and development workers that make organizations like Prakruti effective, perpetuating a simplistic narrative that farmers are ignorant and organic agriculture itself improves lives. Prakruti may, and in many cases does, improve lives—but it does so because they work with farmers to create alternative paths to success in this political economy, not because farmers are poor agricultural managers.

Stories of transformation are also common in development scholarship. As described by critical anthropologists like Arturo Escobar (2011) or Akhil Gupta (1998), agricultural development writ large frames farming problems as scientific and teachable. This is a view of knowledge not as improvised or performed *mêtis* but as *technê*, an application of universal knowledge through technical skills. At times, this has been an awkward and uneven process in India. Not only did the green revolution advances disproportionately help large, high-caste farmers rather than the extreme rural poor (Cullather 2013; Vasavi 2012) but presumably universal technology like pesticides or fertilizers had to be continually reconfigured to function within local hierarchies of caste or gender that defined who knew what and who shared labor with whom. Noting how farmers hybridized the green revolution logic of chemical fertilizers and pesticides with an existing health-based understanding of agronomy, postcolonial scholars (Gupta 1998; Vasavi 1999; Tsing 2005) suggest that we should not expect this process to be smooth. This explains how Jenaram from the previous chapter simultaneously conceives of cow manure as a holistic soil restorer and a micronutrient supplier. Yet Gupta and Vasavi's hybridity lens distracts from the ways in which farmers learn to position themselves within new systems of knowledge. Jenaram leveraged various ways of understanding soil fertility to become a driving force within Prakruti, designing many of the interventions in his village. Because it is focused on development from above, including states or international institutions, hybridity diminishes the local social dynamics within rural communities that govern how knowledge is used and adapted (Agrawal and Sivaramakrishnan 2000).

Gupta (1998, 9) hints at local dynamics when he notes that global development is "reconfigured" in each new context, but Escobar makes these interpersonal adaptations central to his study of agricultural development, knowledge, practice, and claims to authority. Like Kanka above, the farmers that he describes in Colombia "begin to interpret their lives before the program as filled with ignorance and apathy. Before the program, they say, they knew nothing about why their crops died; now they know that the coconut trees are killed by a particular pest that can be combated with chemicals" (Escobar 2011, 51). Escobar is critical of such development programs, but prointervention authors (Duveskog, Friss-Hansen, and Taylor 2011; Mancini, Van Bruggen, and Jiggins 2007) also argue that agricultural interventions are a kind of transformative learning (Mezirow 2000) that changes farmers' outlooks on life. One study from Kenya highlights personal transformations, including renewed confidence, improved work ethic, a shift away from witchcraft toward scientific crop management, and the report from one farmer that in the past they "were just farming carelessly, but now we are farming for business" (farmer participant quoted in Duveskog, Friss-Hansen, and Taylor 2011, 1539). Far more critical of the social context of development, anthropologist Arun Agrawal (2005b) describes transformation as a shifting calculation of self-interest: farmers in North India transformed from forest burners to forest conservators, but only after they came to see environmental discourse as in their own economic interest. Seizing upon this advantage, forest farmers then internalized that economic interest as a form of conservation self-discipline, which he calls environmentality in a nod to Michel Foucault's theory of civic self-discipline, governmentality. This argument explains how environmental self-regulation can be institutionalized, but it minimizes opportunism or local politics by focusing on rational economic behavior (Agrawal 2005a).

Certainly, organic farmers and early adopters like Mahesh, Tulanna, or Jenaram from chapter 5 help to enforce organic regulations in their village, hybridize agricultural knowledge, and come to see themselves differently as a result. Yet I argue that environmentality and hybridity are incomplete lenses through which to understand the lives of these cotton farmers. My ethnographic data is rife with a performance that is reflexive and contingent. By calling these transformations performative, I bring attention to the audiences for whom farmers perform: NGOs, states, companies, other farmers, even the plants, animals, and land itself. To say that this rural life is performed and interactive with an audience is not to diminish its veracity but to contextualize it within a larger sociopolitical fabric of rural life.

Because of its traction in sales and the symbolic work it does in justifying interventions, the notion of transformation can be even more important for organic programs than the actual technology that they promote. To make consumers care about the issues of social change or environmental protections in Ennepad, PANTA director Ramesh explains that his work is as psychological as it is agronomic. PANTA aims to create "a confidence in the people. You see, it's not just about giving [the farmers] seed. By giving them seeds we cannot solve the problem, not unless we create an ecosystem where farmers understand and do it on their own." Rather than accept this transformation at face value, it is illuminating to examine how farmers learn to perform it, and what kinds of social or material rewards they receive in return.

PERFORMING TRANSFORMATION FOR VISITORS

Model farms and farmers hold an important place in agricultural mediation in the twentieth century (Stone 2018; Taylor and Bhasme 2018), showing both an agricultural verisimilitude for uncritical viewers but also life as it *ought* to be. In India, model agriculture was an explicit element in both colonial and postcolonial state visions for agricultural success. The East India Company imported slaveholding landowners from the southern United States to model intensive cotton monocultures in their bid for higher yields and longer fibers (Hazareesingh 2016), while farmers and policymakers toured farms built to demonstrate the merits of the green revolution a century later (Cullather 2013). Model farms sponsored by NGOs promoting the promise of organic agriculture have swayed policymakers in Kerala (Thottathil 2014) and Telangana (Raghupati and Prasad 2009), while corporate projects perform double duty, advertising the promise of a new technology while stressing corporate social responsibility, as with Monsanto's model farms in Visakhapatnam, Andhra Pradesh (Glover 2007).

Through their experience with touring foreigners, farmers participating with formal development programs learn when to speak up and when to defer to their handlers. In May 2014, I accompanied fair-trade representative Gulgoth to Japur, where she met with farmers who traveled to a demonstration farm during the peak of summer. Recorder and camera at the ready, Gulgoth grilled the farmers about their experiences with Prakruti (not unlike the anthropologist seated next to her). Farmers immediately answered that they enjoyed the benefits of extra income and education, an answer that failed to satisfy Gulgoth—she sought a more complicated and less practiced answer.

Her search caused the normal tour performance to falter. The farmers, native speakers of a tribal dialect of Gondi, were uncomfortable with Hindi (Gulgoth did not speak Telugu), leading Prakruti employee Arjuna to summarize the benefits as he sees them. This also corrected the derailed show. Do we benefit from food security? he asks. All agree. Seeds and leadership? he asks. All smile and agree. The conversation shifts back to topics they can explain in Hindi, especially human health and soil health. This discussion is encouraged by Gulgoth's probing on the environment and health, and when she compliments them on their entrepreneurship they agree. When this performance repeated itself in the neighboring town, Gulgoth refused to stop asking questions until farmers voiced their complaints. "As for me I want the truth," she explained to me later. "But if a buyer would come, I would want them to be a bit more enthusiastic [in their responses]. . . . You've been here," she said turning to me on our long ride back to Hyderabad. "What are the benefits beyond the premium?" Unlike Gulgoth, most visitors do not have advanced degrees in development studies and more readily accept the performance.

In other work (Flachs 2017b), I have described how show farmers can perform at different levels. Farmers may be *opportunistic*, recognizing short-term benefits from new intervention programs but dropping away once attention and incentives taper off. "Want to buy some rice?" I was asked during my first day in Ennepad. Over time, opportunistic show farmers may come to enjoy the success and fame they receive by participating in an intervention and become *celebrity* show farmers who enjoy wider acclaim, like Ennepad farmer Mahesh.

Other times, the narrative and transformation are driven less by actors than by the stage itself. Some show spaces are *institutional* in the sense that they have a direct association with shops, programs, companies, or plant science stations. Finally, such stages become entire *show landscapes*. These are particular spaces set up by intervention programs as demonstration or experimental farms. Often maintained by trustworthy show farmers, these show landscapes present an idealized vision of what agriculture could be, parsing out the messiness or illegibility of daily farm life. Show landscapes can convince visiting buyers of the possibilities of their investment, as in Prakruti's Adilabad-based farms. Alternately, show landscapes can show the potential of entire villages, as in Ennepad.

Each of these performances is connected to an intermediary of some kind: show farmers are obvious links between development programs and villagers, but the shops, programs, and farm spaces also offer sites to learn new methods, adapt knowledge, and perform development. When marshalled as part of grand narratives about the promise of GM or organic agriculture, these performances might serve broader interests. It is true, for instance, that Ennepad has not had a single instance of farmer suicide since growing organic cotton. This is not necessarily because Ennepad farmers grow organic, non-GM cotton. Ennepad sidestepped much of Telangana's larger crisis because farmers like Mahesh worked with PANTA to create stability: guaranteed markets, social programs, subsidized inputs, and a cooperative society are far more important to Ennepad's rural sustainability than the seeds themselves.

Most GM cotton farmers' mornings in Kavrupad begin in a huddle. Someone boils milk to brew sweet black tea, and men and women gather around one of the four daily newspapers that service the village. Those who cannot read well demand to hear what has happened as others point to political or sports stories. Inevitably, they turn to the section on agriculture. Because these are local papers, Kavrupad farmers often see stories about farmers in nearby Srigonda. Many Srigonda farmers are ethnic Andhras, who migrated to Telangana from the coast and settled on fertile, dark earth soils well suited to cotton agriculture. Kavrupad farmers in a 2014 focus group celebrated the knowledge and connectivity of those farmers, who have a reputation for honesty and good management, especially Naniram, the manager of Srigonda's cooperative pesticide and fertilizer shop. According to the taxonomy above, Naniram is an institutional show farmer, associated with input companies and the Warangal plant science station because he manages the cooperative shop. His products and suggestions take on special gravitas, as Kavrupad farmer Ramu explains during a focus-group discussion: "In Srigonda there is a shop that gives good chemicals. As [Naniram] is a farmer he will be supplying good rather than false (*nakkili*) chemicals. He's a good man. . . . If you go to a shop, the owner should say correct things to you, and Naniram always says good words." "Because Naniram has been a farmer for many years," added another participant, "he knows what is good and bad. He has good knowledge in agriculture and provides the right fertilizers, pesticides, and information to the famers." This is in contrast to Kavrupad's own shop, in which the focus group agreed that "[shopkeeper] Vikram sells fake products." The Kavrupad farmers distinguish here between trustworthy and dishonest shops, willing to dispense different kinds of knowledge and differentially effective inputs.

In addition to the social emulation where farmers copy their neighbors' seed choices (Stone 2007; Stone, Flachs, and Diepenbrock 2014), Kavrupad or Ralledapalle area farmers would often add that the seed had performed for the Srigonda farmers, who really knew about farming. "Everyone is planting the *Jaadoo* seed," reasoned one Ralledapalle farmer, "but more importantly, last year in Srigonda everyone planted it and got twelve quintals per acre." These yields are reported with questionable veracity in the newspapers for all of the neighboring villages to jealously read. As the head of the cooperative, Naniram is a hub of expert information, a rising tide that raises all boats in Srigonda. "If a farmer goes to a city [to purchase a pesticide], then he doesn't know what is what exactly," explains one Srigonda farmer. "So we prefer to take seeds here instead of going to outside shops. If you go to a city, then they'll link another product along with what you want. Say you want [fertilizer] Nagarjuna urea. Then, the shop owner will attach some other product which is not helpful. But here it is not like that. That's why we've started the cooperative." This is unsurprising for a number of reasons. Not only are there hundreds of possible seed brands but shopkeepers do not always have the time or patience to explain to a skeptical farmer the differences between various brands and chemicals. Even high-caste farmers who are granted more patience in urban shops usually just bring a branch from their afflicted crop and ask shopkeepers what they should buy. As discussed in chapter 4, the institution of the cooperative helps to stabilize GM cotton agriculture, a bulwark against the confusion and unreliability of GM cotton farming for most other Telangana farmers. Naniram uses this success to promote his own shop and works with local university scientists and corporate dealers to stay abreast of new agricultural information.

Performing farmers and performative spaces reinforce a perception that interventions are transforming agriculture on the ground by creating an image of success for an audience of visitors and interested farmers. In the case of the cooperative, part of the performance targets local farmers themselves, asking them to buy into the egalitarian idea of the cooperative because of the authority and knowledge of its organizers. Intervention programs from corporations, government agencies, and NGOs rely on such people and places to prove to outsiders that their methods are working and to convince other farmers that they should follow suit.

INCOMPLETE TRANSFORMATIONS

When organic villages do not see promised yields or infrastructural benefits from their participation, farmers often leave the program or bend the rules. Rule-breaking farmers are by definition marginal to these projects, less personally invested in their success than the show farmers, or less socially connected to the program managers. In 2012, fifteen households in Japur began a mandatory three-year conversion process to transition to certified organic agriculture. By the following year, the farmers were generally irritated with Prakruti. We only do this, one farmer grumbled, "because Prakruti is giving us cheap seeds. But the yields are poor and the profit margins are even worse: a small premium combined with a small yield. Their rules are complicated, they are banning the [fertilizers that would give a] solution [to the yield problem], and if we use them, they won't take our cotton." Prakruti cannot sell organic cotton as such or provide the promised premiums until after the transition period, placing farmers in an uncomfortable double bind where they must suffer comparatively lower yields from non-GM seeds grown without chemical inputs and receive no price premium. Contrary to the farmer's opinion, Prakruti does buy nonorganic cotton and sell it on the open market, but the farmer is correct to note that his family receives no additional income for the trouble of organic production.

In 2013, four of the households maintained Bt cotton on separate fields, affirming to the Prakruti that they used separate farm tools to manage the Bt and non-Bt fields and separated the harvested cotton. In practice this separation is difficult to achieve, and so Prakruti maintains that they certify land, not farmers. Returning to the office after a day of interviews, I mentioned that a number of Japur farmers were planting Bt seeds, an infraction that could violate the letter, if not the spirit, of organic regulation. Arjuna, the NGO's district coordinator, grew irritated and advised me to try other farmers where I could find "better information." "Don't talk to them, they are only transitioning," he informed me. "Oh, it's no problem," I said, feigning ignorance of his discomfort. "This will help me understand how farmers make the jump to organic cotton." The next day in Japur, I asked how farmers justified the transition from input-intensive agriculture. Yields are bad, explained large landowner, head of her women's self-help group, and shop owner Saraswathi, but they were bad in the past as well.* "Now we have the sprays from Prakruti and we know how to plow and properly prepare the cow manure," one farmer told me, espousing his transformation. "The DAP and urea hurt the land and cause it to lose energy," said another, repeating a Prakruti talking point I heard in all the villages. "Now we know better."

A year later, I was back in the office, surprised that all but two of those households had dropped out of the program. "They are defaulters," lamented Arjuna. For three years the farmers took loans; plants; farm equipment, including plastic drums; seeds; and participated in a government assistance program brokered through Prakruti. For three years they claimed that they could not afford to pay back their debts to the program. "We couldn't pay," says Saraswathi. "We lost the entire crop last year and there was nothing to be done." This was a problem for Prakruti, which had invested time and money into Saraswathi's success. As a large farmer and influential person, Saraswathi spoke not just for herself but for the larger needs of the village. Vice versa, her concerns carried extra weight because of this influence. For Saraswathi, the interest-free loans were a saving grace that helped to sustain her shop, the only source of gasoline, oils, and household needs in the village. For Arjuna, this shop was a distraction. Concerned with satisfying visitors and building a demonstration space to show the promise of certified organic agriculture, he was unable to convince Saraswathi to redirect investment from the shop to the village's lost revenue during their transition to organic agriculture, instead asking each year for loans that she never repaid. "They're still interested," mused Arjuna, "but we've stopped giving them things as they aren't paying us back."

---

* Self-help groups throughout India help to organize women's political interests, buying power, and social concerns to advance women's issues and secure financing independent of a patriarchal credit system (Swain and Wallentin 2009). As village political units, their support is helpful for organic development projects like Prakruti and Ennepad, which are interested in empowering women to begin with.

Other farmers refuse to fully commit to the restrictions of organic regulation. Addabad organic farmer Marskonda interrupts my survey to tell me that some of his land is reserved for GM cotton as an insurance against the risk that his organic crops fail. This bet hedging is not uncommon. In her study of Andhra Pradesh fair-trade cotton programs, geographer Rie Makita (2012) found that fair-trade initiatives encouraged some farmers to gamble more on GM cotton, reasoning that fair trade would cushion some of their losses. As the land is separate from his organic field, he assumes that GM crops and chemical inputs present no problem for his organic certification. Prakruti field coordinator Krishna feels differently. "These people are a problem for the certification process," he says. "People try to sell their Bt cotton in with organic cotton and it becomes expensive for us to do any necessary testing. The certifiers take 150 of our 2,500 farmers randomly and do checks. As such it's better to remove any aberrations from our list." Nervously, he asked for the names of those farmers who had taken GM cotton from outside shops, saying that he needed to check up on them. I agreed as I had asked the farmers earlier if I should keep such action secret and they laughed, saying that Krishna ought to know.

In accordance with the letter, if not the spirit, of organic regulation, both are correct as Krishna clarifies the next day: "We certify land, we don't certify the farmer. This way we can register husbands and wives separately to take advantage of government schemes for small farmers." In theory this distinction allows these farmers to maintain separate spaces where they can grow higher-yielding GM cotton with nonorganic inputs. In practice, as Marskonda shows, farmers don't consider these farms to be separate. When questioned, they can attest that their tools do not come into contact with GM cotton, although this would be impossible to police. As smallholder farming occurs at the level of the household, these separate spaces allow farmers to trial different management strategies while leaving the door open to opportunities through organic programs.

An hour's bus ride away in Japur, some farmers devote a minimum of their land to organic agriculture to benefit from free seeds, access to loans, and improvement projects. Their lackluster commitment is justified somewhere between the low yielding organic seeds, which villagers remember as being inferior to Bt seeds, and the organic insistence on not using any chemical fertilizers, which "everyone knows," especially skeptical neighbors, work well. Disgruntled organic farmer Govinder hedges his bets with a separate Bt plot of cotton, voicing the concerns of many that the *digubadi raledu* (the yields never come) with the non-Bt seeds. "The only reason we're still part of organic is because

Prakruti gives cheap seeds," he continued. "Their rules are difficult because they are banning the solution: chemical fertilizers." By this point, Arjuna was used to having these kinds of conversations with me. "There is a problem with fertility," he explains, shifting the blame to inefficient government assistance programs. "We're looking to increase liquid fertilizers, these compost and vermicompost programs, but the government is not working with us. We're giving information, whatever they need. We submit reports, but they are not helping us. . . . The farmers are selling their cattle [to cover seasonal debts], but they need to keep them [for fertilizers and plowing]." Farmers buy or rent tractors to save on labor as children leave the farm, reducing the costs of keeping animals and buying into the promise of modern machine efficiency offered by quick and fun-to-drive tractors.

This is a problem for farmers trying to split their energy between organic and Bt cotton cultivation, like Sitaram, who lives in Japur across the valley from Tulanna, the show farmer profiled in chapter 5. "Now that we have fewer animals," he explained, "the fertility of our land is diminished. Using the chemicals is better." Sitaram and his neighbors plant organic cotton not because they particularly like the program but to maintain access to the rest of the organic program's benefits. Unwilling to learn to use organic methods, farmers like Sitaram or his neighbor Govindrao don't commit fully to organic or nonorganic methods: "It may be a cheaper investment and good for the land but the production is low now," offers Govindrao. "I took it just to remain friendly with the group. We're always willing to cooperate and organic is not so much work. I didn't really have to listen to their instructions—people said, 'Do like this and that,' and they wrote something down, but then they left." Govindrao later showed me that he is switching from a low-density to a higher-density planting system, as he saw it have good yield last year in a neighbor's field, a move not encouraged by Prakruti, as it decreases the overall agrobiodiversity of the farms and promotes monoculture farming.

The combination of heavy rains during that year's harvest and the late El Niño monsoon of 2014 led many farmers to question Prakruti's value, and Arjuna confides that in such difficult years he must keep a closer watch on all the farmers to ensure their compliance. That is, he must make sure that they are following institutional instructions rather than adhering to a more flexible management strategy based on what they themselves think is best. Ultimately, their lackluster support is a distraction from a project Arjuna finds more appealing.

Arjuna is hard at work creating an agricultural landscape that will free him from these awkward contradictions in organic development—improving Prakruti's show farm landscape. Such spaces showcase reliable universal *epistêmê* rather than fickle, improvisational *mêtis*. Have you seen the cooperative land? he asked me.

> We want to make it a better demonstration area but we're having a money problem. We need to show the farmers how to do everything! Even after ten years they are still not always following our rules and they are getting confused. These tribal farmers, you can't just it say once: you have to say two, three times, and you have to show them everything. That's why the land is so important. . . . That support is necessary.

In 2014, only two farmers planted organic, non-Bt seeds. Although Prakruti offered, no other households opted to take seeds from the program. While she was engaged with the Prakruti, Saraswathi's performance of a transformed self in touch with the environmentalist development of Prakruti influenced how she spoke to me and to other visitors, how she farmed, how she framed her decisions about her work and her responsibilities to the larger village, and thus shaped the kinds of knowledge she built. Through this daily practice, she cultivated certain agricultural and social skills. But like all performances, it was contingent to the audiences and needs at hand (Flachs 2018). When the program ceased to offer benefits as she and other important stakeholders in the village recognized them, she began new subjective and agricultural performances. Arjuna's vision of development failed to see farmer practices as performances, and his offhand comment about ST farmers betrays a simmering distrust across this ethnic difference. Frustrated, he is investing in a demonstration space that offers a more controlled vision of organic agriculture.

PERFORMING LIFE, PERFORMING DEATH

Through Prakruti, organic farmers have an option to reframe agriculture as debt minimizing and village sustaining, not simply as profit or yield maximizing. Devarao, who manages five acres, argues that Prakruti has allowed him to avoid the dependencies that he sees in other villages:

We didn't know how to do these things before, but now we're planting in a good way. . . . Before we didn't know about [commercial] sprays or about making our own sprays, and before the investment was much higher without any big difference in yields. Those who work hard can only ever get good yields, including those who take chemicals, but [in that kind of farming] the investment is so high that the yields must also be high at any cost. If I use [chemical fertilizers], they'll work for me this year, but over time what kind of land will be available for my son? After this year if I put ten bags, next year I need to put twenty. . . . Only [cow manure] will fix this situation, and only slowly. In this village almost no one ever used it so we were spared from that, but in my ancestral village the situation is like that.

This transformation hinges on the fertilizer and seed input incentives provided by Prakruti, but also on Devarao's gamble that Prakruti would offer a better way to fulfill the responsibility of caring for land and providing for his household than GM cotton farming. Devarao has come to see cow manure as the best hope to heal land damaged by chemical fertilizers; Tulanna from the previous chapter sees Prakruti as a tool to care for his family, Jenaram, also from the previous chapter, described organic agriculture as making farmwork safe and healthy for his community. Each is frustrated with the status quo and desires a better life as a cotton farmer. These farmers choose to hope that programs like Prakruti might provide an escape, a protest against poisoned landscapes, communities, and farmer bodies. This is the stage upon which daily farmwork and suicides in rural Telangana, sensationally covered in domestic and international press, are performative acts.

Filmmaker Orson Welles famously quipped that we die alone, perhaps building off of German philosopher Martin Heidegger's (2010) assertion that death is final, individual, and unknowable. Because death is nothingness, argued Heidegger, we cannot and do not die for others. The case of farmer suicides in Telangana gives us reason to doubt Heidegger. Others, particularly philosophers Emmanuel Lévinas (2000) and Alphonso Lingis (2000), take exception to Heidegger, arguing instead that we die with and through others. Death affects us through those for whom we care; those whom we empathize with, love, and see suffer; and those who will remember us after we go. Death, they contend, is not the individualistic absence of experience but an interaction that demands a response. Classic anthropological studies of death and mourning (Evans-Pritchard 1976; Malinowski 1992; Scheper-Hughes 1993) have long recognized death as a social act. In Telangana, suicide can be a kind of performance, a reaction that mirrors transformative development as farmers make their deaths meaningful and legible amid global change.

I have described several examples of the slow dangers of pesticides and debt throughout this book to give readers a sense of these persistent anxieties and accepted risks in cotton farming. I knew two people who attempted suicide in the villages where I worked during the time that I was researching the lives of cotton farmers, both from villages where farmers grew GM cotton. Both attempts were complicated, involving young men who ran up high debts, failed to achieve markers of success as cotton farmers or as wage laborers, worried that they would never get married, and saw no way to achieve the image of masculine, modern, individualist success to which they aspired. One attempt was successful.

I was in Ralledapalle the day after Bhadra committed suicide, while his body was being prepared for a funerary procession. I did not watch, but I heard later how his family adorned him in a white cloth and placed flowers over his body. He was buried rather than cremated because he was an unmarried man, in accordance with religious Hindu practices. I had spoken to him only a few days earlier. He was not interested in keeping up with the family's cotton farming, he told me. He was an educated man with aspirations to travel to Hyderabad like so many other educated young people from this area, where he might earn a better living as an information technology consultant. Cotton farming was a temporary holdover, Bhadra told me. After a short life working in those urban enclaves, he hoped to earn enough money to build a more comfortable house for his parents in the Telangana countryside. A dutiful son, he told me of his plans to return to care for them here in Ralledapalle in their old age. As precarious as agrarian life clearly was for Bhadra, Ralledapalle was his home.

Telangana newspapers profile deaths as the result of debts and crop failures, the final stakes in agricultural gambles: farmers who hang themselves from trees on their farms or drink pesticides to escape financial burdens (*Deccan Chronicle* 2018, 2017); farmers who attempt suicide on police station steps to protest spurious seeds (Sarma 2017); farmers who buy pesticides to kill themselves after selling crops at a loss or finding themselves unable to deal with new pests like the Bt-resistant pink bollworm (*Pectinophora gossypiella*) (U. Sudhir 2017; T. S. Sudhir 2017). The staging of farmers who attempt suicide on police station steps is a blatant protest of what farmers see as police apathy, but each of these is a performance of some kind in that these suicides are public deaths (Münster

2015b). Public deaths, argues Münster, are deaths made visible through the state category of farmer suicide. Paradoxically, while success and failure in neoliberal India is an increasingly individual process (Chua 2014), farmers have found a public visibility and political capital through collective self-destruction. Such protests, which include as well fatal self-immolations and hunger strikes, use the body as one final site of public dissent. There, victims assert a modicum of control and reproduce a collective wrong in the form of violence against a single body (Andriolo 2006; McGranahan and Litzinger 2012).

If suicides are a public death, then they are a failure of government policies to address unmitigated economic crisis and structural violence in rural areas. This argument is supported by data showing that farmers with less access to reliable irrigation and electrical infrastructure are more likely to commit suicide (Gutierrez et al. 2015). What word other than *crisis* exists to describe the deaths of over 300,000 farmers since 1995 (National Crime Records Bureau 2014; Menon and Uzramma 2018)? Despite the frustration of statisticians (Plewis 2014) who have shown that farmers are not more prone to suicide than others in India, farmer suicide remains a crisis of public death in India's national consciousness. The ways in which the media and government employ this narrative and the complex reasons that farmers contemplate suicide have even been parodied by India's Bollywood industry in the movie *Peepli Live* (Rizvi 2010).

Münster argues that state statistics and Indian media transform suicides into public deaths, but it is also possible to see suicide as individual and group performances in light of my ethnographic account of farmers' knowledge, practice, and transformations. Farmers consume the same media and know the same suicide statistics as scholars and development policymakers, even as they struggle with the complexities of making a living in Telangana. As I have shown, both organic and GM cotton initiatives target farmers who they feel are at risk of suicide, releasing publications (e.g., Monsanto Company 2017, Eyhorn 2007) arguing that their technology alone can assuage this crisis. What this technological focus can never hope to assuage, however, are the cumulative stakes of aspiration and frustration that farmers perform when engaging with agricultural interventions. Suicides are not just debt, media attention, existential anxiety, unfulfilled aspiration, poor weather, pest attacks, or national statistics. They are all of these things all at once.

GM technology or organic regulations in and of themselves, for example, cannot address the failures of masculinity and stewardship felt by the two farmers above, shared by Australian (L. Bryant and Garnham 2015) and American

(Peter et al. 2009) farmers, and suggested by the statistic that 85 percent of Indian farmer suicides since 1995 have been committed by men (Menon and Uzramma 2018). They cannot address the nebulous concern of debts and aspirations because these are at the core of contemporary India, caught between fabulous wealth and extreme rural precarity. Debts and desperation come from agricultural work, but they also come from extravagant weddings, conspicuous consumption, school and university fees, or the failure to succeed in a new and urban environment when one's family depends on you to succeed (Chua 2014; Linssen, Kempen, and Kraaykamp 2010; Mayer 2010). These anxieties are not more or less valid than the broader narrative of agricultural distress and the need to promote sustainable agriculture. Rather, each is part of the uncertainty of living well in neoliberal Telangana. Since the mid 1990s, India has undergone rapid and profound socioeconomic change, resulting in uneven developments that stem from long-standing inequalities and urban-rural divides. Suicide rates for farmers are high alongside suicide rates for other labor sectors. Yet this signals that the aspiration to lead a good life amid the promises of global change is confronted by the internalized, individual sense of failure and shame when those aspirations fail to materialize in urban (Chua 2014) and rural (Münster 2012; Pandian 2009) India alike.

While agronomic analyses continue to show that the most historically disenfranchised farmers on poor-quality, rainfed land are at greater risk for suicide (Gutierrez et al. 2015; Gupta 2017), anthropologist A. R. Vasavi's (2012) *Shadow Space* adds a layer of social complexity to understand how suicide occurs. Farmers who commit suicide are often trying to capture neoliberal gains of their own. New farmers take over land vacated by larger, higher-caste farmers who benefitted from the green revolution and leveraged their profits to pursue opportunities in urban areas. Unlike those early adopters and early successful farmers, farmers left behind to pursue agricultural success had none of the socioeconomic advantages and fewer of the political connections to university extension groups, shops, or development programs. Given the success of agricultural technologies in the past, Vasavi argues, this new generation of farmers was expected to flourish and grow out of this structural poverty. Farmers themselves aspire to reap high yields and the socioeconomic mobility that comes with them. Lacking shared bodies of knowledge, excluded from social networks in which to share labor and expertise, unable to repay debts, secure credit, or chase the status symbols of neoliberal life, farmers come to see these structural and historical barriers as individual failures.

Even engaged organic development programs like PANTA and Prakruti struggle to combat these deeper social ills, in part because new technologies require everyone involved to create new social relationships. "Before organic we didn't know about these leaf sprays, nobody told us," began Prakruti farmer Soni. "But surely you knew there were insects and that they were eating the cotton," I challenged. Okay, he conceded:

> We knew that the pests were there, but we didn't know what sprays worked for which pests and which different pests were doing what. When I was small there were no insects and no facilities like schools or buses, so everyone did the farm work. We healed ourselves with local medicines from the forests and people weren't sick like today. Now there are hospitals, no one wants to do farm work. They want to leave the village and go to school, they're sick in hospitals not using our own (*desi*) medicines. Before no crops needed fertilizers or pesticides, but now they all need these, these urea and others have made the plants weak.

Soni has had a generally positive experience working with Prakruti, and he appreciates his new scientific understanding of field agronomy. Organic agriculture offers a solution to dropping yields or pest attacks that is not expensive, foreign, or understood to be damaging over the long term. *Desi* as employed by Telugu-speaking farmers refers to a quality that is not simply authentically Indian in contrast to foreign chemicals, but quintessentially of the place and therefore better suited to local problems. Yet neoliberal anxiety persists even here. Scientific ways of understanding agriculture and organic solutions to pest problems have come just as the knowledge and labor base for the next generation is migrating away. Soni speaks nostalgically of a lost, better past when the community was healthy and whole. He has not yet decided if organic agriculture can treat this deeper social ill, in which the next generation questions the value of farming itself. When the products or institutions with which these farmers work do not address systemic concerns, their success or failure with them leaves few remaining options to live well.

If the goal of development is to alleviate this poverty and despair, then knowledge, practice, and performance are the mechanisms by which farmers engage global change. Interventions, then, cannot focus on technologies as though the problem were yields or profits alone, but on ways that farmers learn, the institutions that provide safety nets for new practices, and the alternative possibilities to live well. Transformation is a kind of performance that allows farmers to embrace new opportunities in this global restructuring, but it is always contingent on the ways that farmers can make life meaningful within their local cultural context and make life livable within the larger political economy. Suicide is a performance that remains to farmers not only in India but around the world, when they cannot make this life livable.

TRADING CRISIS FOR TRANSFORMATION

Performance is not insincere. Roles must be learned and practiced, and some farmers, such as the show farmers, are better performers than others. This performance is inextricably linked to the learning process because knowledge and its performers are never separate. The transformation narrative both aligns farmers' experiences with alternative agriculture and allows them to provide a legitimate or legible response to an audience. Soil building and debt resonate so well with these farmers because they are strong justifications for the unusual choice to plant organic cotton when Bt cotton and the search for high yields are virtually universal in Telangana. Organic agriculture is a gamble that some farmers are willing to take if it provides an alternative stage to living or dying by individualist neoliberal seed choices.

This is the insidious danger of the logic of GM seeds as a technological solution to agrarian crisis in Telangana through the pursuit of higher yields. *Manci digubadi*, a good yield, is a logical thing to pursue within the broader framework of neoliberal India, where farmers are asked to make choices about brands and chase yields. But when it becomes by far the most, or the only, important goal of agriculture, farmers' options constrict. The transformations and performances that are logical or even possible in the agricultural regime of GM cotton include new pesticides, different fertilizers, and the hope of newer and better seeds. When *manci digubadi* fails to materialize, farmers have no other way to view success in the cotton market. Transformation within organic development programs allows for a much wider range of success, but only when program guidelines can be adapted to farmers' local needs. Each of these performances is, in turn, structured by local and global social, economic, and political factors. Both GM cottonseeds and organic agriculture are part of an agricultural development apparatus that operates through local hierarchies, like caste and gender, as well as through the global cotton trade, which dictates the rules of organic or GM regulation. In engaging agricultural development, all farmers learn to see themselves and their work in different ways, ranging from the performances of entrepreneurship on GM cotton farms to the performances of show farmers working with development groups.

Ultimately, the role that farmers play depends on the stage they are given: in the presence of economic or material rewards, as well as the added social recognition and sense of celebrity that comes from being regularly interviewed and photographed with visitors, farmers learn to perform and even embody the sense of transformation. This sentiment is then documented by visiting officials and researchers eager to show that their technology is not just improving farms but improving lives. In the absence of reliable and deliverable rewards, or in the absence of consistent and trusted oversight, the transformation of the intervention falls aside in favor of the ways that farmers learn from each other.

The vignette that opens this chapter ranks among the most dramatic and overt performances of transformative sentiment among the farmers that I observed, but it is not an isolated case. In Srigonda, several teams led by agricultural scientist Francesca Mancini (2005, 2007, 2008, 2009) demonstrated that IPM trainings could lead farmers to better lives, enhance well-being, reduce pesticide use and pesticide poisoning, and encourage greater economic resilience. Srigonda farmers who learned IPM as part of an intervention to lower pesticide costs reported "an increased ability and confidence in choosing their management practices on the basis of field observations, resulting in cash savings and higher yields" (Mancini, Van Bruggen, and Jiggins 2007, 106). The farmers doubtlessly performed this transformative sentiment while working with the field school instructors. Through this performance, some may even have incorporated these new ways of relating to agriculture into their improvisational *métis* knowledge. But by 2012, IPM methods had been abandoned. In the words of one farmer, "Bt came, and it gives the same benefit [of lower pesticide use] with less work." This was not, in this sense, a sustainable intervention. Despite earlier comments, the rules of success on cotton farms had changed. In this case, there was no longer any point in learning what this intervention had come to teach. By calling these moments performative, I do not mistake them for evidence of a universally sustainable alternative agriculture.

But the story does not end there—in 2011, eight years after the initial training, Umesh, an agricultural scientist from Warangal, became involved with the same village and offered many of the same IPM suggestions to farmers as part of their GM cotton agriculture. Unlike the previous short-term interventions, Umesh stayed and worked with Naniram to support his fledgling cooperative. Umesh had old family ties to the village, and his pragmatic suggestions have been tested by willing farmers as a means to solve specific incidences of micronutrient deficiency and pest attack. Farmers adapted these suggestions to their own land, keeping some, like bird perches and strategic applications of chicken fertilizer, and abandoning others, such as time-intensive homemade neem pesticides. This flexible, long-term dedication and oversight allows farmers to learn and provides a space to respond to intervention instructions. As Prakruti learned, a failure to listen to concerns about labor or local resources may lead farmers to abandon the identity they perform as part of that intervention. Farmers, like all of us, engage in performances that can change what we know and how we see ourselves. At times, these performances draw upon the contingent gratitude and rule-following of development transformations. During other moments, the slow decline in options to live well can lead farmers to desperation and suicide. Both versions depend upon the knowledge and practice performed in the field.

Performance and transformation do not delegitimize alternative agriculture projects. This is an especially unhelpful conclusion when farmers are considering public suicides. Rather, to understand life and death on these farms, we must understand the audiences and the stages that structure farmers' performances in the fields where they work. Social institutions like Naniram's cooperative and the tireless work of organic show farmers sustain plural visions of living well as a Telangana cotton farmer because they provide opportunities to learn and to adapt agricultural knowledge. The takeaway here is not that these spaces are performative and thus illegitimate and unsustainable. Quite the opposite: the efforts that organic programs or locally managed cooperatives put into underwriting vulnerability, creating social capital, building institutions, and creating new reward structures for farmer success *make* them sustainable.

7

REDEFINING SUCCESS IN TELANGANA COTTON AGRICULTURE

"**WAIT HERE** a moment," said Dasru, a Ralledapalle GM cotton farmer. He set down a paper cup of tea and left our small group of farmers discussing cottonseed trends in the 2014 season to disappear into his mud-brick and palm thatch house. Dasru returned a moment later with several brightly colored seed packets: *Jaadoo*, Telugu for "magic," bearing the image of a chicken laying golden eggs; *ATM*, with a caped cotton boll shooting cash from a slot on its midsection; *Dr. Brent*, stamped with a smiling man wearing a red turban and glasses, presumably the doctor himself. "We don't know how the seeds will fare this year," Dasru sighs. "We have to plant like a blind person, with our eyes closed." A few hours to the north, organic farmers grow seeds without any semblance of choice in a free market, sidestepping the anxiety that such choices entail. "Since we started working with Prakruti," one Addabad farmer says proudly, "we haven't taken any seeds, pesticides, or fertilizers from the outside [shops]. This year we're growing mostly mung bean and pigeon pea." Are you planting organic cottonseeds from Prakruti? I ask, pen ready to compare his choices to those in Ralledapalle. "Well yes, they gave them to us," he answered, laughing. "Why not use them?"

During the worst years of the cotton crisis in the mid-1990s, pesticide use climbed, farmer suicides rose, and India struggled to compete with cotton production in the United States and China. By 2013, suicides plateaued, pesticides aimed at bollworms dropped precipitously, incomes rose, and India's national average yield per hectare had nearly doubled (Cotton Corporation of India 2017; Kranthi 2012; Kouser, Abedullah, and Qaim 2017; Plewis 2014; Vaidyanathan 2006). Over the same time period, Bt cotton came to be planted in more than 95 percent of Indian cotton fields, radically changing the cotton sector by directing farmers toward private hybrid seeds in far greater numbers than had been planted in the past. Non-GM cotton farmers have been relegated to minor niche industries like organic cotton production or high-end surgical cotton grown from *G. arboreum* (Shrivastavi 2015). Organic and GM cotton have offered Telangana farmers different pathways to success and different visions for the future of agriculture, placing yields, ecology, and socioeconomic development at stake. Is anyone's life better?

The biggest champions of GM cotton agriculture in scholarship (Kathage and Qaim 2012; Herring and Rao 2012) and policy (*Economic Times* 2013; Press Trust of India 2018) point to yield increases and seed adoption as evidence that their product is inevitably superior. This is an economic argument—namely, that farmers choose seeds well, they are satisfied with their choices, and the seeds bring farmers and India itself large yields. With the argument framed in these terms, organic agriculture's advocates fire back that organically grown non-GM cotton can provide high yields under the right circumstances (Altenbuchner, Vogel, and Larcher 2017; Forster et al. 2013) and note that India's organic agriculture producer networks are the largest in the world (Willer and Lernoud 2016). In chapter 5, I showed that organic cotton crop yields are dramatically lower than the yields of farmers planting GM cotton in Telangana but that organic farmers have found other advantages through price supports, infrastructure, and social capital. More fundamentally, I have contended in this book that the metrics of yields and adoption do not tell us much about the quality of life for cotton farmers. Organic farmers often plant non-GM versions of commercial hybrid seeds designed for fertilizer and water-intensive agricultural regimens—of course they do not reap higher yields than GM cotton farmers. This comparison misses several larger points. National yield increases are not shared equally or equitably by GM cotton farmers in India's socially stratified countryside (Gutierrez et al. 2015; Stone 2011). Anyway, yields have a complex relationship to Bt seed adoption. When India's Bt adoption climbed past 50 percent, cotton yields plateaued (figure 13). If the seeds were the biggest factor driving yields, then farmers should have seen a continuing uptick in their yields. Finally, irrigation connectivity, the primary agronomic factor associated with

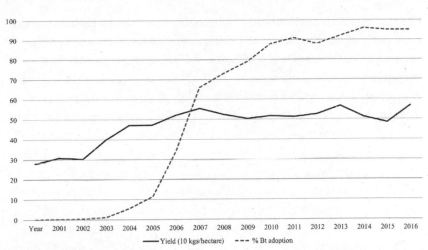

FIGURE 13. Relationship of yields (10 kgs/hectare) to Bt adoption in India. Data compiled from Cotton Corporation of India annual reports.

agrarian distress (Gupta 2017; Gutierrez et al. 2015), reaches only about a third of cotton farmers (Directorate of Cotton Development 2017). In context, yield is a poor metric to judge how seeds change lives.

Both GM and organic cotton make claims to increasing biodiversity and reducing pesticide sprays. Evidence compiled by K. R. Kranthi (2014), former director of the Central Institute of Cotton Research and a leading global expert in Indian cotton, shows that certain pesticide sprays dropped precipitously with the introduction of Bt cotton, particularly the most toxic sprays that targeted bollworms. This is an unambiguously positive development. Yet he also shows that sprays for sucking pests unaffected by Bt toxins have risen just as dramatically. This makes the story more complicated. In fact, the total volume of pesticides now sprayed on Indian cotton exceeds pre-GM levels (figure 14).

Any new pest-control technology would place selective evolutionary pressure on pesticide-resistant organisms and open new niches for nontarget pests. Bt cotton (Tabashnik et al. 2014; K. S. Mohan et al. 2015) is hardly the first pesticide to solve one insect problem while opening the door for another. But the rise in pesticide sprays is troubling to Bt cotton's narrative—why plant a cottonseed modified to kill insects if farmers are now spraying more than they did before? As I've described, a day of spraying pesticides ends with farmers nursing headaches as they wash oil and pesticides from their bare skin. Despite indications that the most harmful pesticides have decreased since Bt cotton's introduction

(Veettil, Krishna, and Qaim 2016), the (mostly) men who spray cotton pesticides and the (mostly) women and children who pluck and hand-weed cotton continue to suffer hair loss, DNA damage, nausea, and skin damage from these persistent pesticides (Venkata et al. 2016). Mixed management strategies like IPM, which advocate planting Bt cotton while also minimizing pesticide and fertilizer applications (Fitt 2000; Mancini, Van Bruggen, and Jiggins 2007), might address these issues, but that management logic has struggled to achieve lasting success in India. In part this is because cotton is a cash crop that farmers strive to see overproduce as I have shown in chapter 4. Yet this struggle intensifies because farmers are increasingly planting their cotton more densely to gain higher yields from a combination of fertilizers, herbicides, pesticides, and herbicide-tolerant GM cotton slated to be approved soon in India (Stone and Flachs 2017). If the goal is to eliminate pesticides, then organic cotton production systems have a clear advantage over GM seeds because they ban such sprays entirely.

By planting a diverse set of different crops, farmers manage entire landscapes. Through agriculture, they build quotidian environmental knowledge, dispersing risk through several subsistence or market crops in case one should fail, diversifying the nutrients taken up and restored by different plants through their life cycles, and helping a wide set of animals, weeds, and fungi to survive. Bt cotton is increasingly unsuited to fostering a diverse farm ecosystem because

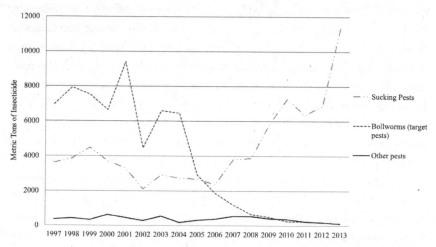

FIGURE 14. Cotton insecticide sprays 1997–2013 (adapted from Flachs 2017a). Data compiled from Kranthi (2014).

the national government and private sector encourage farmers to grow it in increasingly dense monocultures. Some Indian policymakers are promoting a high-density planting system (HDPS), which as much as quadruples the number of cotton plants in a given field by planting cotton much closer together (Madavi 2016; Venugopalan et al. 2014). Doubling down on cotton monocultures, Krishna, Qaim, and Zilberman (2016, 149) argue that, because it increases yields, "adopting Bt may substitute for the insurance function of agrobiodiversity," in which farmers diversify their agricultural risk through different crops. Yet, this treats seed choice in isolation. Several changes happen at once when planting density increases and farmers abandon other crops: herbicides become more cost effective than hand and ox weeders; those same herbicides kill gap-filled vegetables and other economic plants that are still present in many GM cotton farms; breeders select seeds with a tall phenotype suited to dense populations over a branching phenotype suited to more space; pest populations may increase as plants grow closer together; investments and profits may rise from this intensification; and farmers combat later-stage pest resistance to Bt toxins by uprooting their crop after only four months (Stone and Flachs 2017).

DIVERGENT LOGIC ON THE COTTON FARM

I have described how GM and organic cotton fields look, feel, and smell different when one walks through them, but the latest turn to HDPS cotton highlights the differences underlying each system. Pesticides kill soil microbes and predator insects in addition to their target pests (Altieri 2000). Crops with herbicide-tolerant genes are mutually exclusive with polyculture fields (at least until weedy plants evolve herbicide resistance as they have in the United States [Beckie and Hall 2014]). Privatized agribusiness demands international networks of biotechnology expertise, laboratory facilities, and fossil fuels to transport and disseminate these products, as well as regulatory networks capable of defending private investments in new GM technology. This system is not biologically, ecologically, politically, or economically diverse, and it is not intended to be such. Despite early (Fitt 2000) and continuing (Trapero et al. 2016) hopes that it will form part of a biodiverse IPM system, Bt cotton in practice is grown in monocultures with intensive chemical inputs.

Twelve five-year plans have now sought to move farmers out of agricultural work and into urban industrial sectors in the name of development in India, balancing this loss in rural production against new technologies and infrastructures (Cullather 2013; Yapa 1993). The Indian government continues to celebrate GM agriculture as a force for producing more cotton (*Times of India* 2018) and as having been freely chosen by Indian farmers (V. Mohan 2013). Scientists and policymakers are now doubling down on Bt cotton in the face of evolved pest resistance by advocating HDPS (Venugopalan et al. 2014). Until agricultural development focuses more on stability than yields, rural well-being will not improve, least of all for the poorest and most marginal farmers already excluded from green revolution and later multinational and state development projects in rainfed areas. These persistent vulnerabilities are unsolved by an agricultural logic that lives and dies by *manci digubadi*, the Telugu phrase for good yields that dominates farm decisions on GM cotton farms.

The organic agricultural programs that I describe in this book are not biodiverse because of some inherent superiority when compared to Bt cotton cultivation. In fact, organic agriculture is itself not necessarily small or biodiverse, as geographer Julie Guthman (2004) has shown in her study of labor and production on large, monoculture-driven, American organic farms that resemble conventional farms. They are biodiverse because the institutions supporting those farmers proscribe certain kinds of biodiversity, such as trap plants and nitrogen-fixing plants interspersed through cotton fields. These programs incentivize other kinds of biodiversity, such as the free vegetable and grain seeds that offer food security and extra income alongside diverse fields. These human-plant-insect relationships exist because farmers and institutions have worked together to make biodiversity profitable on their own terms. This combination of political and ecological logic explains why Adilabad district organic farms are twice as botanically biodiverse as Warangal district GM cotton farms (Flachs 2016c).

Several states in India have made waves by developing all-organic agricultural development plans, including Kerala (*Hindu* 2010), Sikkim (*Hindu* 2016), and Uttarakhand (Azad 2017). Despite their promise, each of these states has struggled to enact organic agriculture and convince either farmers (Besky 2014; Galvin 2014; D. Sen 2017) or consumers (Doshi 2017; Nazeer 2015) that they can trust organic production. Through these state-level policies, organic agricultural knowledge acts more like a brand than a daily agrarian performance. Time will tell if these projects can be sustained over the long term, but, as I discuss in this book, this is unlikely unless organic agricultural knowledge is adapted at the level of the farm field and supported through local trustworthy institutions.

Though organic agriculture proponents (Shiva 2009) and the biotechnology industry (Monsanto Company 2017) may claim that they hold the solution to suicides, the problems underlying India's agrarian crisis predate Bt cotton technology. Instead, I have argued that the agrarian distress of Indian cotton farmers is more familiar and banal: generational poverty, rising debts, poor irrigation, and narrowing possibilities to live well as a cotton farmer. For a few farmers, especially those who are larger farmers with better connections to agribusiness and university extension, like Naniram and his close friends in Srigonda, Bt cotton works well. That the Bt seed is a commodity in a confusing market is largely irrelevant to them, because they manage their seed with the optimal set of mechanical and chemical inputs and are comfortable solving unexpected problems with help from urban friends and colleagues. For others, especially the poorer, smaller, less-connected farmers in villages like Ralledapalle, Bt cotton has intensified cycles of debt, distress, and hope among rural cash croppers. By underwriting biodiversity and providing plural ways to live well as farmers, organic agriculture can offer more solutions to this underlying distress. As demonstrated by the farmers who left organic projects in chapter 6, it does not always succeed in providing convincing alternative agricultures to farmers, and it is not inevitably sustainable. How we judge the potential of these two mutually exclusive regimes depends on how we measure sustainability or success.

MEASURING COTTON SUCCESS

Rooted in the theoretical framework of political ecology, this book has examined how two legally exclusive agricultural regimes have impacted social, economic, and environmental life in rural Telangana. Despite their presumptions to universal development solutions for Indian farmers, and by extension farmers in the Global South generally, seeds and farming systems have been reworked in new and unexpected ways. Both GM and organic agriculture carry a set of incentives, risks, and pathways to success—a reward structure entangled within local and global political economies. Each reward structure is also dominated by a different social politics, a shifting labyrinth of those with knowledge and influence and those with uncertainty and anxiety.

Success for GM cotton is the culmination of industrial development since the nineteenth century: plant long-staple, annual cotton varieties suited to mechanized spinning (Hazareesingh 2016; S. Guha 2007), cultivate seeds suited to green revolution infrastructure (Cullather 2013; A. K. Basu and Paroda 1995), flood the market with GM brands, (Altenbuchner, Vogel, and Larcher 2017; Desmond 2013), and, most recently, promote HDPS to solve emerging agroecological issues in cotton farming (Stone and Flachs 2017). States and exporters gained by selling and taxing more cotton; urban industrial agribusiness sold more fertilizers, pesticides, seeds, and now herbicides; extension experts rose to the challenge of teaching cotton farmers how to make the most of the new system; and lucky farmers invested their profits from bumper crops in the new neoliberal capitalism of rural India. Through a combination of changes in the political economy and local ecology of cotton farming, GM cotton agriculture in India has transformed a native perennial tree cultivated for millennia into a short-duration annual crop genetically engineered by scientists from Missouri. A history of agrocapitalism that sees the adoption of technology as inevitable might argue that high adoption rates of GM cotton prove GM seeds' inevitable success, or at least their inevitable integration into Telangana smallholder agriculture. This denies farmers' lived experience in this vast, poorly understood seed market, where most farmers are unable to use environmental feedback in the field to make future seed decisions. Unable to build knowledge, faced with heavy debt, and vulnerable to extreme weather events, farmers gamble. Far from smooth or inevitable, *Cultivating Knowledge* describes how instability in the GM seed market, such as the 2012 scarcity, can drive farmers to go to extraordinary and harmful lengths to secure seeds that are abandoned the following year.

Success in certified organic cotton is a more recent development that rests upon elite demand and frustration with large-scale industrial or green revolution agriculture. Here ever-increasing demand, acreage, and regulatory oversight (Guthman 2004; Willer and Lernoud 2016) provide an alternative development model (Thottathil 2014). Organic agriculture's success is a success of agricultural education and market distinction—often achieved by selling stories of transformation like those described in the previous chapter. Telangana organic cotton depends on a network of experts and development projects to educate farmers and build trust in the crowded national and international clothing market. Organic proponents may see India's prowess in organic agricultural production as a clear sign of its potential in fields around the world. This is likely premature, as organic agriculture is highly variable and must be carefully negotiated in each local context. Telangana cotton farmers considering organic agriculture face much lower yields, justified largely by the nonagricultural benefits of learning to perform for visitors and officials. Ignoring the ways that farmers adapt organic proscriptions, cultivate celebrity, or hedge their bets with organic agriculture glosses over the reasons for its success. If organic agriculture inevitably provided farmers with the kinds of lives they wanted to live or built the kinds of biodiverse and sustainable ecologies that consumers hope to support, then Saraswathi and Arjuna from chapter 6 would have been able to work together. Viewing knowledge more as a negotiation and a practice, as did Mahesh and PANTA, allows for a greater flexibility of agricultural course corrections. This maintains the social incentives that make organic agriculture, and its vision for the future, an attractive alternative to GM cotton cultivation.

I have argued that organic and GM development are being made meaningful in ways unintended by organic and GM proponents. The ironies and awkward manifestations of postcolonial development, what anthropologist Anna Tsing (2005) calls "friction," appear when farmers jump from seed to seed, when technology designed to benefit the poor benefits those on optimal land with access to resources (Glover 2010), and when marginal farmers throw up their hands to demand "whatever's popular" in the shop. They appear as well when organic and fair-trade cotton development programs unintentionally provide a safety net that encourages farmers to invest more in GM cotton monocultures (Makita 2012). Intended to teach farmers new methods, organic agriculture often teaches farmers how to benefit from foreign buyers willing to underwrite their costs. Anthropology embraces these ironies. The real story of what happens on these farms is not found in national statistics or progress narratives but in the creative reconfigurations of development, knowledge, and performance.

GM COTTON AND GLOBAL CHANGE

GM cotton agriculture is defined by the expansion of private industry in a traditionally public sector, part of India's larger neoliberalization since the 1990s. To ensure that farmers purchase new seeds each year, all Indian GM cotton is bred into hybrids, which will underperform if replanted. Ironically, many of these hybrids are unsuited to the nonirrigated, nutrient-poor conditions of many small, poor farmers and are thus underperforming (Kranthi 2016). This would be the case even if the slow and intermittently dysfunctional GM regulatory process did not prevent rapid industry responses to agroecological problems (Choudhary et al. 2014; Herring 2014). Public breeders and extension agencies charged with developing new varieties no longer breed cottonseeds locally adapted to district-level farm conditions. Instead, agricultural science stations that I visited rent land to private seed breeding companies and work with them to develop new commercial brands. By collaborating with local extension offices, seed companies gain data on agronomic qualities and access to local germplasm, while scientists receive grant funding, train students, and publish reports. Foreign companies must partner with domestic companies to sell seeds in India, and so domestic Indian seed companies like Nuziveedu or Kaveri develop locally suited hybrid crosses while licensing GM technology from foreign companies like Monsanto.

Farmers experience this complex global change in agricultural technology through levels of local social relationships. Large farmers may recommend seeds to the smaller farmers who work as laborers on their farms, private seed brokers travel to villages to sell the most popular seeds each year, and all farmers look to advertisements and neighbors for seed names that they might seek out in the shop. Farmers hold cooperatives like Naniram's Srigonda shop in high esteem because Naniram provides the authority of a shop without the risk of price gouging always present among farmers who travel to Warangal city to buy seeds. Inside urban stores, the overwhelming brand diversity and seed inconsistency is particularly ill-suited to a socially mediated agriculture that relies on the observation of neighbor choices and the suggestions of local experts who need not be, but often are, high-status individuals. The decision of which seed to plant is a decision that determines if one's neighbors look to a farmer's fields with pity or respect, connected to the ability to pay school fees, buy consumer goods, host weddings, and show off that they are responsible, good farmers. As investments rise, yield and profit become increasingly important. This does little to sustain farmer knowledge, because farmers so frequently plant new and different seeds, but it is a boon to private breeders, seed brokers, and new seed brands.

By March 2016, long after non-GM seeds had disappeared from Telangana store shelves, a rise in pink bollworm (*Pectinophora gossypiella*) resistance throughout India (Aryai 2016; Buradikatti 2015) led to decreased yields, angry farmers, and a political backlash against Monsanto India. "Look at this waste," spat a farmer from Srigonda, gesturing to his cotton plants. "We used to pick the cotton again and again, but now they are telling us to pull it up and burn it after only three pickings." Ripping an unripe cotton boll off of a nearby plant, he peeled back the green outer layers of the fruit to reveal the wriggling, translucent-pink bollworms inside (figure 15). Do the new seeds have any resistance to these insects? I asked. "Those seeds are just old wine in a new bottle,"

FIGURE 15. Pink bollworm in Telangana cotton boll. Photo by Andrew Flachs.

he said, laughing bitterly. The timing of this backlash and rise in pink bollworm attacks was especially poor for Monsanto India. The company had just secured approval for field tests of their herbicide-tolerant (HT) cotton after nearly two years of regulatory impasse following the disbanding of the Genetic Engineering Approval Committee and a moratorium on new GM crops in 2012. On the heels of regulatory victory, Monsanto India faced unexpected criticism for celebrating a new GM HT seed that would not combat pink bollworm resistance. By 2018, this bollworm outbreak had no signs of slowing down (Jadhav 2018).

In early May 2015, the Hyderabad High Court, acting under pressure from the Telangana state government, issued a government order to cap Monsanto's royalty at fifty rupees (approximately eighty cents) (*New Indian Express* 2016). This move initiated a year of arguments and threats between Telangana, India, and Monsanto as they fought a legal battle over the right of states and federal governments to limit licensing fees on technology. After months of review, the Indian central government ultimately slashed Monsanto's royalty fee by 70 percent in early March 2016 (Mulvany 2016; Bhardwaj 2016). In response, Monsanto threatened to leave India and end new research and development programs while researchers at the Central Institute for Cotton Research suggested that Monsanto's new GM technology was no longer necessary for the Indian cotton industry to thrive (Kranthi 2015). Some scientists even suggested that public breeders should make their own GM cotton hybrids without Monsanto's involvement. One Warangal regional newspaper, *Saakshi*, argued that Monsanto's patented Bt modification should never have been approved in the first place, as the resulting licensing fee cost Indian seed companies, and in turn farmers, hundreds of thousands of rupees (*Saakshi* 2016).

Critiques of license fees seemed especially unfair to representatives of Monsanto India. "With all of these costs, why are they focusing on the fee?" Monsanto supply-chain lead Pendyala asked me during a 2016 interview. Seed packets, at ₹930 ($18) per one-acre packet, are a comparatively minor cost next to weeding, picking, sowing, plowing, or spraying pesticides. The outbreak of pink bollworm and the critical response that Monsanto had failed the country is especially irritating to Monsanto officials like Pendyala. Like Monsanto itself (Monsanto Company 2015), Pendyala blames the evolution of Bt resistance on the early use of unapproved Bt seeds and farmer indifference to the non-Bt refugia seeds included in every GM seed packet. These seeds are, in practice, thrown away. Not one farmer that I met over years of cotton planting sowed those seeds as they are directed to do so by the packet, in a border around their field. Not only are these seeds a waste of commercial breeders' time and money but their absence in the field accelerates the evolution of Bt-resistant pests.

Monsanto's solution to Bt resistance, currently held up by government regulation and approval processes, involves placing non-Bt seeds directly in the bag, obviating the need for a non-Bt refuge area. "It's [the regulators'] fault because they held up the solution to resistance," said Pendyala angrily. "We will have to reevaluate our position in India if this continues. Pink bollworm occurred in Gujarat because farmers don't plant the mandated refugia. . . . It's such a shame, such a waste of that seed!" In the wake of this lost revenue, Monsanto representatives announced that they would not introduce the third generation of Bt cotton (Bt-Bollgard III), which provides resistance to pink bollworms, to India in 2017 (Fernandes 2017). Despite the official ban, seed brokers sell Bollgard III and HT seeds to rural farmers (*Hindu* 2018), even selling them online (U. S. Reddy 2018)! This brazen lawbreaking is a source of continued frustration for Monsanto India (K. Kurmanath 2017), which views the unauthorized spread of their technology as theft and bad press. HT and Bollgard III seeds remain illegal in India as I write these words, but it is important to remember that the first Bt seeds were similarly stolen and disseminated throughout India before their legalization—a fact that proponents then used to argue that the seed had to be commercially released because farmers clearly wanted it.

Introduced as a solution to a crisis of pest attacks and low yields, Bt cotton has been judged largely on its promise to raise yields (Herring 2015; Scoones 2006). Through public discourse in newspapers, on television, and in scientific reports, this measure of success has been adopted by Telangana farmers who justify all seed choices in the context of *manci digubadi*. Since 2010, when most farmers had adopted Bt cotton, yields have largely stagnated (Kranthi 2016; Stone 2011), and yet this narrative persists. More than just a rational economic hope, *manci digubadi* encompasses the vision of success in GM cotton agriculture: investing more, earning more, and producing more. This is inextricably linked to the performance of the right kind of farmer (Flachs 2019), who takes advice but chooses freely, makes the right decision, cares for their farm by investing agrochemicals, and reaps the rewards of this hard work.

Unquestioned in this story is why yields would plateau when almost all farmers plant GM cotton, why hybrids are water intensive when so many farmers lack irrigation, why the hybrid seeds are exclusively *G. hirsutum* species so vulnerable to nontarget pests that total insecticide use has now surpassed pre-GM levels (Kranthi 2014), or what farmers will do now that some bollworms are resistant to the Bt toxins. Further unquestioned is why the world needs so much cotton—the planet has produced far more cotton than could be spun into clothing, a glut that has lasted several years (Patwardhan 2015; USDA Foreign Agricultural Service 2016). As farmers produce more and more cotton, Indian and other national governments bear the cost of this surplus by providing minimum support prices. Further down the supply chain, this ever-increasing stock is spun into cheap clothing at the expense of worker rights and safety, exported to wealthy markets in the United States and Europe, and eventually sold back to poorer nations through large-scale donations that suppress domestic industry (Beckert 2014; Brooks 2015).

GM seeds have had a complex impact on the search for sustainable cotton farming, not because of their technological potential but because of their socioeconomic reality. Unexpectedly, these seeds make cotton farming more precarious. This has little to do with their being genetically modified, and everything to do with their being sold in a market in which farmers cannot learn much about their seeds and do not apply that knowledge when they're at the market buying seeds next year. The language of success argued through yields or adoption masks a more serious problem. Farmers do not know much about the seeds they plant and can imagine no alternative futures that guide them off this treadmill of new GM seeds.

ORGANIC COTTON AND A GLOBAL ALTERNATIVE

Success in organic agriculture is a matter of challenging the *manci digubadi* imperative. Despite test plots showing that organic cotton is competitive with GM cotton under the right conditions (Forster et al. 2013), yields are much better on GM farms than on organic farms under the present management conditions in Telangana. Thus, organic groups have to shift the definition of success away from ever-increasing yields to negligible costs, independence from shops or foreign businesses, new visions of stewardship or entrepreneurship, and the cultivation of celebrity. Corporate and NGO organic development groups must themselves adhere to the legal requirements of the organic label institutionalized through APEDA, NPOP, the USDA, or TraceNet. This requires a heavy hand in proscribing agricultural practices and keeping watch for potential rule breakers. Through certifiers, donors, scientists, development project managers, and potential buyers, organic farmers face regular audits and thus enact regular performances.

To alleviate the pressures of this oversight and low yield, organic development projects underwrite agricultural work through free seeds, training programs, part-time employment, price premiums, direct marketing, loan programs, and assistance navigating government bureaucracy. Project field coordinators visit these farmers to distribute these gifts and hold training sessions, checking in to reassure farmers that they are here to help if they face any unexpected problems. Through these interactions, organic agriculture engenders a different kind of performance than GM farming, structured by these different audiences. These performances are contingent on subsidized support, but farmers also adopt new roles as a way to achieve agricultural success and celebrity outside of the possibilities offered by *manci digubadi*. Yields are still important, but farmers gain a sense of expertise and ownership by eschewing predatory credit systems. They avoid chemicals they fear might be poisonous to themselves and to the land that signals their standing in the rural landscape. They pursue celebrity as successful and important intermediaries between program organizers and their local communities. These performances are not necessarily economic calculations but an embracing of an alternative way to be a good farmer.

Organic cotton projects recognize that GM cotton has provided only one possible route to success, one unobtainable for most farmers who spend more on cotton than they receive in profit most years (A. A. Reddy 2017). Instead, these groups have instilled a different kind of safety net and provided a different route to success that does not require farmers to gamble on an exceptional harvest. "Yields are important, but other issues are also important to long-term success," argues Prakruti CEO Chender. This attempt to redefine agricultural success has not always been easy. "Adilabad's [local state agricultural officer] accuses us of promoting subsistence technology over more advanced technology," Chender continues. Advanced technology here means specifically Bt cotton and pesticides. Unusually for a cotton businessman, Chender is happy to see farmers diversifying their agriculture rather than focus on cotton production. Indeed, the Prakruti farmers in the Adilabad district manage an average of twenty-six other crops on their farms, each one taking space away from cotton (Flachs 2016c). These crops provide extra income, food security, and agricultural biodiversity in case the cotton would fail. "People talk about yields, but the real issue is one of productivity," Chender explains. "If the soil is more productive, if the agroforestry is more productive," then one will get a higher income. "What's the point in getting higher yields if you still have to buy all your food and spend all your money on chemicals?" he asks rhetorically.

For a celebrity show farmer like Mahesh from chapter 5, agriculture has benefits far beyond yield. In a district where suicide and debt peaked during the 1990s cotton crisis, Mahesh was able to steer his village away from the pesticide treadmills and predatory credit relationships that plagued other Warangal farmers (Galab, Revathi, and Reddy 2009; Vaidyanathan 2006) and toward a receptive NGO that would guarantee markets and publicize their efforts to the entire country. By performing development and transformation, Mahesh has established a new way to be good farmer in Ennepad, experiments in his remaining cotton fields, has distributed other parcels to his sons as a good father should, and continues to be a popular and useful member of the community in semiretirement. In performing this transformed, hardworking, charismatic farmer self, Mahesh embodies an ideal future offered by agriculture that he promotes.

Just as it would be wrong to view these spaces as illegitimate because they are performative, it would be wrong to think that the successes of organic agriculture can be replicated in other contexts simply because they were successful here. That conclusion would betray an apolitical ecology, viewing organic infrastructure, markets, and regulatory policies as universal and inevitable. If organic governance was infinitely replicable, then Prakruti would not have had difficulties with the incomplete transformations and rule breakers that I describe in the previous chapter. These programs owe their success to the relationships they have built through time and to farmers' iterative adaptations in the field. If anything, certified regulation hinders replication efforts because it establishes rules that can be broken, to the frustration of both parties. That assumption of inevitable success fails to appreciate organic agriculture as a performance. Only by incentivizing these roles, and redefining success in cotton agriculture, are organic programs successful.

IMPLICATIONS FOR THE FUTURE OF FARMING

On all cotton farms in Telangana, farmers perform for an audience of NGOs, neighbors, family members, scientists, and even the environment itself. Show farmers may be the most dramatic example of farmers performing roles to a distinct audience, but local village hierarchies determine who can talk comfortably to whom and who shows deference to whom. By extension, these channels determine how local information flows and which audiences observe the performance of that knowledge. The lens of performance helps to combat a persistent question in Indian cotton agriculture: If GM seeds are not inherently better, why do farmers adopt them? This question, posed in endless variation by economists (Kathage and Qaim 2012; Herring and Rao 2012), critical observers (Kranthi 2016; Stone 2013), and government officials (V. Mohan 2013), presumes an economic rationalism—farmers simply do what's best. Although I have argued at length that knowing what's best is often quite difficult, performance allows us to understand some of the other factors that explain why farmers will choose GM seeds year after year. *Manci digubadi* is about more than just yields. It expresses a search for social recognition, personal satisfaction, relief, and affirmation from the rural Telangana audience of shop owners, agricultural scientists, neighbors, and relatives. Organic agriculture provides an alternative to this search by creating new social values, like celebrity. By recognizing that the ultimate goal of agriculture is as much about the performance of good farming as it is about yield production, we can understand the complexity of agriculture as a social act.

When alternative agricultures, which included GM cotton in its early phases, adhere to a model of quick implementation, quick study, and a quick narrative of success, they reinforce a socioeconomic pattern in which these projects have no staying power. Like many such development schemes, GM cotton and organic cotton projects can be implemented antipolitically (Ferguson 1994), in the sense that poverty, neoliberal crisis, and even cotton agriculture is constructed as a seemingly natural problem rather than a historical and political struggle. Seed companies were never going to solve an endemic agricultural crisis with a new seed, and we should not be surprised or try to obscure, as Sainath (2015) accuses the government of doing, that suicides stubbornly persist in this sector. Sometimes development programs will celebrate show and *pedda* farmers as evidence of their intervention's success, even though most participants learn more about how to use NGO resources or how to work with extension agents than about new agricultural management tools. When development programs ignore or downplay the roles played by intermediaries, or see the most engaged farmers as representative of development work generally, they are likely to miss the reasons that their initiative works.

Yet show and *pedda* farmers can also be involved in longer-term alternative programs that redefine rural success. When given the option to work through local cooperatives or to iteratively adapt management decisions, their performances can help development programs intervene through a series of specific technological fixes to agricultural problems, from pest attacks to new planting densities. Successful reflective practitioners (Schön 1983), like those who worked with Mahesh and Tulanna, recognize that their interventions are not indicative of the inherent superiority of the intervention. They are built upon a shared learning experience and a negotiated set of social and material rewards. This adaptable approach to development can be much more sustainable because it understands farms as dynamic and agrarian distress as social.

I have cited studies from pro- and anti-GM groups throughout this book that claim that one production mode is more or less profitable, socially sustainable, productive, or ecological. These claims are hyperbolic on both sides (Stone 2002a). Yet these misleading data find their way into popular culture and scientific articles, shaping public perceptions of smallholding farmers. Examining the studies and their publicity as texts, geographer Mark Pearson (2006) argues "that there are striking similarities in the narratives utilized by both Monsanto *and* [anti-GM NGO] DDS; both seek to deploy 'objective science' in their efforts to govern smallholder farmers, and both purport to represent transparently the views of farmers and their best interests" (Pearson

2006, 307, emphasis in original). In this book, I hope that I have emphasized the need to examine these claims critically and through empirical ethnographic research.

Had GM cotton remained as a choice between the three varieties approved in 2002, this would likely be a very different book. As part of a slow-moving IPM package integrated into a diverse agriculture, Bt seeds likely would have helped many small farmers earn more as one factor in modest national yield increases. Instead, it has become an aggressively branded commodity in the anarchic agrarian capitalism (Herring 2007) of cotton production. Rice hybrids are not as popular now as cotton hybrids were in the 1990s, and attempts to produce a profitable private rice seed are moving slowly in Telangana. However, cotton's experience as a hybrid GM commodity may foreshadow the spread of a highly commodified GM rice. If GM rice seeds spread like GM cottonseeds—namely, with an initial period of heavy marketing to influential farmers, an explosion of confusing and untrialable seed brands, and the relegation of non-GM varieties to specialty markets dominated by development programs who make farmer knowledge a secondary concern to marketing—then rice seed choices may come to look very much like cottonseed choices. This would be disastrous for the indigenous knowledge now associated with Indian rice cultivation.

Cultivating Knowledge stresses the danger of seeking technological fixes for problems rooted in complex agricultural, political, social, and historical issues. In part, this is because the practice of sustainable agriculture on the farm, let alone the global challenge of feeding or clothing the world, is a social, and not technological, question. The unintended consequences of a new technology create avenues by which some reap benefits at the expense of others: GM seed companies capitalize on the desperation of farmers, organic show farmers engineer the benefits of production to their advantage, alternative agriculture programs earn funds based on false starts, and green consumers at the end of the supply chain consume clothing based on contrived images. More simply, the allure and danger of technological fixes is that they ignore the daily, messy, important, social work of agriculture. Farmers do not make simple cost-benefit analyses when evaluating new technologies and options. Their evaluation of development is a complex and shifting calculation of social meaning, performance, economics, and aspiration. Only by understanding this complicated nexus can we begin to understand sustainable agriculture.

PRAGMATIC SOLIDARITY

During a talk at Washington University in St. Louis, I once heard climate scientist Bill McKibben apologize for being "a professional bummer." Scholars are professional critics and analysts. The arguments that researchers make in scholarly books and articles are part of larger conversations and case studies in our attempt to systematically understand the world. Sometimes we can sound overly critical or negative in the ways that we write, construct arguments, and provide evidence—myself included. This is frustrating for people curious about a topic like sustainable food and agriculture who aren't engaged with these larger academic debates. The main point that I am making in this book is that the spread of GM and organic technologies around the world has changed how farmers learn, and that this change allows for different ways of living well as a farmer. Practice and performance on cotton fields has consequences for development and for long-term environmental management. Because of this line of reasoning, I am critical of simplistic narratives about both GMOs and organic agriculture. I simply don't think they help anyone understand how to move toward a just, sustainable agriculture.

Still, I argue that it is a mistake to treat these two systems with a false equivalence because both are beholden to larger political economies. Spaces that are performative are not therefore inauthentic. Indeed, performance is a force through which farmers can enact sustainable agriculture, and the lack of an engaged audience has left other Telangana cotton farmers exposed to the free market and bereft of socioeconomic support systems. I have been critical of seed selection among GM cotton farmers. But GM seeds are not themselves the root of this problem. Rather, it is the market surrounding them that places rural communities at such risk. As consumers of seeds, farmers often have little basis for choosing the seeds they choose. As producers of cotton, farmers are obligated to invest, and effectively to gamble, in the hope of reaping a large harvest for a global market already facing a cotton glut. This problem stems from the rapid diversification of GM seeds as well as the uncertain local context in which farmers evaluate those seeds. As the performance of knowledge, self, and skill are further squeezed into the limiting script of *manci digubadi* with the growth of herbicides and HDPS, farmers will continue to perform the role of consumers. The effects of innovations have wide-ranging implications beyond farmer decision-making. India's cotton sector has become increasingly capitalized over the past twenty years, first through pesticides and hybrid seeds, and now through herbicides and GM seeds. This drives positives, like increases in urban industrial production, export, and gross domestic product, as well as negatives, like rural inequality, the dissolution of rural safety nets through neo-liberal policies, and farmer suicides. GMOs were not a cause but rather one among many contributing factors to this balance.

This can be a frustrating conclusion for people like myself who want to work toward solutions to complex problems. I hope that readers of this book would not see these pages and give up trying to imagine sustainable futures. Instead, I want readers to consider that technological solutions to complex problems often fall short. These unintended consequences are drawn out by the sociopolitical forces and historical conditions under which people learn. *Cultivating Knowledge* is an argument for a more anthropological engagement with communities in need, one that privileges an understanding of root, social causes over neat, technological solutions.

Two interconnected changes in the way that cotton is grown, herbicide-tolerant GM cotton and high-density cotton planting, will further encourage a capital-intensive cash cropping system. While this shift may ultimately diminish the risk of pesticide exposure for some cotton farmers and laborers (Flachs 2017a), it also accelerates the trend toward smallholder capitalization, rural-urban migration, and monoculture. If cotton producers wanted to truly diminish pesticide risks, they would subsidize climate-appropriate protective clothing or stop selling pesticides dangerous to human life. Herbicides have been historically unpopular in Telangana because of local labor exchanges and ox plowing. However, the rise of pest resistance that shortens the cotton season, high-density planting, and herbicide resistant traits are changing the incentives in Telangana farmer decision-making (Stone and Flachs 2017). Mechanical harvesting and farm consolidation are not far behind these developments, as they are well suited to high-density fields in the context of diminishing rural labor. Under such conditions, Telangana cotton farmers will stop managing a set of useful plants in field gaps (Flachs 2015), losing as well the food security, knowledge, labor exchanges, and agricultural biodiversity associated with this practice. What happens to that labor, knowledge, food, and seeds is a more uncertain question as India continues moving people out of agricultural work and into urban, industrial sectors (Planning Commission, Government of India 2013).

Organic agriculture is not perfect. The system of international regulation incentivizes large producers to grow according to minimum standards (Buck,

Getz, and Guthman 1997; Guthman 2004), consolidates power and capital at the top of the supply chain (Jaffee 2012), and uses labels to elide regional differences between producers across the alienating divide of international capitalism (Galvin 2011; Guthman 2009), while creating fictitious and contrived images of an imagined agrarian life for elite, urban consumers (Besky 2014; R. L. Bryant and Goodman 2004; Guthman 2004). Yet, organic agriculture helps shift the conversation, especially for cotton producers.

Organic agriculture programs provide cotton farmers with a safety net where neoliberalism and heavy investment have eroded previous social contracts. Cotton is different from studies of fair-trade tea (Besky 2014; D. Sen 2017) or coffee (West 2012) in this respect, because these organic and fair-trade programs return stronger benefits to Telangana cotton farmers and do not challenge other equitable paths to justice. Indeed, village-level governments like self-help groups and *panchayats* (village administrative units) are fundamental parts of organic cotton development programs. Socioeconomic returns from organic agriculture in the programs that I document in this book include scholarships, village equipment, school fees, land improvement projects, and public infrastructure. These valuable, locally desired, and locally designed benefits help organic cotton farmers live the kind of lives they would like to live. Farmers and the community at large perform development roles as part of this work, but this is not wholly exploitative or contrived. This performed transformation is a way for show farmers like Mahesh or Tulanna to pursue their own visions of development and modernity, or for less engaged farmers to interact with these programs on their own terms.

Many risks of GM cotton have been overblown in public discourse. Unlike more promiscuous crops, particularly maize (Dyer et al. 2009; Pineyro-Nelso et al. 2009), it is unlikely (although not impossible) for Bt genes to spread from cotton to other plants. Cotton has heavy pollen and tends to self-pollinate rather than disperse its genes to other organisms (Kranthi 2012). Target pests are evolving resistance to the Bt gene (Kranthi 2016; Tabashnik et al. 2014), but this is to be expected of any new pest control method used in isolation. GM cotton was initially introduced as part of an IPM system that would help to reduce agrochemical inputs (Fitt 2000), not just encourage commodity monocultures. Perhaps it can return to this. Finally, the Bt gene does not appear to be harmful to humans, and *Bacillus thuringiensis* itself is a certified organic agricultural management tool selected because of its long, benign history in low-input agriculture (Charles 2001). From an ecological perspective, organic agriculture (Altenbuchner, Vogel, and Larcher 2017; Eyhorn, Ramakrishnan, and Mäder 2007) and GM cotton agriculture (Kouser, Abedullah, and Qaim 2017; Gutierrez et al. 2015) could both claim benefits in reducing the most toxic pesticides used on cotton, a worthy goal for one of the most pesticide-intensive crops (Abhilash and Singh 2009). But only organic cotton seeks to eliminate these altogether, focusing on cows and earthworms as fertilizer sources and agricultural biodiversity and homemade pesticides as a means of pest control.

By working on farms among a mix of cows, invertebrates, people, plants, and microorganisms, farmers cultivate relationships and obligations to a broader community, as well as the diverse skillset necessary to work with these other species. Organic agriculture provides more incentives to continue this work. In agrarian worlds, there can be no knowledge without practice. Organic agriculture gives most farmers lower yields that would make it economically untenable if not for other subsidies that underwrite agricultural costs. If the ultimate goal of farming is to produce as great a quantity of agricultural commodities as possible, then organic agriculture is a failure. If the ultimate goal of agricultural development is to uplift precarious farming communities, then it is reasonable to suggest changes that incentivize rural stability over yields. Organic cotton agriculture is one pathway to accomplish this in Telangana, although it is not the only solution, and not always the best. Bt cotton sold through cooperatives and planted as part of an IPM system may be another.

People wishing to wear clothing have an imperfect choice in an imperfect market. As consumers we can, in some ways, vote with our dollars, buying fair-trade or organic clothing. This requires us to be an informed populous capable of exercising these choices. Like the GM cotton farmers in this book, we do not always have the facts available to us in the dizzying retail world of fast fashion (Beckert 2014; Brooks 2015). Other times, we may be aware that there are some differences, but we may be cynical that the labels we see really signify anything transformative (West 2012), unable to afford these extra costs (Guthman 2009), or in legitimate need of the brand that will signify our status to those in our wider community (Hebdige 1979). And yet, sometimes and if we can, our choices do have measurable impacts on others.

In his landmark study of Mexican migrant labor in the United States, anthropologist Seth Holmes (2013) borrows from the activist and medical anthropologist Paul Farmer to suggest a "pragmatic solidarity" between his readers and the people who bear the consequences of our desire for fresh fruit. Holmes suggests that farms hiring migrant workers could offer courses in English or farm safety to pickers while concerned consumers could visit farms, teach useful classes, and help improve farm infrastructure. I am not suggesting that concerned consumers in the United States or Europe travel to India to investigate cotton farm conditions, although this may be a fair challenge to concerned Indian middle- or upper-class consumers. Teaching farmers' children in local schools is the path that I myself took as a visiting anthropologist when conducting the research for this book. Concerned consumers should do their part to slow fashion down, research where their clothes come from, and ask if this supply chain supports the world they want to live in. For many clothing consumers, it is also possible to completely sidestep the issue and wear second-hand or recycled clothing. Indeed, if the goal of sustainable rural development is to help people live well, rather than to grow as much cotton as possible, a reduction in the global supply of cotton that helps farmers diversify their crops during this glut is likely a net benefit. The fundamental issues of global cotton overproduction and limited choices for rural Indian communities will not be solved by the fashion sense of the readers of this book. I do not think it is possible for ethical consumers to simply buy their way out of global, systemic inequalities between rich and poor, or rural and urban. Yet we can help support institutions like Prakruti and PANTA working toward this kind of transformative change, recognizing that there are still milestones to meet.

The diversification of our clothing consumption offered by organic cotton gives us a choice in this marketplace. This is not the best imaginable choice, nor should it be the final choice that we see in the market. The organic label alone is not a guarantee of any practices or knowledge, although it may be more likely to support an ecologically or socioeconomically beneficial set of practices on farms. Programs that provide safety nets and redefine success in rural communities to include the practice of indigenous technical knowledge deserve our support. In this context, pragmatic solidarity is not a knee-jerk reaction to support organic agriculture or eschew GM cotton. Both of these technologies have the capacity to hide deeper structural problems in the name of easily measured benchmarks or to confront historically rooted social problems with systemic solutions.

Pragmatic solidarity in the current system requires effort on the part of consumers. It takes effort to sift through commercial or development messaging and find out what farmers are actually doing in the field. It takes effort to support organizations and farmers driving sustainable development, and it takes effort to resist the relaxation of governance over ecological and social change. It takes effort to understand that GM crops do not inherently solve pest problems because these plants do not grow themselves. In short, it requires an anthropological commitment. Clothing has always signified status, and it is not always possible to completely buck this system. It is not always appropriate or possible to wear secondhand T-shirts and jeans in lieu of a crisp business suit or professional blazer. If and when we can, readers of this book will have a small part in this pragmatic solidarity—not because our consumption or lack thereof will lead to transformative change, but because we might support larger institutions that change the rules of cotton agriculture and incentivize local knowledge, management, and technology that allows rural communities to live well, on their terms, as farmers.

REFERENCES

Abhilash, P. C., and Nandita Singh. 2009. "Pesticide Use and Application: An Indian Scenario." *Journal of Hazardous Materials* 165 (1–3): 1–12. https://doi.org/10.1016/j .jhazmat.2008.10.061.

Agrawal, Arun. 2005a. "Environmentality: Community, Intimate Government, and the Making of Environmental Subjects in Kumaon, India." *Current Anthropology* 46 (2): 161–90. https://doi.org/10.1086/427122.

Agrawal, Arun. 2005b *Environmentality: Technologies of Government and the Making of Subjects*. Durham, N.C.: Duke University Press.

Agrawal, Arun, and K. Sivaramakrishnan, eds. 2000. *Agrarian Environments: Resources, Representations, and Rule in India*. Durham, N.C.: Duke University Press.

Altenbuchner, Christine, Stefan Vogel, and Manuela Larcher. 2017. "Social, Economic and Environmental Impacts of Organic Cotton Production on the Livelihood of Smallholder Farmers in Odisha, India." *Renewable Agriculture and Food Systems* 33 (4): 373–85. https://doi.org/10.1017/S174217051700014X.

Altieri, Miguel A. 2000. "Ecological Impacts of Industrial Agriculture and the Possibilities for Truly Sustainable Farming." In *Hungry for Profit: The Agribusiness Threat to Farmers, Food, and the Environment*, edited by Fred Magdoff, John Bellamy Foster, and Frederick H. Buttel, 77–92. New York: Monthly Review Press.

Andriolo, Karin. 2006. "The Twice-Killed: Imagining Protest Suicide." *American Anthropologist* 108 (1): 100–113. https://doi.org/10.1525/aa.2006.108.1.100.

APEDA. 2011. "India Organic Tracability." Paper presented at Meeting of the Working Group on Agriculture: "Enhancing Competitiveness on Sustainable Sourcing and Tracing of Agri-Food Products in the GMS," Siem Reap, Cambodia.

APEDA. 2012. "National Programme for Organic Production (NPOP)." Accessed February 9, 2019. http://www.apeda.gov.in/apedawebsite/organic/index.htm.

Aristotle. 2016. *Nicomachean Ethics.* Translated by W. D. Ross. Digireads.com.

Arya, Shishir. 2016. "Is Bt Cotton No Longer Safe Against Pink Bollworm?" *Times of India,* February 13, 2016. http://timesofindia.indiatimes.com/city/nagpur/Is-Bt-Cotton-no-longer-safe-against-pink-bollworm/articleshow/50967835.cms.

Azad, Shivani. 2017. "Uttarakhand to Roll out Organic Agriculture Act in January." *Times of India,* December 29, 2017. https://timesofindia.indiatimes.com/city/dehradun/uttarakhand-to-roll-out-organic-agriculture-act-in-jan/articleshow/62285262.cms.

Bagla, Pallava, and Richard Stone. 2012. "India's Scholar-Prime Minister Aims for Inclusive Development." *Science* 335 (6071): 907–8. https://doi.org/10.1126/science.335.6071.907.

Bardone, Ester. 2013. "My Farm Is My Stage: A Performance Perspective on Rural Tourism and Hospitality Services in Estonia." PhD diss., University of Tartu. http://dspace.utlib.ee/dspace/handle/10062/34504.

Basu, A. K., and R. S. Paroda. 1995. *Hybrid Cotton in India: A Success Story.* Bangkok: Asia-Pacific Association of Agricultural Research Institutions.

Basu, Soutrik, and Cees Leeuwis. 2012. "Understanding the Rapid Spread of System of Rice Intensification (SRI) in Andhra Pradesh: Exploring the Building of Support Networks and Media Representation." *Agricultural Systems* 111 (1): 34–44. https://doi.org/10.1016/j.agsy.2012.04.005.

Batterbury, Simon P. J. 1996. "Planners or Performers? Reflections on Indigenous Dryland Farming in Northern Burkina Faso." *Agriculture and Human Values* 13 (3): 12–22. https://doi.org/10.1007/BF01538223.

Beck, Ulrich. 1992. *Risk Society: Towards a New Modernity.* London: SAGE.

Beckert, Sven. 2014. *Empire of Cotton: A Global History.* New York: Knopf.

Beckie, Hugh J., and Linda M. Hall. 2014. "Genetically-Modified Herbicide-Resistant (GMHR) Crops a Two-Edged Sword? An Americas Perspective on Development and Effect on Weed Management." *Crop Protection* 66 (December): 40–45. https://doi.org/10.1016/j.cropro.2014.08.014.

Behere, P. B., and M. C. Bhise. 2009. "Farmers' Suicide: Across Culture." *Indian Journal of Psychiatry* 51 (4): 242–43. https://doi.org/10.4103/0019-5545.58286.

Berkes, Fikret, Johan Colding, and Carl Folke. 2000. "Rediscovery of Traditional Ecological Knowledge as Adaptive Management." *Ecological Applications* 10 (5): 1251–62.

Besky, Sarah. 2014. *The Darjeeling Distinction: Labor and Justice on Fair-Trade Tea Plantations in India.* Berkeley: University of California Press.

Bhardwaj, Mayank. 2016. "India Cuts Monsanto Cottonseed Royalties Despite Threat to Quit." Reuters, March 9, 2016. http://www.reuters.com/article/us-india-monsanto-idUSKCN0WB1X8.

Bikhchandani, Sushil, David Hirshleifer, and Ivo Welch. 1992. "A Theory of Fads, Fashion, Custom, and Cultural Change as Informational Cascades." *Journal of Political Economy* 100 (5): 992–1026.

Bikhchandani, Sushil, David Hirshleifer, and Ivo Welch. 1998. "Learning from the Behavior of Others: Conformity, Fads, and Informational Cascades." *Journal of Economic Perspectives* 12 (3): 151–70.

Boyd, Robert, and Peter J. Richerson. 1988. *Culture and the Evolutionary Process.* Chicago: University of Chicago Press.

Boyd, Robert, Peter J. Richerson, and Joseph Henrich. 2011. "The Cultural Niche: Why Social Learning Is Essential for Human Adaptation." *Proceedings of the National Academy of Sciences* 108 (Supplement 2): 10918–25. https://doi.org/10.1073/pnas.1100290108.

Bradburn, Christopher. 2014. "Thousands of Plant Breeders: Women Conserving in Situ Crop Genetic Resources." Master's thesis, Swedish University of Agricultural Sciences.

Brookfield, Harold C. 2001. *Exploring Agrodiversity.* New York: Columbia University Press.

Brooks, Andrew. 2015. *Clothing Poverty: The Hidden World of Fast Fashion and Second-Hand Clothes.* London: Zed Books.

Bryant, Lia, and Bridget Garnham. 2015. "The Fallen Hero: Masculinity, Shame and Farmer Suicide in Australia." *Gender, Place, and Culture* 22 (1): 67–82. https://doi.org/10.1080/0966369X.2013.855628.

Bryant, Raymond L., and Michael K. Goodman. 2004. "Consuming Narratives: The Political Ecology of 'Alternative' Consumption." *Transactions of the Institute of British Geographers* 29 (3): 344–66. https://doi.org/10.1111/j.0020-2754.2004.00333.x.

Buck, Daniel, Christina Getz, and Julie Guthman. 1997. "From Farm to Table: The Organic Vegetable Commodity Chain of Northern California." *Sociologia Ruralis* 37 (1): 3–20. https://doi.org/10.1111/1467-9523.00033.

Buradikatti, Kumar. 2015. "Pink Bollworm a Nightmare for Bt Cotton Growers." *Hindu,* December 5, 2015. http://www.thehindu.com/news/national/karnataka/pink-bollworm-a-nightmare-for-bt-cotton-growers/article7950687.ece.

Butler, Judith. 1990. *Gender Trouble: Feminism and the Subversion of Identity.* New York: Routledge.

Charles, Daniel. 2001. *Lords of the Harvest: Biotech, Big Money, and the Future of Food.* New York: Basic Books.

Chaudhuri, K. N. 1985. *Trade and Civilisation in the Indian Ocean: An Economic History from the Rise of Islam to 1750.* New York: Cambridge University Press.

Chernev, Alexander, Ulf Böckenholt, and Joseph Goodman. 2015. "Choice Overload: A Conceptual Review and Meta-Analysis." *Journal of Consumer Psychology* 25 (2): 333–58. https://doi.org/10.1016/j.jcps.2014.08.002.

Choudhary, Bhagirath, Godelieve Gheysen, Jeroen Buysse, Piet van der Meer, and Sylvia Burssens. 2014. "Regulatory Options for Genetically Modified Crops in India." *Plant Biotechnology Journal* 12 (2): 135–46. https://doi.org/10.1111/pbi.12155.

Chua, Jocelyn Lim. 2014. *In Pursuit of the Good Life: Aspiration and Suicide in Globalizing South India.* Berkeley: University of California Press.

Coexist Campaign. 2016. "Why We Chose Our T-Shirt Factory." *Coexist Campaign* (blog). June 2, 2016. https://coexistcampaign.com/chose-t-shirt-factory/.

Conford, Philip. 2011. *The Development of the Organic Network: Linking People and Themes, 1945–95*. Edinburgh: Floris Books.

Cote, Muriel, and Andrea J. Nightingale. 2012. "Resilience Thinking Meets Social Theory: Situating Social Change in Socio-Ecological Systems (SES) Research." *Progress in Human Geography* 36 (4): 475–89. https://doi.org/10.1177/0309132511425708.

Cotton Corporation of India. 2014. *44th Annual Report 2013–2014*. Annual Report 44. Mumbai: Cotton Corporation of India.

Cotton Corporation of India. 2016. "Current Cotton Scenario." Last modified May 2, 2016. https://cotcorp.org.in/current_cotton.aspx.

Cotton Corporation of India. 2017. "Statistics" Accessed February 20, 2018. https://cotcorp.org.in/statistics.aspx.

Cotton Corporation of India. 2018. "National Cotton Scenario." National Cotton Scenario. Accessed February 20, 2018. https://cotcorp.org.in/national_cotton.aspx.

Crane, T. A., C. Roncoli, and G. Hoogenboom. 2011. "Adaptation to Climate Change and Climate Variability: The Importance of Understanding Agriculture as Performance." In "Technography and Interdisciplinarity: Performance, Practices and Experiments," special issue, *NJAS—Wageningen Journal of Life Sciences* 57 (3–4): 179–85. https://doi.org/10.1016/j.njas.2010.11.002.

Cullather, Nick. 2013. *The Hungry World: America's Cold War Battle Against Poverty in Asia*. Cambridge, Mass.: Harvard University Press.

Davidson, Osha Gray. 1996. *Broken Heartland: The Rise of America's Rural Ghetto*. Iowa City: University of Iowa Press.

Dawson, Andrew H., Michael Eddleston, Lalith Senarathna, Fahim Mohamed, Indika Gawarammana, Steven J. Bowe, Gamini Manuweera, and Nicholas A. Buckley. 2010. "Acute Human Lethal Toxicity of Agricultural Pesticides: A Prospective Cohort Study." *PLoS Med* 7 (10): e1000357. https://doi.org/10.1371/journal.pmed.1000357.

Deb, U., N. Nagaraj, R. Kumar, M. Bhattarai, R. Padmaja, P. Parthasarathy Rao, and C. Bantilan. 2014. "Dynamics of Rural Labor Markets in India: Implications for Inclusive Development Strategy." *ICRISAT Policy Brief* 27 (September): 1–12.

Deccan Chronicle. 2017. "Telangana: Failure of Cotton Crop Takes Another Life." December 17, 2017. https://www.deccanchronicle.com/nation/crime/171217/telangana-failure-of-cotton-crop-takes-another-life.html.

Deccan Chronicle. 2018. "Telangana: Farmer Loses Crop, Hangs Himself." February 15, 2018. https://www.deccanchronicle.com/nation/current-affairs/150218/telangana-farmer-loses-crop-hangs-himself.html.

Department of Commerce. 2005. *National Programme for Organic Production*. New Delhi: Ministry of Commerce and Industry.

Deshpande, R. S., and Saroj Arora. 2010. "Editor's Introduction." In *Agrarian Crisis and Farmer Suicides*, edited by R. S. Deshpande and Saroj Arora, 1–42. Land Reforms in India 12. New Delhi: SAGE Publications India.

Deshpande, Vivek. 2010. "Fraud Charges Cloud Indian Rise in Organic Cotton Production." *Indian Express*, February 7, 2010. http://www.indianexpress.com/news/fraud-charges-cloud-indian-rise-in-organic-cotton-production/576678/0.

Desmond, Elaine. 2013. "The Legitimation of Risk and Democracy: A Case Study of Bt Cotton in Andhra Pradesh, India." PhD diss., University College Cork. https://cora .ucc.ie/handle/10468/1688.

Desmond, Elaine. 2017. "Risk Definition and the Struggle for Legitimation: A Case Study of Bt Cotton in Andhra Pradesh, India." *Journal of Risk Research* 20 (1): 135–50. https://doi.org/10.1080/13669877.2015.1042504.

Desmond, Elaine. 2016. "The Legitimation of Development and GM Crops: The Case of Bt Cotton and Indebtedness in Telangana, India." *World Development Perspectives* 1 (March): 23–25. https://doi.org/10.1016/j.wdp.2016.05.008.

Dillehay, Tom D., Jack Rossen, Thomas C. Andres, and David E. Williams. 2007. "Preceramic Adoption of Peanut, Squash, and Cotton in Northern Peru." *Science* 316 (5833): 1890–93. https://doi.org/10.1126/science.1141395.

Directorate of Cotton Development. 2017. "Status Paper of Indian Cotton." Nagpur, India: Ministry of Agriculture and Farmers Welfare.

Doshi, Vidhi. 2017. "Sikkim's Organic Revolution at Risk as Local Consumers Fail to Buy into Project." *Guardian*, January 31, 2017. https://www.theguardian.com/ global-development/2017/jan/31/sikkim-india-organic-revolution-at-risk-as-local -consumers-fail-to-buy-into-project.

Durkheim, Émile. 1897. *Le suicide: Étude de sociologie.* Paris: F. Alcan.

Duveskog, Deborah, Esbern Friss-Hansen, and Edward W Taylor. 2011. "Farmer Field Schools in Rural Kenya: A Transformative Learning Experience." *Journal of Development Studies* 47 (10): 1529–44.

Dyer, George A., J. Antonio Serratos-Hernández, Hugo R. Perales, Paul Gepts, Alma Piñeyro-Nelson, Angeles Chávez, Noé Salinas-Arreortua, Antonio Yúnez-Naude, J. Edward Taylor, and Elena R. Alvarez-Buylla. 2009. "Dispersal of Transgenes Through Maize Seed Systems in Mexico." *PLoS ONE* 4 (5): e5734. https://doi.org/10.1371/ journal.pone.0005734.

Economic Times. 2010. "India Aims to Export $1 Bn Organic Products in Next 5 Yrs." May 15, 2010. https://economictimes.indiatimes.com/news/economy/foreign-trade/ india-aims-to-export-1-bn-organic-products-in-next-5-yrs/articleshow/5934473.cms.

Economic Times. 2012. "Biotechnology Sector to Have More M&A Activity Due to Fund Crunch: Report." February 15, 2012. https://economictimes.indiatimes.com/industry/ healthcare/biotech/biotechnology-sector-to-have-more-ma-activity-due-to-fund -crunch-report/articleshow/11895715.cms.

Economic Times. 2013. "Farmers Prefer Growing Genetically Modified Crops: Sharad Pawar." August 27, 2013. https://economictimes.indiatimes.com/news/economy/ agriculture/farmers-prefer-growing-genetically-modified-crops-sharad-pawar/ articleshow/22095086.cms.

Ecouterre Staff. 2010. "H&M, Other Brands Guilty of 'Organic Cotton Fraud'?" *Ecouterre*, January 25, 2010. http://www.ecouterre.com/hm-other-brands-guilty-of -organic-cotton-fraud/.

Escobar, Arturo. 2012. *Encountering Development: The Making and Unmaking of the Third World.* Princeton, N.J.: Princeton University Press.

Evans-Pritchard, E. E. 1976. *Witchcraft, Oracles and Magic Among the Azande.* Oxford: Oxford University Press.

Eyhorn, Frank. 2007. *Organic Farming for Sustainable Livelihoods in Developing Countries? The Case of Cotton in India.* Zürich: vdf Hochschulverlag AG.

Eyhorn, Frank, Mahesh Ramakrishnan, and Paul Mäder. 2007. "The Viability of Cotton-Based Organic Farming Systems in India." *International Journal of Agricultural Sustainability* 5 (1): 25–38. https://doi.org/10.1080/14735903.2007.9684811.

Faria, Neice Müller Xavier, Cesar Gomes Victora, Stela Nazareth Meneghel, Lenine Alves de Carvalho, and João Werner Falk. 2006. "Suicide Rates in the State of Rio Grande Do Sul, Brazil: Association with Socioeconomic, Cultural, and Agricultural Factors." *Cadernos de Saúde Pública* 22 (12): 2611–21. https://doi.org/10.1590/S0102-311X2006001200011.

Ferguson, James. 1994. *The Anti-Politics Machine: "Development," Depoliticization and Bureaucratic Power in Lesotho.* Minneapolis: University of Minnesota Press.

Fernandes, Vivian. 2017. "Monsanto Not to Introduce Bollgard-3, Some Other GM Crops in India over Regulatory Clouds." *Financial Express,* May 11, 2017. http://www.financialexpress.com/opinion/monsanto-not-to-introduce-bollgard-3-some-other-gm-crops-in-india-over-regulatory-clouds/663069/.

Fitt, Gary P. 2000. "An Australian Approach to IPM in Cotton: Integrating New Technologies to Minimise Insecticide Dependence." *Crop Protection,* XIVth International Plant Protection Congress, 19 (8–10): 793–800. https://doi.org/10.1016/S0261-2194(00)00106-X.

Fitzgerald, Deborah. 1993. "Farmers Deskilled: Hybrid Corn and Farmers' Work." *Technology and Culture* 34 (2): 324–43. https://doi.org/10.2307/3106539.

Fitzgerald, Deborah. 2003. *Every Farm a Factory: The Industrial Ideal in American Agriculture.* New Haven, Conn.: Yale University Press.

Flachs, Andrew. 2015. "Persistent Agrobiodiversity on Genetically Modified Cotton Farms in Telangana, India." *Journal of Ethnobiology* 35 (2): 406–26. https://doi.org/10.2993/etbi-35-02-406-426.1.

Flachs, Andrew. 2016a. "Cultivating Knowledge: The Production and Adaptation of Knowledge on Organic and GM Cotton Farms in Telangana, India." PhD diss., Washington University, St. Louis, Mo.

Flachs, Andrew. 2016b. "Redefining Success: The Political Ecology of Genetically Modified and Organic Cotton as Solutions to Agrarian Crisis." *Journal of Political Ecology* 23 (1): 49–70.

Flachs, Andrew. 2016c. "The Economic Botany of Organic Cotton Farms in Telangana, India." *Journal of Ethnobiology* 36 (3): 683–713. https://doi.org/10.2993/0278-0771-36.3.683.

Flachs, Andrew. 2017a. "Transgenic Cotton: High Hopes and Farming Reality." *Nature Plants* 3 (January): 16212. https://doi.org/10.1038/nplants.2016.212.

Flachs, Andrew. 2017b. "'Show Farmers': Transformation and Performance in Telangana, India." *Culture, Agriculture, Food and Environment* 39 (1): 25–34. https://doi.org/10.1111/cuag.12085.

Flachs, Andrew. 2018. "Development Roles: Contingency and Performance in Alternative Agriculture in Telangana, India." *Journal of Political Ecology* 25 (1): 716–31. http://dx.doi.org/10.2458/v25i1.22387.

Flachs, Andrew. 2019. "Planting and Performing: Anxiety, Aspiration, and 'Scripts' in Telangana Cotton Farming." *American Anthropologist* 121 (1): 48–61. https:// 10.1111/aman.13175.

Flachs, Andrew, and Paul Richards. 2018. "Playing Development Roles: The Political Ecology of Performance in Agricultural Development." *Journal of Political Ecology* 25 (1): 638–46. http://dx.doi.org/10.2458/v25i1.23089.

Flachs, Andrew, and Glenn Davis Stone. 2018. "Knowledge Across the Commodification Spectrum: Seeds and Agricultural Skill in Telangana, India." *Journal of Agrarian Change*. Published online September 28. https://doi.org/10.1111/joac.12295.

Flachs, Andrew, Glenn Davis Stone, and Christopher Shaffer. 2017. "Mapping Knowledge: GIS as a Tool for Spatial Modeling of Patterns of Warangal Cottonseed Popularity and Farmer Decision-Making." *Human Ecology* 45 (2): 143–59. https://doi.org/10.1007/s10745-016-9885-y.

Forster, Dionys, Christian Andres, Rajeev Verma, Christine Zundel, Monika M. Messmer, and Paul Mäder. 2013. "Yield and Economic Performance of Organic and Conventional Cotton-Based Farming Systems—Results from a Field Trial in India." *PLoS ONE* 8 (12): e81039. https://doi.org/10.1371/journal.pone.0081039.

Forsyth, Timothy. 2002. *Critical Political Ecology: The Politics of Environmental Science.* London: Routledge.

Foster, John Bellamy, and Fred Magdoff. 2000. "Liebig, Marx, and the Depletion of Soil Fertility: Relevance for Today's Agriculture." In *Hungry for Profit: The Agribusiness Threat to Farmers, Food, and the Environment*, edited by Fred Magdoff, John Bellamy Foster, and Frederick H. Buttel, 43–60. New York: Monthly Review Press.

Fouilleux, Eve, and Allison Loconto. 2017. "Voluntary Standards, Certification, and Accreditation in the Global Organic Agriculture Field. A Tripartite Model of Techno-Politics." *Agriculture and Human Values* 34 (1): 1–14. https://doi.org/10.1007/s10460-016-9686-3.

Franz, Martin, and Markus Hassler. 2010. "The Value of Commodity Biographies: Integrating Tribal Farmers in India into a Global Organic Agro-Food Network." *Area* 42 (1): 25–34. https://doi.org/10.1111/j.1475-4762.2009.00893.x.

Freidberg, Susanne. 2004. *French Beans and Food Scares: Culture and Commerce in an Anxious Age.* New York: Oxford University Press.

Galab, S., E. Revathi, and P. Prudhvikar Reddy. 2009. "Farmers' Suicides and Unfolding Agrarian Crisis in Andhra Pradesh." In *Agrarian Crisis in India*, edited by D. Narasimha Reddy and Srijit Mishra, 164–98. New Delhi: Oxford University Press.

Galt, Ryan E. 2009. "'It Just Goes to Kill Ticos': National Market Regulation and the Political Ecology of Farmers' Pesticide Use in Costa Rica." *Journal of Political Ecology* 16 (1): 1–33.

Galvin, Shaila Seshia. 2011. "Nature's Market? A Review of Organic Certification." *Environment and Society* 2 (1): 48–67.

Galvin, Shaila Seshia. 2014. "Organic Designs and Agrarian Practice in Uttarakhand, India." *Culture, Agriculture, Food and Environment* 36 (2): 118–28. https://doi.org/10.1111/cuag.12039.

Galvin, Shaila Seshia. 2018. "The Farming of Trust: Organic Certification and the Limits of Transparency in Uttarakhand, India." *American Ethnologist* 45 (4): 495–507. https://doi.org/10.1111/amet.12704.

GEAC. 2012. "Yearwise List of Commercially Released Varieties of Bt Cotton Hybrids by GEAC (Year 2002–Up to May 2012)." Standing committee report. Delhi: Department of Biotechnology of India.

Glover, Dominic. 2007. "Monsanto and Smallholder Farmers: A Case Study in CSR." *Third World Quarterly* 28 (4): 851–67. https://doi.org/10.1080/01436590701336739.

Glover, Dominic. 2010. "Is Bt Cotton a Pro-Poor Technology? A Review and Critique of the Empirical Record." *Journal of Agrarian Change* 10 (4): 482–509. https://doi.org/10.1111/j.1471-0366.2010.00283.x.

Glover, Dominic. 2011. "Science, Practice and the System of Rice Intensification in Indian Agriculture." In "Between the Global and the Local, the Material and the Normative: Power Struggles in India's Agrifood System," special issue, *Food Policy* 36 (6): 749–55. https://doi.org/10.1016/j.foodpol.2011.07.008.

Goffman, Erving. 1956. "The Nature of Deference and Demeanor." *American Anthropologist* 58 (3): 473–502. https://doi.org/10.1525/aa.1956.58.3.02a00070.

Goffman, Erving. 1959. *The Presentation of Self in Everyday Life.* New York: Anchor.

Gold, Ann Grodzins. 2003. "Vanishing: Seeds' Cyclicality." *Journal of Material Culture* 8 (3): 255–72. https://doi.org/10.1177/13591835030083002.

Goldschmidt, Walter Rochs. 1978. *As You Sow: Three Studies in the Social Consequences of Agribusiness.* Montclair, N.J.: Allanheld, Osmun.

Goodman, David, Bernardo Sorj, and John Wilkinson. 1987. *From Farming to Biotechnology: A Theory of Agro-Industrial Development.* Oxford: Basil Blackwell.

Graß, Therese. 2013. "H&M—a Role Model for Organic Cotton Use in Textile Processing?" *Journal of European Management and Public Affairs Studies* 1 (1): 23–26.

Griliches, Zvi. 1957. "Hybrid Corn: An Exploration in the Economics of Technological Change." *Econometrica* 25 (4): 501–22. https://doi.org/10.2307/1905380.

Griliches, Zvi. 1980. "Hybrid Corn Revisited: A Reply." *Econometrica* 48 (6): 1463–65. https://doi.org/10.2307/1912818.

Gruère, Guillaume, and Debdatta Sengupta. 2011. "Bt Cotton and Farmer Suicides in India: An Evidence-Based Assessment." *Journal of Development Studies* 47 (2): 316–37. https://doi.org/10.1080/00220388.2010.492863.

Gudynas, Eduardo. 2011. "Buen Vivir: Today's Tomorrow." *Development* 54 (4): 441–47. https://doi.org/10.1057/dev.2011.86.

Guha, Ramachandra. 2008. *India After Gandhi: The History of the World's Largest Democracy.* New York: Harper Collins.

Guha, Smit. 2007. "Genetic Change and Colonial Cotton Improvement in Nineteenth and Twentieth Century India." In *Situating Environmental History*, edited by Ranjan Chakrabarti, 307–22. New Delhi: Manohar.

Gunnell, David, Michael Eddleston, Michael R. Phillips, and Flemming Konradsen. 2007. "The Global Distribution of Fatal Pesticide Self-Poisoning: Systematic Review." *BMC Public Health* 7 (1): 357. https://doi.org/10.1186/1471-2458-7-357.

Gupta, Akhil. 1998. *Postcolonial Developments: Agriculture in the Making of Modern India.* Durham, N.C.: Duke University Press.

Gupta, Akhil. 2017. "Farming as Speculative Activity: The Ecological Basis of Farmers' Suicides in India." In *The Routledge Companion to the Environmental Humanities*, edited by Ursula K. Heise, Jon Christensen, and Michelle Niemann, 185–93. London: Routledge.

Guthman, Julie. 2004. *Agrarian Dreams: The Paradox of Organic Farming in California.* Berkeley: University of California Press.

Guthman, Julie. 2009. "Unveiling the Unveiling: Commodity Chains, Commodity Fetishism, and Ethical Food Labels." In *Frontiers of Commodity Chain Research*, edited by Jennifer Bair, 190–206. Stanford, Calif.: Stanford University Press.

Gutierrez, Andrew Paul, Luigi Ponti, Hans R. Herren, Johann Baumgärtner, and Peter E. Kenmore. 2015. "Deconstructing Indian Cotton: Weather, Yields, and Suicides." *Environmental Sciences Europe* 27 (1): 12. https://doi.org/10.1186/s12302-015-0043-8.

Harvey, David. 1991. *The Condition of Postmodernity: An Enquiry into the Origins of Cultural Change.* Oxford: Wiley-Blackwell.

Harvey, David. 2007. *A Brief History of Neoliberalism.* Oxford: Oxford University Press.

Hazareesingh, Sandip. 2016. "'Your Foreign Plants Are Very Delicate': Peasant Crop Ecologies and the Subversion of Colonial Cotton Designs in Dharwar, Western India, 1830–1880." In *Local Subversions of Colonial Cultures: Commodities and Anti-Commodities in Global History*, 1–10. Cambridge Imperial and Post-Colonial Studies Series. Hampshire, UK: Palgrave MacMillan.

Hebdige, Dick. 1979. *Subculture, the Meaning of Style.* New Accents. New York: Methuen.

Heidegger, Martin. 2010. *Being and Time.* Albany: SUNY Press.

Heinemann, Jack. 2012. *Suggestions on How to Apply International Safety Testing Guidelines for Genetically Modified Organisms.* Christchurch, New Zealand: Centre for Integrated Research in Biosafety.

Heller, Alison. 2018. *Fistula Politics: Birthing Injuries and the Quest for Continence in Niger.* New Brunswick, N.J.: Rutgers University Press.

Henrich, Joseph. 2001. "Cultural Transmission and the Diffusion of Innovations: Adoption Dynamics Indicate That Biased Cultural Transmission Is the Predominate Force in Behavioral Change." *American Anthropologist* 103 (4): 992–1013. https://doi.org/10.1525/aa.2001.103.4.992.

Herring, Ronald J. 2006. "Why Did 'Operation Cremate Monsanto' Fail?" *Critical Asian Studies* 38 (4): 467–93. https://doi.org/10.1080/14672710601073010.

Herring, Ronald J. 2007. "Stealth Seeds: Bioproperty, Biosafety, Biopolitics." *Journal of Development Studies* 43 (1): 130–57. https://doi.org/10.1080/00220380601055601.

Herring, Ronald J. 2014. "On Risk and Regulation: Bt Crops in India." *GM Crops and Food* 5 (3): 204–9. https://doi.org/10.4161/21645698.2014.950543.

Herring, Ronald J. 2015. "State Science, Risk and Agricultural Biotechnology: Bt Cotton to Bt Brinjal in India." *Journal of Peasant Studies* 42 (1): 159–86. https://doi.org/10.1080/03066150.2014.951835.

Herring, Ronald J., and Ann Grodzins Gold. 2005. "Biology and Utility, Meanings and Histories." *Economic and Political Weekly* 40 (38): 4117–20.

Herring, Ronald J., and N. Chandrasekhara Rao. 2012. "On the 'Failure of Bt Cotton': Analysing a Decade of Experience." *Economic and Political Weekly* 47 (18): 45–53.

Hindu. 2010. "Organic Farming Policy Announced." May 18, 2010. http://www.hindu.com/2010/05/18/stories/2010051853630400.htm.

Hindu. 2012. "Fear of Seed Shortage Grips Farmers." June 20, 2012. http://www.thehindu.com/todays-paper/tp-national/tp-andhrapradesh/article3549752.ece.

Hindu. 2013. "Use of Bt. Cotton Increased Yield, Farmers' Income: Pawar." August 29, 2013. http://www.thehindu.com/news/national/use-of-bt-cotton-increased-yield-farmers-income-pawar/article5069072.ece.

Hindu. 2016. "Sikkim Becomes India's First Organic State." January 14, 2016. https://www.thehindu.com/news/national/Sikkim-becomes-India%E2%80%99s-first-organic-state/article13999445.ece.

Hindu. 2017. "Spurious Cottonseeds Seized." June 9, 2017. http://www.thehindu.com/news/national/telangana/spurious-cotton-seeds-seized/article18869248.ece.

Hindu. 2018. "49 Special Squads to Check Spurious, HT Cottonseed." March 18, 2018. http://www.thehindu.com/todays-paper/tp-national/tp-telangana/49-special-squads-to-check-spurious-ht-cotton-seed/article23283757.ece.

Hirsch, Jameson K. 2006. "A Review of the Literature on Rural Suicide." *Crisis* 27 (4): 189–99. https://doi.org/10.1027/0227-5910.27.4.189.

Holmes, Seth. 2013. *Fresh Fruit, Broken Bodies: Migrant Farmworkers in the United States.* Berkeley: University of California Press.

Illge, Lydia, and Lutz Preuss. 2012. "Strategies for Sustainable Cotton: Comparing Niche with Mainstream Markets." *Corporate Social Responsibility and Environmental Management* 19 (2): 102–13. https://doi.org/10.1002/csr.291.

Ingold, Tim. 2011. "Making, Growing, Learning: Two Lectures Presented at UMFG, Belo Horizonte, October 2011." *Educação Em Revista* 29 (3): 301–23.

ISAAA. 2016. "Global Status of Commercialized Biotech/GM Crops: 2016." ISAAA Brief 52. Ithaca, N.Y.: International Service for the Acquisition of Agri-biotech Applications.

Iyengar, Sheena S., Gur Huberman, and Wei Jang. 2004. "How Much Choice Is Too Much? Contributions to 401(k) Retirement Plans." In *Pension Design and Structure: New Lessons from Behavior Finance,* edited by Olivia S. Mitchell and Steve Utkus, 83–95. Oxford: Oxford University Press.

Iyengar, Sheena S., and Mark R. Lepper. 2000. "When Choice Is Demotivating: Can One Desire Too Much of a Good Thing?" *Journal of Personality and Social Psychology* 79 (6): 995–1006. https://doi.org/10.1037/0022-3514.79.6.995.

Jadhav, Rajendra. 2018. "India's Cotton Plantings to Fall as Pest Dents Farmers' Income." Reuters, March 20, 2018. https://www.reuters.com/article/india-cotton-area/indias-cotton-plantings-to-fall-as-pest-dents-farmers-income-idUSL3N1R2355.

Jaffee, Daniel. 2012. "Weak Coffee: Certification and Co-Optation in the Fair Trade Movement." *Social Problems* 59 (1): 94–116. https://doi.org/10.1525/sp.2012.59.1.94.

James, Clive. 2015. *20th Anniversary (1996 to 2015) of the Global Commercialization of Biotech Crops and Biotech Crop Highlights in 2015.* ISAAA Brief 51. Ithaca: International Service for the Acquisition of Agri-Biotech Applications.

James, Erica Caple. 2010. *Democratic Insecurities: Violence, Trauma, and Intervention in Haiti.* California Series in Public Anthropology 22. Berkeley: University of California Press.

Jasanoff, Sheila. 2005. *Designs on Nature: Science and Democracy in Europe and the United States.* Princeton, N.J.: Princeton University Press.

Jayaraman, K. S. 2001. "Illegal Bt Cotton in India Haunts Regulators." *Nature Biotechnology* 19 (12): 1090. https://doi.org/10.1038/nbt1201-1090.

Johnson, Jennifer L., Laura Zanotti, Zhao Ma, David J. Yu, David R. Johnson, Alison Kirkham, and Courtney Carothers. 2018. "Interplays of Sustainability, Resilience, Adaptation and Transformation." In *Handbook of Sustainability and Social Science Research,* edited by Walter Leal Filho, Robert W. Marans, and John Callewaert, 3–25. World Sustainability Series. Cham: Springer International. https://doi.org/10.1007/978-3-319-67122-2_1.

Joshua, Anita, and B. Muralidhar Reddy. 2014. "15th Lok Sabha Holds Nerve, Passes Telangana Bill." *Hindu,* February 18, 2014. http://www.thehindu.com/news/national/15th-lok-sabha-holds-nerve-passes-telangana-bill/article5702134.ece.

Judd, Fiona, Henry Jackson, Caitlin Fraser, Greg Murray, Garry Robins, and Angela Komiti. 2006. "Understanding Suicide in Australian Farmers." *Social Psychiatry and Psychiatric Epidemiology* 41 (1): 1–10. https://doi.org/10.1007/s00127-005-0007 1.

Kathage, Jonas, and Matin Qaim. 2012. "Economic Impacts and Impact Dynamics of Bt (Bacillus Thuringiensis) Cotton in India." *Proceedings of the National Academy of Sciences* 109 (29): 11652–56. https://doi.org/10.1073/pnas.1203647109.

Kennedy, Jonathan, and Lawrence King. 2014. "The Political Economy of Farmers' Suicides in India: Indebted Cash-Crop Farmers with Marginal Landholdings Explain State-Level Variation in Suicide Rates." *Globalization and Health* 10 (March): 16. https://doi.org/10.1186/1744-8603-10-16.

Kloppenburg, Jack. 2004. *First the Seed: The Political Economy of Plant Biotechnology 1492–2000.* Madison: University of Wisconsin Press.

Kothari, Uma. 2005. "Authority and Expertise: The Professionalisation of International Development and the Ordering of Dissent." *Antipode* 37 (3): 425–46. https://doi.org/10.1111/j.0066-4812.2005.00505.x.

Kouser, Shahzad, Abedullah, and Matin Qaim. 2017. "Bt Cotton and Employment Effects for Female Agricultural Laborers in Pakistan." *New Biotechnology* 34 (January): 40–46. https://doi.org/10.1016/j.nbt.2016.05.004.

Kouser, Shahzad, and Matin Qaim. 2011. "Impact of Bt Cotton on Pesticide Poisoning in Smallholder Agriculture: A Panel Data Analysis." *Ecological Economics,* Special Section—Earth System Governance: Accountability and Legitimacy, 70 (11): 2105–13. https://doi.org/10.1016/j.ecolecon.2011.06.008.

Kranthi, K. R. 2012. *Bt Cotton Q&A*. Mumbai: Indian Society for Cotton Improvement.

Kranthi, K. R. 2014. "Cotton Production Systems—Need for a Change in India." *Cotton Statistics and News*, no. 38, 4–7.

Kranthi, K. R. 2015. "Technologies Are Breaking Down—What Next?" *Cotton Statistics and News*, no. 19, 4.

Kranthi, K. R. 2016. "Technology and Agriculture: Messed in India!" *Indian Express* (blog). March 10, 2016. http://indianexpress.com/article/india/india-news-india/technology-and-agriculture-messed-in-india/.

Krishna, Vijesh, Matin Qaim, and David Zilberman. 2016. "Transgenic Crops, Production Risk, and Agrobiodiversity." *European Review of Agricultural Economics* 43 (1): 137–64.

Kumar, Richa. 2015. *Rethinking Revolutions: Soyabean, Choupals, and the Changing Countryside in Central India*. New Delhi: Oxford University Press.

Kumbamu, Ashok. 2009. "Subaltern Strategies and Autonomous Community Building: A Critical Analysis of the Network Organization of Sustainable Agriculture Initiatives in Andhra Pradesh." *Community Development Journal* 44 (3): 336–50. https://doi.org/10.1093/cdj/bsp024.

Kurmanath, K. V. 2013. "Telangana Will Show Its Might in Cotton, Maize." *Hindu Business Line*, August 2, 2013. http://www.thehindubusinessline.com/industry-and-economy/agri-biz/telangana-will-show-its-might-in-cotton-maize/article4982372.ece.

Kurmanath, K. V. 2017. "Bollworm, Bt3: Telangana Farmers Want Monsanto Compensate Their Losses." *Hindu Business Line*, December 19, 2017. https://www.thehindubusinessline.com/economy/agri-business/bollworm-bt3-telangana-farmers-want-monsanto-compensate-their-losses/article9996971.ece.

Lalita, Ke, Kannabiran Vasantha, Rama S Melkote, Uma Maheshwari, Susie J. Tharu, and Veen Shatrugna. 1989. *We Were Making History: Life Stories of Women in the Telangana People's Struggle*. London: Zed Books.

Lansing, John Stephen. 2006. *Perfect Order: Recognizing Complexity in Bali*. Princeton Studies in Complexity. Princeton, N.J.: Princeton University Press.

Leach, Melissa, Andrew Charles Stirling, Ian Scoones, Andrew Charles Stirling, and Ian Scoones. 2010. *Dynamic Sustainabilities: Technology, Environment, Social Justice*. London: Routledge.

Lee, Henry. 1887. *The Vegetable Lamb of Tartary: A Curious Fable of the Cotton Plant. To Which Is Added a Sketch of the History of Cotton and the Cotton Trade*. London: S. Low, Marston, Searle, and Rivington.

Leslie, Paul, and J. Terrence McCabe. 2013. "Response Diversity and Resilience in Social-Ecological Systems." *Current Anthropology* 54 (2): 114–43. https://doi.org/10.1086/669563.

Lévinas, Emmanuel. 2000. *God, Death, and Time*. Palo Alto, Calif.: Stanford University Press.

Lingis, Alphonso. 2000. "To Die with Others." *Diacritics* 30 (3): 106–13. https://doi.org/10.1353/dia.2000.0020.

Linssen, Rik, Luuk van Kempen, and Gerbert Kraaykamp. 2010. "Subjective Well-Being in Rural India: The Curse of Conspicuous Consumption." *Social Indicators Research* 101 (1): 57–72. https://doi.org/10.1007/s11205-010-9635-2.

Ludden, David. 1999. *An Agrarian History of South Asia.* Cambridge: Cambridge University Press.

MacIntyre, Alasdair C. 2007. *After Virtue: A Study in Moral Theory.* 3rd ed. Notre Dame, Ind.: University of Notre Dame Press.

Madavi, B. 2016. "Impact of High Density Planting and Weed Management Practices on Growth and Yield of Bt Cotton." Master's thesis, Professor Jayashnakar Telangana State Agricultural University.

Maertens, Annemie. 2017. "Who Cares What Others Think (or Do)? Social Learning and Social Pressures in Cotton Farming in India." *American Journal of Agricultural Economics* 99 (4): 988–1007. https://doi.org/10.1093/ajae/aaw098.

Magdoff, Fred, John Bellamy Foster, and Frederick H. Buttel, eds. 2000. *Hungry for Profit: The Agribusiness Threat to Farmers, Food, and the Environment.* New York: Monthly Review Press.

Makita, Rie. 2012. "Fair Trade and Organic Initiatives Confronted with Bt Cotton in Andhra Pradesh, India: A Paradox." *Geoforum* 43 (6): 1232–41. https://doi.org/10.1016/j.geoforum.2012.03.009.

Malinowski, Bronislaw. 1992. *Magic, Science and Religion and Other Essays.* Prospect Heights, Ill.: Waveland Press.

Malmberg, Aslög, Sue Simkin, and Keith Hawton. 1999. "Suicide in Farmers." *British Journal of Psychiatry* 175 (2): 103 5. https://doi.org/10.1192/bjp.175.2.103.

Mancini, Francesca, and Ariena H. C. van Bruggen. 2005. "Acute Pesticide Poisoning Among Female and Male Cotton Growers in India." *International Journal of Occupational and Environmental Health* 11 (3): 221–32.

Mancini, Francesca, Janice L. S. Jiggins, and Michael O'Malley. 2009. "Reducing the Incidence of Acute Pesticide Poisoning by Educating Farmers on Integrated Pest Management in South India." *International Journal of Occupational and Environmental Health* 15 (2): 143–51.

Mancini, Francesca, Aad J. Termorshuizen, Janice L. S. Jiggins, and Ariena H. C. van Bruggen. 2008. "Increasing the Environmental and Social Sustainability of Cotton Farming Through Farmer Education in Andhra Pradesh, India." *Agricultural Systems* 96 (1–3): 16–25. https://doi.org/10.1016/j.agsy.2007.05.001.

Mancini, Francesca, Ariena H. C. van Bruggen, and Janice L. S. Jiggins. 2007. "Evaluating Cotton Integrated Pest Management (IPM) Farmer Field School Outcomes Using the Sustainable Livelihoods Approach in India." *Experimental Agriculture* 43 (1): 97–112. https://doi.org/10.1017/S001447970600425X.

Martineau, Belinda. 2001. *First Fruit: The Creation of the Flavr Savr Tomato and the Birth of Biotech Foods.* New York: McGraw-Hill.

Maumbe, Blessing M., and Scott M. Swinton. 2003. "Hidden Health Costs of Pesticide Use in Zimbabwe's Smallholder Cotton Growers." *Social Science and Medicine* 57 (9): 1559–71. https://doi.org/10.1016/S0277-9536(03)00016-9.

Mayer, Peter. 2010. *Suicide and Society in India.* New York: Routledge.

McGranahan, Carole, and Ralph Litzinger. 2012. "Self-Immolation as Protest in Tibet." Hot Spots, *Cultural Anthropology,* April 9, 2012. https://culanth.org/fieldsights/93-self-immolation-as-protest-in-tibet.

McMichael, Philip D. 2007. "Globalization and the Agrarian World." In *The Blackwell Companion to Globalization*, edited by George Ritter, 216–38. Malden, Mass.: Blackwell Publishing.

Meemken, Eva-Marie, and Matin Qaim. 2018. "Organic Agriculture, Food Security, and the Environment." *Annual Review of Resource Economics* 10 (1): 39–63. https://doi.org/10.1146/annurev-resource-100517-023252.

Menon, Meena, and Uzramma. 2018. *A Frayed History: The Journey of Cotton in India.* Oxford: Oxford University Press.

Merriott, Dominic. 2016. "Factors Associated with the Farmer Suicide Crisis in India." *Journal of Epidemiology and Global Health* 6 (4): 217–27. https://doi.org/10.1016/j.jegh.2016.03.003.

Mezirow, Jack. 2000. *Learning as Transformation: Critical Perspectives on a Theory in Progress.* Jossey-Bass Higher and Adult Education Series. San Francisco, Calif.: Jossey-Bass.

Mines, Diane P. 2005. *Fierce Gods: Inequality, Ritual, and the Politics of Dignity in a South Indian Village.* Bloomington: Indiana University Press.

Mintz, Sidney W. 1986. *Sweetness and Power: The Place of Sugar in Modern History.* New York: Penguin.

Mitra, Amit, and M. Somasekhar. 2013. "Textile Mills Will Suffer Once Telangana Turns Cotton Hub." *Hindu Business Line*, August 18, 2013. http://www.thehindubusinessline.com/industry-and-economy/textile-mills-will-suffer-once-telangana-turns-cotton-hub/article5035378.ece.

Mohan, Komarlingam S., Kadanur C. Ravi, Pennadam J. Suresh, Douglas Smerford, and Graham P. Head. 2015. "Field Resistance to the Bacillus Thuringiensis Protein Cry1Ac Expressed in Bollgard® Hybrid Cotton in Pink Bollworm, *Pectinophora gossypiella* (Saunders), Populations in India." *Pest Management Science* 72 (4): 738–46. https://doi.org/10.1002/ps.4047.

Mohan, Vishwa. 2013. "Sharad Pawar Bats for GM Crops in House, Holds up Bt Cotton as Success Story." *Times of India*, August 28, 2013. http://timesofindia.indiatimes.com/india/Sharad-Pawar-bats-for-GM-crops-in-House-holds-up-Bt-cotton-as-success-story/articleshow/22109722.cms.

Mohanty, B. B. 2005. "'We Are Like the Living Dead': Farmer Suicides in Maharashtra, Western India." *Journal of Peasant Studies* 32 (2): 243–76. https://doi.org/10.1080/03066150500094485.

Monsanto Company. 2012. "India Cotton Success." Accessed March 19, 2019. https://web.archive.org/web/20170528154138/http://www.monsanto.com/improvingagriculture/pages/celebrating-bollgard-cotton-india.aspx.

Monsanto Company. 2015. "Pink Bollworm Resistance to GM Cotton in India." Accessed March 19, 2019. https://web.archive.org/web/20150714073504/http://www.monsanto.com/newsviews/pages/india-pink-bollworm.aspx.

Monsanto Company. 2017. "Is Bt or GMO Cotton the Reason for Indian Farmer Suicides?" Last modified April 6, 2017. https://monsanto.com/company/commitments/human-rights/statements/indian-suicides-bt-gmo-not-responsible/.

Mukherji, Rahul. 2014. *Globalization and Deregulation.* Delhi: Oxford University Press.

Mulvany, Lydia. 2016. "India Cuts Monsanto Modified Cotton-Seed Royalty Fees by 70%." *Bloomberg News*, March 9, 2016. http://www.bloomberg.com/news/articles/2016-03-09/india-cuts-monsanto-modified-cotton-seed-royalty-fees-by-70.

Münster, Daniel. 2012. "Farmers' Suicides and the State in India: Conceptual and Ethnographic Notes from Wayanad, Kerala." *Contributions to Indian Sociology* 46 (1–2): 181–208. https://doi.org/10.1177/006996671104600208.

Münster, Daniel. 2015a. "'Ginger Is a Gamble': Crop Booms, Rural Uncertainty, and the Neoliberalization of Agriculture in South India." *Focaal* 2015 (71): 100–113. https://doi.org/10.3167/fcl.2015.710109.

Münster, Daniel. 2015b. "Farmers' Suicides as Public Death: Politics, Agency and Statistics in a Suicide-Prone District (South India)." *Modern Asian Studies* 49 (5): 1580–1605. https://doi.org/10.1017/S0026749X14000225.

Naik, Dhanasing B. 2000. *The Art and Literature of Banjara Lambanis: A Socio-Cultural Study*. New Delhi: Abhinav.

Narayanan, S. 2005. "Organic Farming in India: Relevance, Problems, and Constraints." Occasional Paper 38. Mumbai: Department of Economic Analysis and Research National Bank for Agriculture and Rural Development.

National Cotton Council of America. 2018. "What Can You Make from a Bale of Cotton?" Accessed February 20, 2018. https://www.cotton.org/pubs/cottoncounts/what-can-you-make.cfm.

National Crime Records Bureau. 2014. "Accidental Deaths & Suicides in India 2013." Annual Report 47. Accidental Deaths and Suicides in India. New Delhi: Ministry of Home Affairs.

National Public Radio. 2013. "Planet Money's T-Shirt Project." *Planet Money* (blog). December 2, 2013. https://www.npr.org/series/248799434/planet-moneys-t-shirt-project.

Nazeer, Mohamed. 2015. "Organic Farming Caught in 'Quality vs. Quantity' Debate." *Hindu*, August 30, 2015. http://www.thehindu.com/news/national/kerala/organic-farming-caught-in-quality-vs-quantity-debate/article7594299.ece.

Netting, Robert McC. 1993. *Smallholders, Householders: Farm Families and the Ecology of Intensive, Sustainable Agriculture*. Stanford, Calif.: Stanford University Press.

New Indian Express. 2012. "A Mayhem Called Mahyco Seed Shortage." June 25, 2012. http://newindianexpress.com/states/andhra_pradesh/article550368.ece.

New Indian Express. 2016. "Hyderabad HC to Intervene If Centre Fails to Fix Bt Cottonseed Price." March 9, 2016. http://www.newindianexpress.com/cities/hyderabad/Hyderabad-HC-to-Intervene-if-Centre-Fails-to-Fix-Bt-Cotton-Seed-Price/2016/03/09/article3317815.ece.

Newell, Peter. 2003. "Biotech Firms, Biotech Politics: Negotiating GMOs in India." IDS Working Paper 201. Brighton: Institute of Development Studies.

Nicholls, Clara Ines, and Miguel A. Altieri. 1997. "Conventional Agricultural Development Models and the Persistence of the Pesticide Treadmill in Latin America." *International Journal of Sustainable Development and World Ecology* 4 (2): 93–111. https://doi.org/10.1080/13504509709469946.

Nussbaum, Martha C. 2002. "Capabilities and Social Justice." *International Studies Review* 4 (2): 123–35.

Nussbaum, Martha C. 2006. "Capabilities as Fundamental Entitlements." In *Capabilities Equality*, edited by Alexander Kaufman, 44–70. New York: Routledge.

Nussbaum, Martha C., and Amartya Sen, eds. 1993. *The Quality of Life*. New York: Oxford University Press.

Oosterhuis, Derrick M., and Judy Jernstedt. 1999. "The Origin and Domestication of Cotton." In *Cotton: Origin, History, Technology, and Production*, edited by C. Wayne Smith and J. Tom Cothren, 175–206. New York: Wiley.

Ortner, Sherry. 2005. "Subjectivity and Cultural Critique." *Anthropological Theory* 5 (1): 31–52. https://doi.org/10.1177/1463499605050867.

Paarlberg, Robert L. 2001. *The Politics of Precaution: Genetically Modified Crops in Developing Countries*. Baltimore, Md.: Johns Hopkins University Press.

Paarlberg, Robert L. 2002. "The Real Threat to GM Crops in Poor Countries: Consumer and Policy Resistance to GM Foods in Rich Countries." *Food Policy* 27 (3): 247–50.

Pandian, Anand. 2009. *Crooked Stalks: Cultivating Virtue in South India*. Durham, N.C.: Duke University Press.

Pandian, Anand. 2011. "Ripening with the Earth: On Maturity and Modernity in South India." In *Modern Makeovers: A Handbook of Modernity in South Asia*, edited by Saurabh Dube, 157–169. New Delhi: Oxford University Press.

Panneerselvam, P., Niels Halberg, Mette Vaarst, and John Erik Hermansen. 2012. "Indian Farmers' Experience with and Perceptions of Organic Farming." *Renewable Agriculture and Food Systems* 27 (2): 157–69. https://doi.org/10.1017/S1742170511000238.

Parsai, Gargi. 2012. "Protests Mark 10th Anniversary of Bt Cotton." *Hindu*, March 27, 2012. http://www.thehindu.com/sci-tech/agriculture/article3248530.ece.

Parthasarathy, G., and Shameem. 1998. "Suicides of Cotton Farmers in Andhra Pradesh: An Exploratory Study." *Economic and Political Weekly* 33 (13): 720–26.

Patwardhan, Mayank. 2015. "Global Glut in Cotton to Persist." *Business Standard India*, June 10, 2015. http://www.business-standard.com/article/markets/global-glut-in-cotton-to-persist-115061000904_1.html.

Pearson, Mark. 2006. "'Science,' Representation and Resistance: The Bt Cotton Debate in Andhra Pradesh, India." *Geographical Journal* 172 (4): 306–17.

Peled, Micha, dir. 2011. *Bitter Seeds*. DVD. San Francisco, Calif.: Teddy Bear Films.

Perkins, John H. 1997. *Geopolitics and the Green Revolution: Wheat, Genes, and the Cold War*. New York: Oxford University Press.

Perrière, Robert Ali Brac De La, and Franck Seuret. 2000. *Brave New Seeds: The Threat of GM Crops to Farmers*. New York: Zed.

Peter, Gregory, Michael Mayerfeld Bell, Susan Jarnagin, and Donna Bauer. 2009. "Coming Back Across the Fence: Masculinity and the Transition to Sustainable Agriculture." *Rural Sociology* 65 (2): 215–33. https://doi.org/10.1111/j.1549-0831.2000.tb00026.x.

Pineyro-Nelso, A., J. van Heerwaarden, H. R. Perales, J. Antonio Serratos-Hernández, A. Rangel, M. B. Hufford, Paul Gepts, A. Garay-Arroyo, R. Rivera-Bustamante, and

Elena R. Alvarez-Buylla. 2009. "Transgenes in Mexican Maize: Molecular Evidence and Methodological Considerations for GMO Detection in Landrace Populations." *Molecular Ecology* 18 (4): 750–61. https://doi.org/10.1111/j.1365-294X.2008.03993.x.

Planning Commission, Government of India. 2013. "Twelfth Five Year Plan (2012–2017): Faster, More Inclusive and Sustainable Growth." Five Year Plans 12. New Delhi: Planning Commission, Government of India.

Plewis, Ian. 2014. "Indian Farmer Suicides: Is GM Cotton to Blame?" *Significance* 11 (1): 14–18. https://doi.org/10.1111/j.1740-9713.2014.00719.x.

Ploeg, Jan Douwe van der. 2013. *Peasants and the Art of Farming: A Chayanovian Manifesto.* Agrarian Change and Peasant Studies. Winnipeg: Fernwood. https://library.wur.nl/WebQuery/wurpubs/441695.

Pollan, Michael. 2002. *The Botany of Desire.* New York: Random House.

Pollan, Michael. 2006. *The Omnivore's Dilemma: A Natural History of Four Meals.* New York: Penguin Group.

Prabu, M. J. 2013. "Organic Cultivation: Learning from the Enabavi Example." *Hindu*, August 22, 2013. http://www.thehindu.com/sci-tech/agriculture/organic-cultivation-learning-from-the-enabavi-example/article5045359.ece.

Prakash, C. S. 1999. "Feeding a World of Six Billion." *AgBioForum: The Journal of Agrobiotechnology Management and Economics* 2 (3/4): Article 13.

Prashanth, P., M. J. M. Reddy, and I. S. Rao. 2013. "Organic Cotton Farming in Andhra Pradesh—a Constraint Analysis." *Journal of Cotton Research and Development* 27 (1): 138–43.

Press Trust of India. 2018. "Bt Cotton Doubled Production since 2002, Minimised Harm by Pest: Govt." *Business Standard India*, February 5, 2018. http://www.business-standard.com/article/economy-policy/bt-cotton-doubled-production-since-2002-minimised-harm-by-pest-govt-118020500963_1.html.

Qaim, Matin. 2003. "Bt Cotton in India: Field Trial Results and Economic Projections." *World Development* 31 (12): 2115–27. https://doi.org/10.1016/j.worlddev.2003.04.005.

Qaim, Matin. 2010. "Benefits of Genetically Modified Crops for the Poor: Household Income, Nutrition, and Health." *New Biotechnology* 27 (5): 552–57. https://doi.org/10.1016/j.nbt.2010.07.009.

Quartz, Julia. 2010. "Creative Dissent with Technoscience in India: The Case of Non-Pesticidal Management (NPM) in Andra Pradesh." *International Journal of Technology and Development Studies* 1 (1): 55–92.

Raghupati, Tarakarama Rao, and Jay Shankar Prasad. 2009. "Enabavi—The Road Ahead in Agriculture." In *The Poor and the Private Sector: Public Private Community Partnership: Cases from the Field*, edited by Shoba Ramachandran, 60–70. New Delhi: ACCESS Development Services.

Rahnema, Majid, and Victoria Bawtree, eds. 1997. *The Post-Development Reader.* London: Zed.

Ram, M. Kodanda. 2007. "Movement for Telangana State: A Struggle for Autonomy." *Economic and Political Weekly* 42 (2): 90–94.

Ramamurthy, Priti. 2000. "The Cotton Commodity Chain, Women, Work and Agency in India and Japan: The Case for Feminist Agro-Food Systems Research." *World Development* 28 (3): 551–78. https://doi.org/10.1016/S0305-750X(99)00137-0.

Ramamurthy, Priti. 2003. "Material Consumers, Fabricating Subjects: Perplexity, Global Connectivity Discourses, and Transnational Feminist Research." *Cultural Anthropology* 18 (4): 524–50. https://doi.org/10.1525/can.2003.18.4.524.

Ramamurthy, Priti. 2011. "Rearticulating Caste: The Global Cottonseed Commodity Chain and the Paradox of Smallholder Capitalism in South India." *Environment and Planning A: Economy and Space* 43 (5): 1035–56. https://doi.org/10.1068/a43215.

Rao, P. Narasimha, and K. C. Suri. 2006. "Dimensions of Agrarian Distress in Andhra Pradesh." *Economic and Political Weekly* 41 (16): 1546–52.

Raynolds, Laura T. 2004. "The Globalization of Organic Agro-Food Networks." *World Development* 32 (5): 725–43. https://doi.org/10.1016/j.worlddev.2003.11.008.

Reddy, A. Amarender. 2017. "Agrarian Economy of Telangana." Paper presented at the Telangana Economic Association meeting, Hyderabad.

Reddy, B. Muralidhar. 2014. "Telangana to Come into Existence on June 2." *Hindu*, March 5, 2014. http://www.thehindu.com/news/national/andhra-pradesh/telangana -to-come-into-existence-on-june-2/article5751092.ece.

Reddy, U. Sudhakar. 2018. "BT Cottonseeds Sold Online Despite Ban." *Times of India*, March 12, 2018. https://timesofindia.indiatimes.com/city/hyderabad/bt-cotton-seeds -sold-online-despite-ban/articleshow/63266522.cms.

Reding, Nick. 2009. *Methland: The Death and Life of an American Small Town*. New York: Bloomsbury.

Richards, Paul. 1985. *Indigenous Agricultural Revolution: Ecology and Food Production in West Africa*. Boulder: Westview.

Richards, Paul. 1989. "Agriculture as a Performance." In *Farmer First: Farmer Innovation and Agricultural Research*, edited by Robert Chambers, Arnold Pacey, and Lori Ann Thrupp, 39–42. London: Intermediate Technology.

Richards, Paul. 1993. "Cultivation: Knowledge or Performance?" In *An Anthropological Critique of Development: The Growth of Ignorance*, edited by Mark Hobart, 61–78. New York: Routledge.

Richerson, Peter J., and Robert Boyd. 2008. *Not by Genes Alone: How Culture Transformed Human Evolution*. Chicago: University of Chicago Press.

Rizvi, Anusha, dir. 2010. *Peepli Live*. DVD. Mumbai: Aamir Khan Productions.

Rogers, Everett M. 2003. *Diffusion of Innovations*. 5th ed. New York: Free Press.

Roitman, Janet. 2013. *Anti-Crisis*. Durham, N.C.: Duke University Press.

Ross, Eric B. 1998. *The Malthus Factor: Poverty, Politics, and Population in Capitalist Development*. New York: Zed.

Roy, Devparna, Ronald J. Herring, and Charles C. Geisler. 2007. "Naturalising Transgenics: Official Seeds, Loose Seeds and Risk in the Decision Matrix of Gujarati Cotton Farmers." *Journal of Development Studies* 43 (1): 158–76. https://doi.org/10 .1080/00220380601055635.

Rupa, D. S., P. P. Reddy, and O. S. Reddi. 1991. "Reproductive Performance in Population Exposed to Pesticides in Cotton Fields in India." *Environmental Research* 55 (2): 123–28. https://doi.org/10.1016/S0013-9351(05)80168-9.

Ryan, Bryce, and Neal C. Gross. 1943. "The Diffusion of Hybrid Seed Corn in Two Iowa Communities." *Rural Sociology* 8 (1): 15–24.

Saakshi. 2016. "In Cotton Business, Monsanto's Monopoly Has Come to an End." March 8, 2016. https://www.sakshi.com/news/hyderabad/valid-on-the-seed-hegemony-320902.

Sainath, P. 2013. "Over 2,000 Fewer Farmers Every Day." *Hindu*, May 2, 2013. http://www.thehindu.com/opinion/columns/sainath/over-2000-fewer-farmers-every-day/article4674190.ece.

Sainath, P. 2015. "The Slaughter of Suicide Data." *P. Sainath: Rural Reporter* (blog). August 5, 2015. https://psainath.org/the-slaughter-of-suicide-data/.

Sarma, Ch. R. S. 2017. "Spurious Seeds Playing Havoc with Farmers' Lives in AP, Telangana." *Hindu Business Line*, December 15, 2017. https://www.thehindubusinessline.com/economy/agri-business/spurious-seeds-playing-havoc-with-farmers-lives-in-ap-telangana/article9992518.ece.

Scheibehenne, Benjamin, Rainer Greifeneder, and Peter M. Todd. 2010. "Can There Ever Be Too Many Options? A Meta Analytic Review of Choice Overload." *Journal of Consumer Research* 37 (3): 409–25. https://doi.org/10.1086/651235.

Scheper-Hughes, Nancy. 1993. *Death Without Weeping: The Violence of Everyday Life in Brazil.* Berkeley: University of California Press.

Schieffelin, Edwaard L. 1998. "Problematizing Performance." In *Ritual, Performance, Media*, edited by Felicia Hughes-Freeland, 199–212. New York: Routledge.

Schmid, Otto. 2007. "Development of Standards for Organic Farming." In *Organic Farming: An International History*, edited by William Lockeretz, 152–74. Cambridge: CABI.

Schön, Donald A. 1983. *The Reflective Practitioner: How Professionals Think in Action.* New York: Basic Books.

Schurman, Rachel, and William A. Munro. 2010. *Fighting for the Future of Food: Activists Versus Agribusiness in the Struggle Over Biotechnology.* Minneapolis: University of Minnesota Press.

Scoones, Ian. 2006. *Science, Agriculture and the Politics of Policy: The Case of Biotechnology in India.* New Delhi: Orient Blackswan.

Scoones, Ian. 2008. "Mobilizing Against GM Crops in India, South Africa, and Brazil." *Journal of Agrarian Change* 8 (2 and 3): 315–44.

Scott, James C. 1998. *Seeing Like a State: How Certain Schemes to Improve the Human Condition Have Failed.* New Haven, Conn.: Yale University Press.

Sen, Amartya. 2005. "Human Rights and Capabilities." *Journal of Human Development* 6 (2): 151–66. https://doi.org/10.1080/14649880500120491.

Sen, Debarati. 2017. *Everyday Sustainability: Gender Justice and Fair Trade Tea in Darjeeling.* Albany: State University of New York Press.

Sen, Debarati, and Sarasij Majumder. 2011. "Fair Trade and Fair Trade Certification of Food and Agricultural Commodities: Promises, Pitfalls, and Possibilities." *Environment and Society* 2 (1): 29–47.

Seufert, Verena, and Navin Ramankutty. 2017. "Many Shades of Gray—The Context-Dependent Performance of Organic Agriculture." *Science Advances* 3 (3): e1602638. https://doi.org/10.1126/sciadv.1602638.

Seufert, Verena, Navin Ramankutty, and Tabea Mayerhofer. 2017. "What Is This Thing Called Organic?—How Organic Farming Is Codified in Regulations." *Food Policy* 68 (April): 10–20. https://doi.org/10.1016/j.foodpol.2016.12.009.

Shetty, P. K. 2004. "Socio-Ecological Implications of Pesticide Use in India." *Economic and Political Weekly* 39 (49): 5261–67.

Shiva, Vandana. 1993. *The Violence of the Green Revolution: Third World Agriculture, Ecology, and Politics.* 2nd ed. Atantic Highlands, N.J.: Third World Network.

Shiva, Vandana. 1997. *Biopiracy: The Plunder of Nature and Knowledge.* Boston, Mass.: South End Press Collective.

Shiva, Vandana. 2009. "From Seeds of Suicide to Seeds of Hope: Why Are Indian Farmers Committing Suicide and How Can We Stop This Tragedy?" *Huffington Post*, May 29, 2009. https://www.huffingtonpost.com/vandana-shiva/from-seeds-of-suicide-to_b_192419.html.

Shiva, Vandana, Afsar H. Jafri, Ashok Emani, and Manish Pande. 2002. *Seeds of Suicide.* 2nd ed. New Delhi: Research Foundation for Science, Technology, and Ecology.

Shrivastavi, Snehlata. 2015. "Desi Cotton, a Profitable Option for Marginal Farmers of Region." *Times of India*, December 3, 2015. http://timesofindia.indiatimes.com/city/nagpur/Desi-cotton-a-profitable-option-for-marginal-farmers-of-region/articleshow/50034374.cms.

Sillitoe, Paul. 1998. "The Development of Indigenous Knowledge: A New Applied Anthropology." *Current Anthropology* 39 (2): 223–52.

Sneyd, Adam. 2016. *Cotton.* Malden, Mass.: John Wiley and Sons.

Sridhar, V. 2006. "Why Do Farmers Commit Suicide? The Case of Andhra Pradesh." *Economic and Political Weekly* 41 (16): 1559–65.

Srinivasan, N. 2010. *Microfinance India: State of the Sector Report 2009.* New Delhi: SAGE Publications India.

Stallones, Lorann. 1990. "Suicide Mortality Among Kentucky Farmers, 1979–1985." *Suicide and Life-Threatening Behavior* 20 (2): 156–63. https://doi.org/10.1111/j.1943-278X.1990.tb00098.x.

Stark, C., Deborah Gibbs, P. Hopkins, Alan Belbin, A. Hay, and Sivasubramaniam Selvaraj. 2006. "Suicide in Farmers in Scotland." *Rural and Remote Health* 6 (1): 509.

Stoll, Steven. 2002. *Larding the Lean Earth: Soil and Society in Nineteenth-Century America.* New York: Hill and Wang.

Stone, Glenn Davis. 2002a. "Both Sides Now: Fallacies in the Genetic-Modification Wars, Implications for Developing Countries, and Anthropological Perspectives." *Current Anthropology* 43 (4): 611–30.

Stone, Glenn Davis. 2002b. "Commentary: Biotechnology and Suicide in India." *Anthropology News* 43 (5): 5–5. https://doi.org/10.1111/an.2002.43.5.5.2.

Stone, Glenn Davis. 2007. "Agricultural Deskilling and the Spread of Genetically Modified Cotton in Warangal." *Current Anthropology* 48 (1): 67–103.

Stone, Glenn Davis. 2011. "Field versus Farm in Warangal: Bt Cotton, Higher Yields, and Larger Questions." *World Development* 39 (3): 387–98.

Stone, Glenn Davis. 2013. "A Response to Herring and Rao." *Economic and Political Weekly* 48 (33): 70–72.

Stone, Glenn Davis. 2014. "Theme Park Farming in Japan." *Fieldquestions* (blog). June 5, 2014. http://fieldquestions.com/2014/06/05/theme-park-farming-in-japan/.

Stone, Glenn Davis. 2016. "Towards a General Theory of Agricultural Knowledge Production: Environmental, Social, and Didactic Learning." *Culture, Agriculture, Food and Environment* 38 (1): 5–17.

Stone, Glenn Davis. 2018. "Agriculture as Spectacle." *Journal of Political Ecology* 25 (1): 656–85.

Stone, Glenn Davis. 2019. "Commentary: New Histories of the Indian Green Revolution." *Geographical Review*. Published online February 21. https://doi.org/10.1111/geoj.12297.

Stone, Glenn Davis, and Andrew Flachs. 2014. "The Problem with the Farmer's Voice." *Agriculture and Human Values* 31 (4): 649–653. https://doi.org/10.1007/s10460-014-9535-1.

Stone, Glenn Davis, and Andrew Flachs. 2017. "The Ox Fall down: Path-Breaking and Technology Treadmills in Indian Cotton Agriculture." *Journal of Peasant Studies* 45 (7): 1272–96. https://doi.org/10.1080/03066150.2017.1291505. http://www.tandfonline.com/eprint/TbaXt6cAx3JV8WVBUJkM/full.

Stone, Glenn Davis, Andrew Flachs, and Christine Diepenbrock. 2014. "Rhythms of the Herd: Long Term Dynamics in Seed Choice by Indian Farmers." *Technology in Society* 36 (1): 26–38. https://doi.org/10.1016/j.techsoc.2013.10.003.

Strathern, Marilyn. 2000. "New Accountabilities: Anthropological Studies in Audit, Ethics, and the Academy." In *Audit Cultures: Anthropological Studies in Accountability, Ethics and the Academy*, edited by Marilyn Strathern, 1–18. London: Routledge.

Subramanian, Ajantha. 2009. *Shorelines: Space and Rights in South India*. Stanford, Calif.: Stanford University Press.

Sudhir, T. S. 2017. "Amid Rising Farmer Suicides, Telangana to Send 1,000 Officials for Israel 'Study Tour.'" *News Minute*, November 17, 2017. https://www.thenewsminute.com/article/amid-rising-farmer-suicides-telangana-send-1000-officials-israel-study-tour-71777.

Sudhir, Uma. 2017. "After Selling Crop at a Loss, Telangana Farmers Return Home with Pesticide." *NDTV*, November 17, 2017. https://www.ndtv.com/telangana-news/after-selling-crop-at-a-loss-telangana-farmers-return-home-with-pesticide-1776673.

Suri, K. C. 2006. "Political Economy of Agrarian Distress." *Economic and Political Weekly* 41 (16): 1523–29.

Swain, Ranjula Bali, and Fan Yang Wallentin. 2009. "Does Microfinance Empower Women? Evidence from Self-Help Groups in India." *International Review of Applied Economics* 23 (5): 541–56. https://doi.org/10.1080/02692170903007540.

Tabashnik, Bruce E., David Mota-Sanchez, Mark E. Whalon, Robert M. Hollingworth, and Yves Carrière. 2014. "Defining Terms for Proactive Management of Resistance to Bt Crops and Pesticides." *Journal of Economic Entomology* 107 (2): 496–507. https://doi.org/10.1603/EC13458.

Taylor, Marcus. 2011. "'Freedom from Poverty Is Not for Free': Rural Development and the Microfinance Crisis in Andhra Pradesh, India." *Journal of Agrarian Change* 11 (4): 484–504. https://doi.org/10.1111/j.1471-0366.2011.00330.x.

Taylor, Marcus. 2013. "Liquid Debts: Credit, Groundwater and the Social Ecology of Agrarian Distress in Andhra Pradesh, India." *Third World Quarterly* 34 (4): 691–709. https://doi.org/10.1080/01436597.2013.786291.

Taylor, Marcus. 2014. *The Political Ecology of Climate Change Adaptation: Livelihoods, Agrarian Change and the Conflicts of Development*. New York: Routledge Earthscan.

Taylor, Marcus, and Suhas Bhasme. 2018. "Model Farmers, Extension Networks and the Politics of Agricultural Knowledge Transfer." *Journal of Rural Studies* 64 (November): 1–10. https://doi.org/10.1016/j.jrurstud.2018.09.015.

Tewari, Ananya. 2017. "A Certified Problem." *Down to Earth*, October 15, 2017. http://www.downtoearth.org.in/news/a-certified-problem-58797.

Thaindian News. 2008. "Genetic Engineering Can Help Solve Food Crisis: US Expert." July 29, 2008. http://www.thaindian.com/newsportal/sci-tech/genetic-engineering-can-help-solve-food-crisis-us-expert_10077548.html.

Thottathil, Sapna E. 2014. *India's Organic Farming Revolution*. Iowa City: University of Iowa Press.

Times of India. 2018. "Bt Cotton Doubled Production, Minimised Harm by Pest." February 5, 2018. https://timesofindia.indiatimes.com/home/science/bt-cotton-doubled-production-minimised-harm-by-pest-govt/articleshow/62792163.cms.

Trapero, Carlos, Iain W. Wilson, Warwick N. Stiller, and Lewis J. Wilson. 2016. "Enhancing Integrated Pest Management in GM Cotton Systems Using Host Plant Resistance." *Crop Science and Horticulture* 7: 500. https://doi.org/10.3389/fpls.2016.00500.

Tripp, Robert. 2005. *Self-Sufficient Agriculture: Labour and Knowledge in Small-Scale Farming*. London: Earthscan.

Tsing, Anna Lowenhaupt. 2005. *Friction: An Ethnography of Global Connection*. Princeton, N.J.: Princeton University Press.

Tsing, Anna Lowenhaupt. 2015. *The Mushroom at the End of the World: On the Possibility of Life in Capitalist Ruins*. Princeton, N.J.: Princeton University Press.

Turner, B. L., Roger E. Kasperson, Pamela A. Matson, James J. McCarthy, Robert W. Corell, Lindsey Christensen, Noelle Eckley, et al. 2003. "A Framework for Vulnerability Analysis in Sustainability Science." *Proceedings of the National Academy of Sciences* 100 (14): 8074–79. https://doi.org/10.1073/pnas.1231335100.

Turner, Victor. 1970. *The Forest of Symbols: Aspects of Ndembu Ritual*. Ithaca, N.Y.: Cornell University Press.

Turner, Victor. 1980. "Social Dramas and Stories About Them." *Critical Inquiry* 7 (1): 141–68.

Upasana. 2017. "Preserving Resources—Road to Redemption." *Upasana Blog* (blog). January 23, 2017. https://www.upasana.in/blogs/2017/01/23/preserving-resources-road-to-redemption/.

USDA Foreign Agricultural Service. 2015. *Cotton: World Markets and Trade.* World Production, Markets, and Trade Reports. July 10. Washington, D.C.: United States Department of Agriculture.

USDA Foreign Agricultural Service. 2016. *China and Hong Kong: Challenges and Opportunities.* International Agriculture Trade Reports. September 6. Washington, D.C.: United States Department of Agriculture.

Vaidyanathan, A. 2006. "Farmers' Suicides and the Agrarian Crisis." *Economic and Political Weekly* 41 (38): 4009–13.

Vakulabharanam, Vamsi. 2004. "Agricultural Growth and Irrigation in Telangana: A Review of Evidence." *Economic and Political Weekly* 39 (13): 1421–26.

Vanclay, Frank, and Gareth Enticott. 2011. "The Role and Functioning of Cultural Scripts in Farming and Agriculture." *Sociologia Ruralis* 51 (3): 256–71. https://doi.org/10.1111/j.1467-9523.2011.00537.x.

Vasavi, A. R. 1999. *Harbingers of Rain: Land and Life in South Asia.* New Delhi: Oxford University Press.

Vasavi, A. R. 2012. *Shadow Space: Suicides and the Predicament of Rural India.* Gurgaon: Three Essays Collective.

Veblen, Thorstein. 1899. *The Theory of the Leisure Class.* New York: Oxford University Press.

Veettil, Prakashan Chellattan, Vijesh V. Krishna, and Matin Qaim. 2017. "Ecosystem Impacts of Pesticide Reductions Through Bt Cotton Adoption." *Australian Journal of Agricultural and Resource Economics* 61 (1): 115–34. https://doi.org/10.1111/1467-8489.12171.

Venkata, Rekhadevi Perumalla, M. F. Rahman, M. Mahboob, S. Indu Kumari, Srinivas Chinde, Bhanuramya M, Naresh Dumala, and Paramjit Grover. 2016. "Assessment of Genotoxicity in Female Agricultural Workers Exposed to Pesticides." *Biomarkers* 22 (5): 446–54. https://doi.org/10.1080/1354750X.2016.1252954.

Venugopalan, M. V., K. R. Kranthi, D. Blaise, Shubhangi Lakde, and K. Sankaranarayana. 2014. "High Density Planting System in Cotton—The Brazil Experience and Indian Initiatives." *Cotton Research Journal* 5 (2): 172–85.

Vernant, Jean-Pierre, and Marcel Detienne. 1991. *Cunning Intelligence in Greek Culture and Society.* Translated by Janet Lloyd. Chicago: University of Chicago Press.

Wadke, Rahul. 2012. "Mahyco Denies It Sold Its Seeds in Black Market." *Hindu.* July 19, 2012. http://www.thehindubusinessline.com/industry-and-economy/agri-biz/article3658632.ece?homepage=true&ref=wl_home.

Walsh, Catherine. 2010. "Development as Buen Vivir: Institutional Arrangements and (de)Colonial Entanglements." *Development* 53 (1): 15–21. https://doi.org/10.1057/dev.2009.93.

Weber, Thomas. 2015. *Gandhi at First Sight*. New Delhi: Roli Books.

Wendel, Jonathan F., and Corrinne Grover. 2015. "Taxonomy and Evolution of the Cotton Genus, *Gossypium*." In *Cotton*, 2nd ed., edited by David D. Fang and Richard G. Percy, 25–44. Agronomy Monograph 57. Madison, Wis.: American Society of Agronomy; Crop Science Society of America; Soil Science Society of America.

West, Paige. 2012. *From Modern Production to Imagined Primitive: The Social World of Coffee from Papua New Guinea*. Durham, N.C.: Duke University Press.

Wilken, Gene C. 1987. *Good Farmers: Traditional Agricultural Resource Management in Mexico and Central America*. Berkeley: University of California Press.

Willer, Helga, and Julia Lernoud, eds. 2016. *The World of Organic Agriculture: Statistics and Emerging Trends 2016*. Bonn: Research Institute of Organic Agriculture (FiBL); Frick; IFOAM – Organics International.

Wood, Ellen Meiksins. 2000. "The Agrarian Origins of Capitalism." In *Hungry for Profit: The Agribusiness Threat to Farmers, Food, and the Environment*, edited by Fred Magdoff, John Bellamy Foster, and Frederick H Buttel, 23–42. New York: Monthly Review Press.

World Commission on Environment and Development. 1987. *Report of the World Commission on Environment and Development: Our Common Future*. Brundtland Report. Oxford: United Nations World Commission on Environment and Development. https://doi.org/10.1080/07488008808408783.

Yapa, Lakshman. 1993. "What Are Improved Seeds? An Epistemology of the Green Revolution." *Economic Geography* 69 (3): 254–73. https://doi.org/10.2307/143450.

Zohary, Daniel, Maria Hopf, and Ehud Weiss. 2012. *Domestication of Plants in the Old World: The Origin and Spread of Domesticated Plants in Southwest Asia, Europe, and the Mediterranean Basin*. New York: Oxford University Press.

Zubrzycki, John. 2007. *The Last Nizam: The Rise and Fall of India's Greatest Princely State*. Sydney: Pan Macmillan.

INDEX

*Indicates a pseudonym.

*Addabad, 121, 130, 138, 160, 171
agrarian crisis: certified organic farming,
  9; civil bureaucracy and, 10; debt and,
  71; debts and, 177; fertilizers and, 36;
  genetically modified organisms and, 7,
  9; journalists and, 10; *PANTA and, 125;
  performances and, 42, 57; pesticides and,
  14; political ecology and, 8, 11–13, 67, 150;
  predatory insects and, 9–10; suicides
  and, 6, 9–10, 12, 16, 47, 70–71, 125, 177;
  yield problems and, 9
agricultural knowledge: certified organic
  farming and, 7–8; fad seeds and, 44,
  91; fertilizers and, 40, 65, 79, 152–53, 157,
  169–170; genetically modified organisms
  and, 7–8; in *Kavrupad, 93, 96, 111, 147–
  48, 156–57; new technologies and, 8–9;
  *PANTA and, 143, 147, 179; performances
  and, 14, 37, 48–52, 56–57, 83, 111, 135, 137,
  142, 146, 162, 168–170, 183, 186–87; pesticides and, 86, 132, 135, 157; *Prakruti and,
  132–33, 159, 161–62, 167; *Ralledapalle

and, 111, 148, 157; rice and, 105–6, 120, 138,
  143–44, 188; seed choices and, 83, 90, 112;
  seed shops and, 39, 96, 111, 148; sustainability and, 8, 37, 112, in Warangal, 141.
  See also learning
ATM, 3–5, 89, 99, 171
Australia, 73
biodiversity, 10, 13, 31, 38, 55, 122, 138, 141, 161,
  173, 175–77, 185, 190, 192
black market, 102–4, 107–10
bollworms, 5, 16, 19, 29–30, 82, 113, 138, 164,
  171–73, 180–83
Brazil, 9–10, 73
Bt cotton: pesticides and, 29, 47, 129, 173–74;
  suicides and, 16. See also genetically
  modified organisms
Bunny, 133
capitalism, 7
caste system: backward castes (BC), 21–
  22; cultural preservation and, 53–54;
  discrimination and, 21–22, 38–39, 49,
  67–68, 89, 92–97, 99, 112, 145–46, 162, 168;

distribution of labor and, 29; distinctions within, 21; genetically modified organisms and, 18; the green revolution and, 152, 166, 176; harijans, 21; history of, 67–68; in *Kavrupad, 22, 107–8; open castes (OC), 21–22; opportunities and, 21–22, 38–39, 49, 67–68, 92–97; *PANTA and, 139; peace between, 68; pesticides and, 152; political ecology and, 150; *Prakruti and, 120–21, 139; scheduled castes (SC) and, 21–22; scheduled tribes (ST) and, 21–22, 99; seed shops and, 97, 99, 111, 157; success of farm and, 17; untouchables, 21

castor (*Ricinus communis* L.), 171

certified organic farming: agrarian crisis in Indian and, 7; agricultural knowledge and, 7–8; cotton and, 3; debts and, 126–27, 129, 137, 162; fair trade and, 191; fertilizers and, 13, 19, 40, 79, 115, 118, 128, 132, 158, 160–61, 192; learning and, 116–17, 133–34, 138–140; loans and, 140, 144, 184; *PANTA and, 121, 139, 146; performances and, 33, 56, 73, 117, 137, 155, 168, 176, 184, 186–87, 189; pesticides and, 13, 19, 79, 118, 173; political ecology and, 139, 177, 185–86; *Prakruti and, 116, 121, 124, 127–29, 131, 158–160, 186; of rice, 120, 140; seed choices and, 133, 135–36; subsidies and, 192; suicides and, 126–27, 138–39, 156, 177, 187; sustainability and, 45, 83; in Warangal, 116, 128, 141; yield from, 8

China, 9–10

choice overload, 103–7

climate change, 120

cotton: agricultural history of, 9; in Brazil, 9; capitalism and, 7; certified organic farming and, 3; in China, 9; commodification of, 9; commodity chain studies of, 6–7; costs of growing of, 4–5; cycle of clothing and, 6–7; debts and, 6, 68; distribution of labor and, 24; fiber length of, 9–10; genetically modified organisms and, 3; globalization and, 6–7; growing

cycle of, 5; hybrids of, 9–10; inequalities and, 3; pesticides and, 5, 10; predatory insects and, 4–5, 9–10; profits and, 5; rural well-being and, 7; saving seeds and, 16; seeds per acre, 4–5; seed varieties of, 3–5, 135–36; slavery and, 9; suicide and, 3; in the U.S., 9–10; varieties of, 9–10, 66–67; yield from, 6, 8–10, 172–73

death, 163–64

debts: agrarian crisis and, 71, 177; agricultural inputs and, 37–38, 67, 115; certified organic farming and, 126–27, 129, 137, 162; chronic, 125; costs of, 87; cotton and, 68; dangers of, 164; disparities and, 72, 80; genetically modified organisms and, 73, 129, 164, 177–78; inability to pay, 87, 101, 115, 159, 166; income to debt ratio, 101; neoliberal capitalism and, 71; performances and, 145; pesticides and, 68; poor access to, 6; responses to, 70–71; seasonal, 69, 126, 161; seed choice and, 112; seed choices and, 7; suicides and, 6, 30, 67–68, 70, 72, 81, 115, 125–26, 164–65; in Warangal, 185; as widespread, 28

Diwali, 5

Dr. Brent, 85, 89, 99, 101, 171

droughts, 36, 70–71, 103

education, 22, 121–22, 132–33, 159

El Nino, 161

*Ennepad, 120–21, 125, 128, 130, 134–35, 140–41, 143, 146–47, 149, 154–56, 159, 185

environmental learning, 43–46, 55–57, 112–13, 133–34, 136, 139. *See also* agricultural knowledge

epistêmê, 46, 49–50, 57, 162

fad seeds: agricultural knowledge and, 44, 91; expanded use of, 105; in *Kavrupad, 94, 103; learning and, 44; pattern of use of, 85, 89–90, 93–94; popularity of, 97, 101; in *Ralledapalle, 94, 103; seed shortages and, 101, 103; social status and, 93, 97, 103; subsidies and, 105; in Warangal, 85, 92; yields from, 84–90, 92 fair trade: benefits of, 126; benefits to producers of, 8; certifications for, 122, 124; certified organic farming and, 191; consumers of, 151; genetically modified organisms and, 124; postcolonialism and, 179; *Prakruti and, 124; producers of, 151, 160; supply chains of, 18

Fair Trade UK, 124, 151

famine, 11, 59, 65

fertilizers: agrarian crisis and, 36; agricultural knowledge and, 16–17, 40, 65, 79, 152–53, 157; American hybrid and, 9–10; application of, 5; availability of, 64; certified organic farming and, 13, 19, 40, 79, 115, 118, 128, 132, 158, 160–61, 192; commodification of, 65; cost of, 5–6, 10, 12–13, 15–16, 27, 39, 65, 109, 115, 129; cotton yields and, 10, 12; customization of, 136, 152; debts and, 67; distribution of labor and, 24; ecological damage from, 10, 132, 163, 167; effectiveness of, 47, 65, 128–29; genetically modified organisms and, 13, 15–16, 28, 40, 66, 75, 118, 163, 168, 172, 174; globalization and, 9, 26–27; the green revolution and, 27, 65, 152–53; growth of, 26, 64–65; increased use of, 9, 12, 64, 66–67, 178; integrated pest management and, 174; as a management strategy, 90, 174; manufacturing and, 64; natural, 40, 80, 115, 129, 132, 142, 146–47, 153, 157, 159, 163, 167; overuse of, 10, 12, 163, 167; profits from, 39–40, 66, 178; risks of, 10; saved seeds and, 16; seed choices and, 91–92; seed shops and, 3–4, 16, 39–40, 98–101, 156–57; seed varieties and, 98–100, 128–29; sources of, 16; strike, 36; subsidies and, 27, 65–66, 69; suicides and, 67; in the U.S., 26–27, 40; yields and, 37–38, 40, 47, 64–65. See also manure; urea

food security, 31, 36, 55, 136, 138, 144, 176, 185

generational poverty, 56, 59, 66–70, 80–81, 116, 177

genetically modified organisms: agrarian crisis in India and, 7; agricultural knowledge and, 7–8; caste system and, 18; costs of, 15–16; cotton and, 3; debt and, 73; debts and, 129, 164, 177–78; effectiveness of, 4; fertilizers and, 13, 15–16, 28, 40, 66, 75, 118, 163, 168, 172, 174; in *Kavrupad, 138; learning and, 83–84, 86, 90, 92–94, 96–100, 103–8, 111–14, 117, 140; Monsanto leases for, 76; *PANTA and, 149; performances and, 56, 73, 83, 155, 168, 184, 186–87, 189; pesticides and, 13, 15–16, 19, 25–31, 35–38, 65, 82, 118, 123, 131, 168–69, 173–74, 192; political ecology and, 177; profits and, 4; in *Ralledapalle, 171, 177; *Ralledapalle and, 111; rice and, 188; seed market and, 7–8; subsidies and, 41, 84, 184; suicides and, 19, 25–31, 73, 138–39, 148, 177, 187; sustainability and, 45, 83, 112; in Warangal, 116, 128; yield from, 8. See also Bt cotton

globalization, 3, 6–7, 9, 12, 26–27, 167–68

green revolution: agrarian crisis and, 12; agricultural yield and, 65; caste system and, 152, 166, 176; globalization and, 12; impact of, 32, 41–42, 59, 65; modifications to, 152–55; origins of, 26–27, 65; seed hybridization and, 177–78

historical marginalization, 166–67

Hyderabad, 17, 20, 53, 68–69, 120–21, 123, 132, 155, 164, 181

identity, 14, 51–52, 54, 111, 135, 137, 170, 184

imidacloprid, 5

integrated pest management, 8, 110, 120, 169, 174–75, 188, 191–92

Jaadoo, 3–4, 89–90, 96, 99, 157, 171. See also Kaveri Seeds

Jackpot, 89, 93, 99

journalists, 10

Kaveri Seeds, 76, 90, 180. See also Jaadoo

*Kavrupad: agricultural knowledge and, 93; agricultural knowledge in, 96, 111, 147–48, 156–57; black market seeds in, 103, 107–8;

caste system in, 22, 107–8; debts in, 101; description of, 22, 54; distribution of labor in, 113; education in, 22; fad seeds in, 94, 103; genetically modified organisms and, 138; monocultures in, 113, 137; neoliberal capitalism in, 137; pesticide use in, 148; rice in, 138; seed choices and, 90, 92, 94; seed choices in, 156–57; seed shops of, 22, 39, 101, 103, 109, 156–57; transportation in, 89

leafhoppers (*Amrasca biguttula biguttula*), 16, 89

learning: certified organic farming and, 116–17, 133–34, 138–140; choice overload and, 103–7; environmental learning as, 43–47, 55–57, 84, 112–14, 133–34, 139; fad seeds and, 44; genetically modified organisms and, 83–84, 86, 90, 92–94, 96–100, 103–8, 111–14, 117, 140; globalization and, 32; kinds of, 8, 23, 43; marketing and, 84, 97–100, 103–7, 117; new technologies and, 9, 42–45; political ecology and, 47–50; postcolonialism and, 56; practice-based learning as, 44–47; the process of, 52, 56, 74, 83, 86, 108, 111, 137–39, 168; seed choices and, 38, 55–56, 66, 84, 103–7, 112, 117; shared, 187; social learning as, 43–44, 56–57, 92–94, 96, 112, 136–37, 139; success and, 32, 38, 139; sustainability and, 90, 187; as transformative, 153. *See also* agricultural knowledge

lenders, 68, 70

loans: certified organic farming and, 140, 144, 184; cost of, 51, 102; inability to pay, 70, 159; interest free, 108, 116, 159; *Prakruti and, 142, 159; seasonal, 28, 67; subsidies and, 131; suicides and, 70

Mahyco, 85, 90, 101–2. *See also* Neeraja

Mallika, 133. *See also* Nuziveedu

management strategies, 15, 54, 90, 116, 160, 174

manci digubadi: concerns about, 128–29; importance of, 176; meaning of, 189;

performances and, 50, 52, 186; roles for, 186; seed choices and, 23, 56, 87–88, 183; seed switching and, 38, 88; success and, 138, 168, 183–84

manure, 5, 40, 80, 115, 129, 132, 142, 146–47, 153, 159, 163

marketing: learning and, 84, 97–100, 103–7, 117; *PANTA and, 123, 137, 146, 151; performances and, 73, 158, 189; pesticides and, 151; of *Prakruti, 151–52, 155–56; in Warangal, 4

Medak, 20, 141

mêtis, 46, 49–50, 53–55, 57, 111, 137, 142, 144, 146, 152, 162, 169

monocultures, 11–12, 16, 63, 67, 111–13, 137, 154, 161, 175–76, 179, 190–91

Monsanto: cottonseeds of, 73–74; in India, 76; leasing rights to genes by, 76

Monsanto India, 76

monsoons, 4, 10, 161

mung beans (*Vigna radiata* [L.] R. Wilczek), 53, 171

National Agriculture Bank for Rural Development, 137

National Public Radio, 6–7

neem (*Azdirachta indica* A. Juss.), 40, 54, 115–16, 132, 135, 170

Neeraja, 85, 89–90, 96, 99, 101–2. *See also* Mahyco

neoliberal capitalism, 12, 49, 69–72, 129, 137, 166, 190

newspapers, 71, 163–64

nonpesticide management (NPM). *See also* agricultural knowledge

Nuziveedu, 76, 101, 135, 180. *See also* Mallika

organic farming. *See* certified organic farming

*PANTA: agrarian crisis and, 125; agricultural knowledge and, 143, 147, 179; assistance from, 120–21, 135, 139, 143, 151–52, 154, 156; certified organic farming and, 121, 139, 146; description of, 120; farmers and, 121, 134, 137; flexibility and,

179; genetically modified organisms and, 149; history, 120–21; integrated pest management and, 120; marketing and, 123, 137, 146, 151; partner villages of, 120; pesticides and, 125; recruitment by, 121, 151–52; rice and, 120–21, 143–44; seed choices and, 135; social networks and, 166–67; success of, 129, 136, 143, 154, 156, 193; suicides and, 125, 156

performances: agrarian crisis and, 8–9, 42, 57; agricultural knowledge and, 14, 37, 48–52, 56–57, 83, 111, 135, 137, 142, 146, 162, 168–170, 183, 186–87; audience response and, 52, 54–55, 142, 144–45, 155–56, 162; certified organic farming and, 33, 56, 73, 117, 137, 155, 168, 176, 184, 186–87, 189; debts and, 145; definition of, 51; in the everyday, 144–49; failure and, 52; fear and, 137; genetically modified organisms and, 56, 73, 83, 155, 168, 184, 186–87, 189; globalization and, 167–68; identity and, 14, 51–52, 54, 57, 111, 135, 137, 170, 184; importance of, 14; improvisation and, 49, 51–52, 57, 111; as iterative, 56, 189; management strategies and, 57; marketing and, 73, 150, 189; as a metaphor, 51; metis and, 54–55, 111, 142, 169; moral values and, 49, 57, 144; pesticides and, 95–96, 145; political ecology and, 13–14, 38, 83, 113–14; postcolonialism and, 38, 48, 52–53; power and, 51; seed choices and, 8–9, 38, 83, 186, 189; success and, 56, 135; suicides as, 8, 42, 144–45, 163–65, 168, 170; sustainability and, 188–89; transformation and, 144, 150, 154, 162, 167–170; types of, 144; well-being and, 14, 145; yields and, 51, 56, 183, 186

pesticides: agrarian crisis and, 14; agricultural knowledge and, 86, 98–99, 132, 135, 157; biodiversity and, 192; bollworms and, 16; Bt cotton and, 29, 47, 129, 173–74; caste system and, 152; certified organic farming and, 13, 19, 79, 118, 173; contamination from, 29; costs of, 4–6, 90, 109,

115, 146, 148, 182; cotton varieties and, 66–67; dangers of, 3, 5, 29–31, 72, 113, 123, 129, 138, 148, 164, 169, 173–74, 190; debts and, 68; distribution of labor and, 24, 173–74; ecological damage from, 10; effectiveness of, 146, 148, 173–74; expired, 40, 108, 148; exposure from, 60; genetically modified organisms and, 13, 15–16, 19, 25–31, 35–38, 65, 82, 118, 123, 131, 168–69, 173–74, 192; the green revolution and, 26–27, 65, 152–53; increased use of, 9–10, 12–16, 66–67, 69, 72, 113, 150, 167, 169, 171, 173–74, 190; long-term poisoning from, 29–31; manufacturing and, 64; marketing and, 151; monocultures and, 16; motorized sprayers and, 5; natural, 54, 115–16, 132, 135, 170; as a necessity, 29–31; overuse of, 6, 10; *PANTA and, 125; performances and, 95–96, 145; pervasive use of, 16, 66–67, 113, 138, 150–52, 173–74; *Prakruti and, 131; profits from, 39, 189–190; risks of, 5–6, 10; seed shops and, 16, 31, 40, 99–101, 108, 156–57; subsidies and, 66, 69; success of, 66; suicides and, 6, 10, 25–31, 35, 67–68, 73, 129, 145, 171–72; suppliers of, 40; treadmills of, 12, 67, 184–85; ubiquity of, 10, 30–31; use of, 5; yields and, 128. *See also* neem (*Azdirachta indica* A. Juss.); nonpesticide management (NPM)

pigeon peas (*Cajanus cajan*), 53–54, 103, 138, 171

Planet Money T-shirt project, 6–7

planting density, 16, 161, 175, 190

police, 164–65

political ecology: agrarian crisis and, 8, 11–13, 67, 150; caste system and, 150; certified organic farming and, 139, 177, 185–86; definition of, 11; denaturalization and, 11–14, 31; genetically modified organisms and, 177; learning and, 14, 47–50; performances and, 13–14, 38, 83, 113–14; seed choices and, 8; suicides and, 71; well-being and, 14

postcolonialism, 38, 48, 52–53, 56, 179
*Prakruti: in *Addabad, 138; agricultural
    knowledge and, 132–33, 159, 161–62, 167;
    agricultural success and, 116; assistance
    from, 116, 121, 139–142, 159, 162–63;
    biodiversity and, 122, 136, 138–140, 185;
    caste system and, 121; certified organic
    farming and, 116, 121–22, 124, 127–29, 131,
    158–160, 186; cotton yields and, 127–28;
    criticisms of, 158, 160–61; debts and, 159,
    162–63; description of, 115, 121–22, 151–52;
    donations from, 122; education and, 121–
    22, 132–33, 159; fair trade and, 124; farmer
    suicides and, 125; farm of, 122–23, 136;
    historical marginalization and, 166–67;
    investments in, 122–24, 126–27, 151–52,
    155–56, 193; loans and, 142; marketing
    of, 151–52, 155–56; monuments of, 149;
    pesticides and, 131; planting density and,
    161; recruitment by, 121; rice and, 140;
    seed choices and, 121, 130, 133, 135–36, 158,
    160–61, 171; success of, 136, 139–142, 152,
    155, 162–63, 167, 171; water and, 121
*Ralledapalle: agricultural knowledge and,
    111, 148, 157; description of, 22; fad seeds
    and, 103; fad seeds in, 94; farmer suicides
    in, 164; genetically modified organisms
    and, 111, 171, 177; seed choices and, 99,
    103, 157, 171; seed shops and, 99; yield
    and, 94; yields and, 96
rice: in *Addabad, 138; agricultural knowl-
    edge and, 105–6, 120, 138, 143–44, 188;
    certified organic farming and, 140;
    certified organic farming of, 120; crop
    rotations and, 20; cultural preservation
    with, 50, 53–54, 143–44; in *Ennepad, 143;
    genetically modified organisms and, 188;
    hybrids of, 188; importance of, 53, 106;
    in *Kavrupad, 138; manci digubadi and,
    138; in Medak, 20; *PANTA and, 120–21,
    143–44; *Prakruti and, 140; price for, 148;
    saving seeds and, 140; seed choices in,
    188; seed shops and, 39; in Telangana,

20; varieties of, 121, 188; in Warangal, 20;
    water, 121; water usage and, 120–21
rural well-being, 7–8, 13, 19–20, 36–37, 112,
    131–32, 138, 141, 176. See also well-being
saving seeds: rice and, 140; sorghum and, 140
seed choices: agricultural knowledge and,
    83, 90, 112; certified organic farming and,
    133, 135–36; debts and, 112; fertilizers and,
    91–92; in *Kavrupad, 90, 92, 94, 156–57;
    learning and, 38, 55–56, 66, 84, 103–7, 112;
    in Mahesh, 6; manci digubadi and, 23;
    *PANTA and, 135; performances and, 38,
    83, 186, 189; *Prakruti and, 121, 130, 133,
    135–36, 158, 160–61, 171; in *Ralledapalle,
    171; *Ralledapalle and, 157; rice in, 188;
    seed shops and, 179; social status and, 93;
    sustainability and, 83; in Warangal, 84,
    92, 101–5
seed shops: agricultural inputs and, 39,
    101; agricultural knowledge and, 39,
    96, 111, 148; black market and, 102–3;
    caste system and, 97, 99, 111, 147–48;
    complaints about, 109; corruption in,
    108; costs of, 102; credit in, 131; fake
    seeds and, 109–10, 157; fertilizers and,
    3, 16, 39, 98–99, 101, 156–57; importance
    of, 108–9; in *Kavrupad, 22, 39, 101, 103,
    108, 156–57; pesticides and, 31, 39, 101,
    108, 156–57; *Prakruti and, 121; rice in,
    39; seed choices and, 179; seed prices
    and, 102, 108; seed shortages and, 101–2;
    seed varieties and, 39, 99, 143, 180; social
    status and, 98–99; trust in, 39–40, 96,
    108–9, 147, 156–57, 180; of Warangal, 3–4,
    98–100, 102, 108–9, 180
seed shortages, 47, 101, 103–4, 109, 118
slavery, 9, 58
social learning, 43–44, 56–57, 92–94, 96, 112,
    136, 139. See also agricultural knowledge
social status: fad seeds and, 93, 97, 103; seed
    choices and, 93; seed shops and, 98–100
sorghum (Sorghum bicolor [L.] Moench), 20,
    53–54, 121, 140

subsidies: certified organic farming and, 192;
cooperatives and, 110; fad seeds and, 105;
fertilizers and, 27, 65–66, 69; genetically
modified organisms and, 41, 84, 184; the
green revolution and, 41; loans and, 130;
low cotton yield and, 126; neoliberal
capitalism and, 51; *PANTA and, 121, 156;
pesticide risks and, 190; *Prakruti and,
141–42; seed choice and, 39; seeds, 110,
133–36; seed varieties and, 102
sugar, 7
suicides: agrarian crisis and, 6, 9–10, 12,
16, 47; agrarian crisis and, 70–71, 177;
agricultural costs and, 129; anxiety and,
35, 165; in Australia, 73; in Brazil, 73;
Bt cotton and, 16; causes of, 3, 33, 70,
72, 129, 145, 164–66; certified organic
farming and, 126–27, 138–39, 156, 177,
187; competitiveness and, 47; cotton
and, 3; debts and, 6, 30, 67–68, 70, 72,
81, 115, 125–26, 165; droughts and, 70;
failure and, 33, 39, 49, 111, 115, 138–39; of
farmers, 6, 10, 49, 70, 73, 80–81, 115, 165–
66, 190; fertilizers and, 67; generational
poverty and, 70; genetically modified
organisms and, 19, 25–31, 73, 138–39, 148,
177, 187; governmental response to, 71–
72, 165, 187; in Hyderabad, 68; impact of,
71, 129, 163; in India, 80; in Indian farmers, 6; loans and, 70; in Mahesh, 185; in
the media, 165; neoliberal capitalism
and, 12, 49, 69–72, 129, 166, 190; newspapers and, 71, 163–64; *PANTA and,
125, 156; as a performance, 8, 42, 144–45,
163–65, 168, 170; pesticides and, 10,
25–31, 35, 67–68, 73, 129, 145, 171–72; at
police stations, 164–65; political ecology
and, 8, 71; *Prakruti and, 125; prevention
of, 71, 82–83; in public, 144–45, 164–65,
168, 170; in *Ralledapalle, 164; rates of,

6, 10, 49, 70–72, 115, 125–26, 139, 145, 165–
66, 171–72, 187; in the United Kingdom,
73; in the U.S., 73; in Vidarbha, 115; in
Warangal, 26, 115; water and, 125; yield
problems and, 8–9
sustainability: agricultural knowledge and,
8, 37, 112; benchmark and, 45, 177; caste
system and, 112; certified organic farming and, 45, 83; definition of, 35–37; early
adopters and, 131–34; environmental, 69;
flexibility and, 46–47; genetically modified organisms and, 45, 83, 112; learning
and, 90, 187; long-term, 46–47, 119–120;
performances and, 188–89; rural well-
being and, 36–37; seed choices and, 83
system of rice intensification (SRI), 120
techné, 45–46, 49–50, 152
trap plants, 138, 176
United Kingdom, 73
urea, 115, 129, 157, 159, 167
U.S., 9–10, 40–41, 65, 73
U.S. Civil War, 9–10, 63–64
vermicompost pits, 116, 132
Vidarbha, 115
Warangal: agricultural knowledge in, 141;
biodiversity in, 176; black market seeds
in, 103–4, 109–10; certified organic
farming and, 116, 128, 141; crop rotations
in, 20; debt issues in, 185; debts and, 185;
fad seeds in, 85, 92; farmer suicides in,
26, 115; genetically modified organisms
in, 116, 128; rice in, 20; rural well-being
in, 141; seed choices in, 85, 92, 101–5; seed
marketing in, 4; seed shops of, 3–4, 22,
40, 98–100, 102, 108–9, 180; seed shortages and, 101–4
well-being, 7, 14, 36–37, 112, 117, 145, 169. *See
also* rural well-being
whiteflies (*Bemisia tabaci*), 5, 16
Yuva, 89

ABOUT THE AUTHOR

Andrew Flachs is an assistant professor of anthropology at Purdue University. Trained as an environmental anthropologist, his research spans sustainable agriculture, food studies, the anthropology of knowledge, and political ecology.